W9-BVD-018

AROUND THE WORLD
IN 2,000 PICTURES

Braniff Super Convair 340

Matson Lines Lurline

Sabena Belgian Helicopt

Italian Line Cristoforo Colombo

United States welcomed to New York—United States Lines

TWA Constellation

Holland-America Nieuw Amsterdam

French Railroads "Blue Train"

American Export Independen

Swissair DC-6B

Canadian Pacific Empress of Britain

Scandinavian Airlines DC-6

Furness Queen of Bermuda

Air France Constellations

Norwegian America Oslofjo

AROUND THE WORLD IN 2,000 PICTURES

"AROUND THE WORLD" AND "AROUND THE U. S. A." NOW IN ONE VOLUME

Edited by A. MILTON RUNYON and VILMA F. BERGANE

20 MAPS BY RAFAEL PALACIOS

DOUBLEDAY & COMPANY, INC.

Garden City, N.Y.

Pan American 707 Jet

Europabus

Swedish American Kungsholm

Grace Line Santa Rosa

Trans-Canada "Viscount"

Cunard Line Caronia

This book was originally published
in two volumes under the titles
**AROUND THE WORLD
IN 1,000 PICTURES**
and
**AROUND THE U. S. A.
IN 1,000 PICTURES**
Revised Edition, • Printed in the United States

ACKNOWLEDGMENTS

The editors wish to thank *The New York Times* and the authors for permission to reprint the following articles, copyright 1954 by *The New York Times: New England,* by John H. Fenton; *The Midsouth,* by Stacy V. Jones; *The South,* by John Popham; *The Midwest,* by Richard J. H. Johnston; *The Plains States,* by Seth S. King; *The Rocky Mountains,* by Marshall Sprague; *The Southwest,* and *Southern California,* by Gladwin Hill; *California — The Golden Gate,* by Lawrence E. Davies; *The Northwest,* by Richard L. Neuberger. All other rights in these articles are specifically reserved to the authors.

CONTENTS

THE LURE OF WORLD TRAVEL
by Richard Joseph

Mr. Joseph is Travel Editor of Esquire Magazine *and author of* WORLD WIDE TRAVEL GUIDE, YOUR TRIP TO BRITAIN, WORLD WIDE MONEY CONVERTER AND TIPPING GUIDE, *and with Muriel E. Richter,* WORLD WIDE TRAVEL REGULATIONS MADE EASY.

In the catalog of man's dreams, taking a trip around the world ranks with making a million dollars, being elected President of the United States or inheriting a South Sea island. It's the ultimate travel experience, and next to it even the most fabulous junket fades into insignificance.

Like so many dreams, a world-tour can become a reality for only a comparatively few people, even though you can now fly around the world for about two thousand dollars, and one airline already is promoting round-the-world flights for the two-week vacationist. Nevertheless the odds are still strongly against your visiting most of the places covered in the following pages.

That being the case, this book is a working substitute for a trip around the world. The well-over-a-thousand pictures which follow will give you many of the sights and evoke some of the sounds, smells, tastes and moods of those far-away places with the fabulous names. They cover all the free world outside the limits of the fifty U. S. states which can be reached conveniently by American pleasure travelers. You'll sense some of the space of the far Pacific, see the breeze rustling the leaves of the palm trees of Sumatra, smell the delicate fragrance of jasmine tea handed you in a fragile cup by a geisha girl in Kyoto. You will feel the life pulsating through the pack-jammed sampans in Hong Kong harbor, absorb the peace of a Buddhist shrine in Thailand, understand the loneliness of Africa's vast open places, and come back to the world you know in the street scenes of western Europe.

The photographs are arranged in a number of tours, following the same itineraries a traveler would take in seeing the world in a series of different trips. And they've been chosen to give you the best possible idea of what you'd actually see on your world travels rather than dealing with impossibly remote spots or esoteric subjects available to the correspondent and professional photographer but not to the average pleasure traveler.

That's why you'll see many pictures of ordinary people the world over, but none of political leaders or celebrities of any sort. The photos will reveal to you the usual life of the various countries of the world; they won't take you for a weekend at the country home of an Indian Maharajah or English Viscount, backstage at a rehearsal of the *Folies Bergère* or between the spokes of a wheel in a tractor factory.

The things you'll see in these pictures, in other words, are the things you'd really see on a tour of the world. And the pictures are the same sort of pictures that can be and frequently are taken by the average traveler (I've been able to contribute quite a few myself), although they've been carefully selected for subject interest and photographic excellence. The editors have screened out the fuzzy prints, and the shots of Grandma with the doorman of the Grande Hotel; nevertheless you'll recognize photos of some of the places you've been to as duplicates of some of the better pictures you've taken yourself.

That, for me, is one of the charms of the book, the identification the traveler will feel for many of the pictures he'll see. This volume really has a three-fold attraction: it will give the intending traveler a preview of some of the fantastic things he'll see in various parts of the globe, it will treat the man who has been there to some wonderfully nostalgic memories of what he's seen and experienced, and it will give the armchair traveler a knowledge of the world and an intimate feeling of having been to most of the colorful places on earth.

There's a proverb, allegedly ancient Chinese, to the effect that *"The world is a book, and he who stays at home reads only one page."* Read all the pages of this book, though, and you will have seen the world.

GREAT BRITAIN AND IRELAND

Going by an English ship—Cunard's great *Queen Mary, Queen Elizabeth, Mauretania, Caronia* or one of the others—is perhaps the best introduction to Britain because you're surrounded by English tradition and atmosphere as soon as you step aboard. But there are plenty of delightful ways to get to England. Some ships put you off by tender at Plymouth, others dock at Liverpool, many at the great port of Southampton for the short train ride to London. If you're going to Ireland, take a ship that lands you at Cobh.

Flying across the Atlantic has its delights too. You can go direct to Shannon, for Ireland, or to Glasgow for Scotland, or to London Airport.

When you get there, hiring one of the easy-to-manage English cars is an excellent way to get about because the distances are so short. You'll readily get used to driving on the "wrong" side of the road, and you'll find many charming places for "tea" and for overnight stops. If you prefer, England is well covered by the British Railways network, and there are good bus lines. Most distances are too short for air travel, but the plane from London to Dublin avoids a possibly rough crossing of the 130-mile-wide Irish Sea.

The greatest appeal of England to many Americans is the great abundance of historic "things you've heard about" . . . Shakespeare's Stratford, the great mystery of Stonehenge, Westminster Abbey, the Houses of Parliament and Big Ben, the Tower of London, the Lake Country beloved of the poets, changing of the guard at Buckingham Palace, Peter Pan in Kensington Gardens, and Eros in Piccadilly. With the accession to the throne of young Elizabeth II, royalty takes on new glamor. Theater is at its best in London, and there are music, art, golf and other sports.

S.S. CARONIA LEAVES NEW YORK

England is but 500 miles long, and so narrow that it is nowhere possible to be as much as one hundred miles from the sea. The climate, affected by the Gulf Stream, is temperate.

All in all, with its many differences, England offers a common language and the closest thing to home that you will find anywhere abroad . . . a great common heritage.

Photo: Cunard Line

Great Britain and Ireland
LONDON
HYDE PARK
GREEN PARK
ST. JAMES'S PARK
THAMES RIVER
1 TOWER BRIDGE
2 TOWER OF LONDON
3 BUCKINGHAM PALACE
4 PICCADILLY CIRCUS
5 TRAFALGAR SQUARE
6 BRITISH MUSEUM
7 ST. PAUL'S CATHEDRAL
8 WESTMINSTER ABBEY
9 HOUSES OF PARLIAMENT
Atlantic Ocean
North Sea
Irish Sea
English Channel
SCOTLAND
Inverness
TROSSACHS
LOCH LOMOND
Glasgow
Edinburgh
GIANT'S CAUSEWAY
Londonderry
NORTHERN IRELAND
Belfast
Durham
LAKE DISTRICT
Windermere
York
ENGLAND
Liverpool
Llandudno
Rhyl
Chester
Caernarvon
Dublin
IRELAND
ARAN ISLANDS
SHANNON R.
WALES
Aberystwyth
Stratford-on-Avon
Norwich
Ely
Cambridge
Colchester
Oxford
London
COTSWOLD HILLS
THAMES R.
Salisbury
Canterbury
Brighton
Exeter
ISLE OF WIGHT
FRANCE
Scale of Miles
0 20 60 100

LOVERS SIT BY THE THAMES, ON TOWER WALK, BESIDE THE BRIDGE.

Photo: Henri Cartier-Bresson (Magnum)

Westminster Abbey has been the setting for the coronation of English monarchs from the year 1066, which saw the crowning of Harold II, last of the Saxon kings, and William the Conqueror, down to the recent coronation of Elizabeth II. The Abbey, officially called *Collegiate Church of St. Peter in Westminster,* is one of the finest examples of Early English architecture in England. Poets' Corner (Longfellow is the only American poet included) is one of the high spots for visitors. Another is Henry VII's magnificent chapel. The third is the old Coronation Chair.

Photo: British Travel Association

Buckingham Palace is residence of the Royal Family in London. When the Queen is there, the changing of guard ceremony takes place every other day at 10:30 a.m.

The Houses of Parliament, by the Thames, with Big Ben in the tower make the most celebrated landmark in England. Probably you've heard chimes of Big Ben by radio.

Photos: British Travel Association

England LONDON

St. James's Palace was built by Henry VIII in 1532. Changing of the guard ceremony takes place here when Queen is not in residence at Buckingham Palace.

10 Downing Street is the home of Prime Minister, equivalent of U.S. White House.

Chelsea Arts Ball at Royal Albert Hall, New Year's Eve, is England at its gayest.

Photos: British Travel Association; bottom right, Pan American World Airways

The Tower Bridge spans the Thames just below the Tower of London. The great

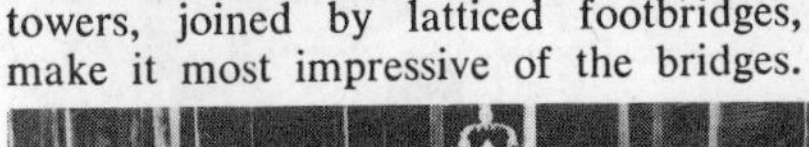

towers, joined by latticed footbridges, make it most impressive of the bridges.

Tower of London, guarded by the famous beefeaters, is a "must" for all visitors.

Crown Jewels, on display in the Tower, include the biggest diamond in existence.

The Orb of England and the Queen's Orb are among historic regalia in the display.

Photos: British Travel Association; bottom left, A. Milton Runyon

St. Paul's Cathedral, Renaissance masterpiece of Sir Christopher Wren, stands on summit of Ludgate Hill, a landmark for miles. Visit the "whispering gallery."

Photo: British Travel Association

Hyde Park has an area of 361 acres. Together with Kensington Gardens it makes a continuous park of more than 600 acres, favorite place for mass meetings.

Crowds of workers cross London Bridge on foot or by bus, on way to their shops and offices. Peak hour for the thousands of travelers is from 8:30 to 9:15 a.m.

Photos: British Travel Association; bottom, Henri Cartier-Bresson (Magnum)

Trafalgar Square, seen through terrace columns of the National Gallery, is a favorite site for political demonstrations. On south side towers Nelson Monument.

Photo: British Travel Association

Library in the House of Lords contains works of legal and historical character.

Chamber of the House of Commons, rebuilt in same style after 1941 bombing.

The British Museum is unrivaled for the variety of its exhibits, Elgin Marbles, Rosetta Stone, one of four copies of the Magna Charta, four-million-book library.

Photos: British Travel Association

Ceremony of Trooping the Color is held at the Horse Guards Parade, Whitehall.

When you've lost your car, or your way, ask the policeman at Piccadilly Circus.

Madame Tussaud's Exhibition of Waxworks attracts many visitors including the Pan American stewardess shown here looking at the tableau of Henry VIII.

Photos: William E. Reinhardt, Jr.; top right, Henri Cartier-Bresson (Magnum); bottom, British Travel Association

Piccadilly Circus is one of city's best-known features. It's a circle formed by the junction of five streets. The statue of Eros stands atop the central fountain.

Photo: British Travel Association

Hampton Court Palace, for over two centuries a royal residence, was started in 1514 by Cardinal Wolsey. Visit celebrated Maze in the gardens, the picture gallery.

Photo: British Travel Association

The Knights of the Garter Procession enters St. George's Chapel, Windsor—a building of which it has been said, "Such perfection is scarcely of this world."

Through Henry VIII's gateway at Windsor Castle, we watch the royal guard.

Arundel, Sussex, is on a hillside below the twelfth-century Arundel Castle.

Photos: British Travel Association; bottom left, A. Milton Runyon; bottom right, Charles Marschalek

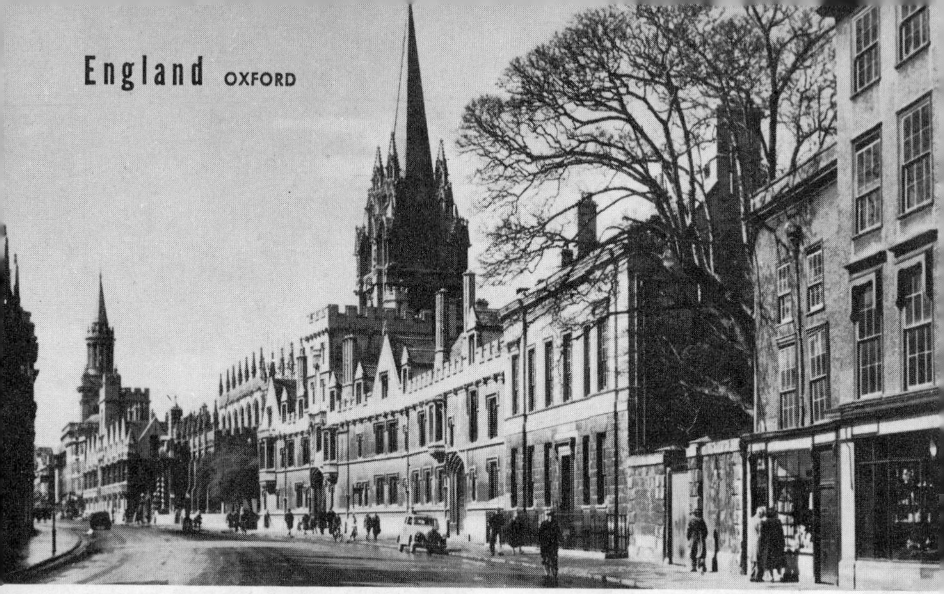

England OXFORD

Oxford University has 21 colleges for men, 4 for women. It dates back to 12th century. High Street is known to Oxford grads all over the world as "The High."

Christ Church, familiarly known as "the House," is the largest college in Oxford.

Magdalen Tower, bell-tower of Magdalen College, is setting of May Morning Hymn.

Photos: British Travel Association

Cambridge University, on the River Cam, is the other great seat of learning.

On way to Cambridge, visit Audley End, palatial Jacobean Renaissance mansion.

The "Backs" are the lovely tree-shaded grounds on left bank of the River Cam.

St. John's College, founded 1511, is one of the 20 colleges; 2 are for women.

Boating, or "punting," on the Cam is one of the delights of idyllic Cambridge.

Photos: British Travel Association;

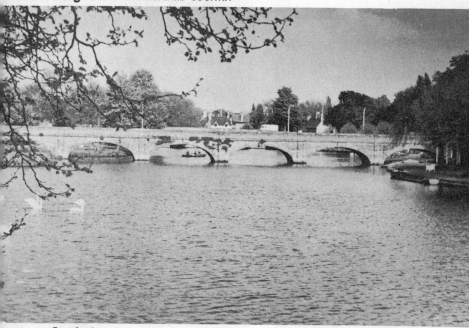

Stratford-on-Avon was the birthplace, in 1564, of William Shakespeare. It at-

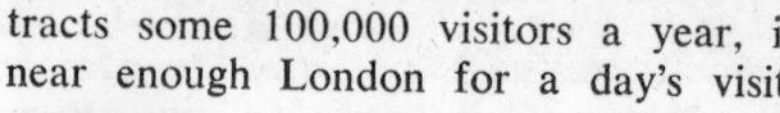
tracts some 100,000 visitors a year, is near enough London for a day's visit

Shakespeare's birthplace was originally part of a long row of terrace cottages.

Anne Hathaway's cottage, birthplace of Shakespeare's wife, has thatched roof

Photos: Richard Joseph; bottom, British Travel Association

Shakespeare Memorial Theatre is large, modern, seems out of keeping with the rest of Stratford, but is well suited to fine presentation of bard's great plays.

This view from Warwick Castle indicates charm of this medieval baronial castle.

Tintern Abbey, founded by Cistercians in 1131, is now romantic, roofless ruin.

Photos: British Travel Association; bottom left, Richard Joseph

Canterbury, one of most revered shrines, has been called "The Mother City of the Anglo-Saxon Race." Splendid cathedral, begun in 1070, was completed in 1503.

Photo: British Travel Association

'anterbury was stormed by Julius Caesar. /ar bombings uncovered Roman ruins.

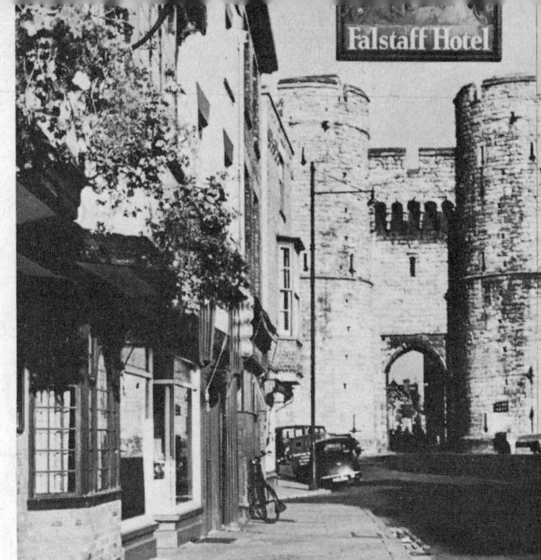

Visitors to Canterbury pass through the city gates, follow route of pilgrims of old.

Iermaid Row in Rye is peaceful English cene that attracts visitors and artists.

Knole, one of finest baronial mansions, has 365 rooms, is now open to visitors.

Dast houses, these odd conelike structures n Penshurst, are used for drying hops.

Dover Castle was built in 12th century by Henry II. Nearby is Roman lighthouse.

'hotos: Top left, Richard Joseph; thers, British Travel Association

Salisbury Cathedral is the most perfect realization of pure English Gothic, possibly because it was built in 38 years with the 404-foot steeple added later

Stonehenge, a mass of stones set on end, is one of Britain's greatest curiosities.

Druid ceremony at dawn on Midsumme Day is one of the rituals held regularly

Photos: British Travel Associatio

Brighton, one hour by electric train from London, is England's largest and most famous seaside resort. Often crowded, it is referred to as "London by the Sea."

Winchester, with its red brick Georgian buildings, has true English personality.

Once capital of kingdom, Winchester is famous for its cathedral and its school.

The Isle of Wight is just off the south coast, below Southampton. The town of Ventnor, built on terraces above the sea, is one of the best-known health resorts.

Photos: Winchester by Richard Joseph; others by British Travel Association

Exeter, County town of Devon, has enough historic buildings to give you the feeling that it's one of the traditional centers of the lovely West of England.

Ancient Guild Hall in Exeter has pillared façade projecting over the sidewalk.

Royal Clarencé Hotel, near Exeter Cathedral, has old-fashioned, quiet charm.

Photos: Richard Joseph

Clovelly, delightfully situated in a narrow rift in the cliffs of north Devon, descends in steps to a little cove. The picturesque houses have green trim.

Menabilly is home of Daphne du Maurier, author of *Jamaica Inn* and *Rebecca.*

Chapel of Gyllyngdune, in Falmouth, is said to be the smallest church in England.

In typical country "pubs" you'll find a darts game in progress most of the time. English "pubs" have taken on many of the American "country store" qualities.

Photos: William E. Reinhardt, Jr.; center left, Doubleday; center right, Richard Joseph, bottom, Robert Capa (Magnum)

Fifteenth-century George Inn, Norton St. Philip, in Somerset, is called "the oldest licensed house in England." It's like hundreds of other country "pubs."

Somerset's lush fields make dairying a major industry. Its cheeses are famous.

Broadway, pretty village in Cotswold hills, is home of many artists, writers.

Photos: Richard Joseph

One of the show places of Hertfordshire is Hatfield House, Jacobean mansion built for Robert Cecil, Earl of Salisbury, Secretary of State to Queen Elizabeth.

The Norman town of Chepstow guards Wye River. This gate is part of old wall.

Wye Valley is one of the most beautiful corners of Britain, with Forest of Dean.

Photos: British Travel Association

Ely Cathedral dominates the treeless fens for miles around. The striking West Tower, except for its octagonal top and turrets, is of Transition Norman period.

In Tolleshunt D'Arcy is home of Margery Allingham, famous for mystery novels.

Norwich, capital of Norfolk, is an ancient city with many beautiful houses.

Photos: British Travel Association; bottom left, A. Milton Runyon; bottom right, Richard Joseph

The Norfolk Broads, an area of shallow lagoons and placid streams, are near Norwich.

Colchester High Street was thoroughfare of the first Roman colony in Britain.

This gateway is all that's left of 11th-century Benedictine Abbey of St. John.

"Norwich Mercury" is said to be oldest English paper still using original name.

Norwich Cathedral is majestic structure, with graceful, tapering 313-ft. spire.

Photos: Top, Richard Joseph; others, British Travel Association

England YORKSHIRE AND THE EASTERN BORDER

York Minster is largest of England's medieval cathedrals. Its chief glory is its stained glass, contained in 120 windows. Most famous are West and "Five Sisters."

York has maze of narrow streets with names like Shambles (above), Gillygate, Whip-ma-whop-ma-gate. The city walls, with four gates, are mostly 14th century.

Photos: British Travel Association

The Royal Scot, British Railways' famous express, ascends Shap Fell, Westmoreland,

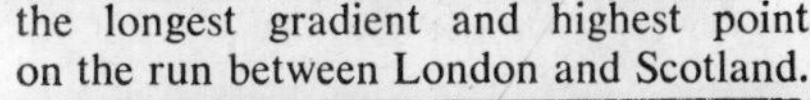

the longest gradient and highest point on the run between London and Scotland.

Hadrian's Wall, seen here at Housesteads, was built by Romans in second century.

Haworth, Yorkshire, was the Vicarage home of the celebrated Brontë family.

Durham Cathedral contains coffin of St. Cuthbert, carried on famous wanderings.

Harrowgate, high on Yorkshire moors, in center of England, is a beautiful resort.

Photos: top, British Railways; others, British Travel Association

The Anglican Cathedral at Liverpool is one of the most modern churches, under construction since 1904. When completed, it will be the fourth largest in the world.

Liverpool has 6 miles of docks. Several of transatlantic ships land you there.

The swashbuckling John of Gaunt built one of the gateways in Lancaster Castle.

Photos: British Travel Association

Chester, with its well-preserved walls, is most medieval-looking town in England.

Steps give easy access to the walls, and you can walk along them for two miles.

"The Rows" are unique Chester feature: arcades, built high to avoid muddy roads. They form continuous passage from shop to shop without going down to the street.

Photos: Richard Joseph

England THE LAKE DISTRICT

Ullswater, second in size, is said to be grandest of the English lakes in scenery.

Buttermere is one of the smaller lakes. There are 16 lakes, in 35 square miles.

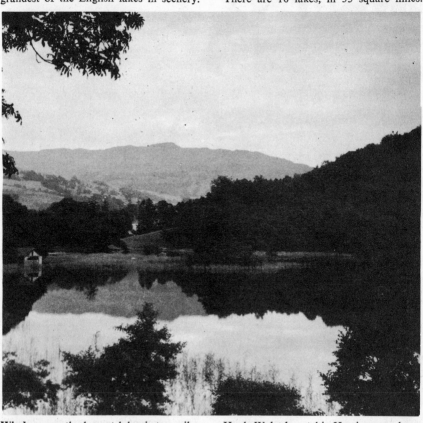

Windermere, the largest lake, is ten miles long, so narrow it looks like a river. Hugh Walpole set his Herries saga here; home also of Keats, Shelley, Wordsworth.

Photos: British Travel Association; bottom, Richard Joseph

The hamlet of Seatoller is one of the charming Cumberland villages that are best appreciated on a walking tour. Make your headquarters at a place like Keswick.

Grasmere, one of Lakeland's loveliest, was for 14 years the home of William Wordsworth. Visit Dove Cottage, where he lived, and the Wordsworth Museum.

Photos: British Travel Association

Eton boys: You tell their standing by whether their collars are "turned down."

At Epsom Downs, the "Derby" and "Oaks" attract the fashionable crowds.

Chimney sweep of Lancaster might have stepped right out of a Dickens' novel.

Oxford student is one of 8,000 undergrads. There are 590 teachers, called fellows.

Photos: British Travel Association; top right, Richard Joseph

DAILY CHANGING OF THE GUARD AT EDINBURGH CASTLE IS COLORFUL.

SCOTLAND MEANS HILLS AND HISTORY

When you talk of Scotland, some people think of Bobbie Burns, some think of Mary, Queen of Scots, and some of Ben Hogan's victory at Carnoustie. For Scotland is a land of great diversity, of great cities like Edinburgh and Glasgow, of hills and lochs, of poets and novelists and golfers, of unwavering national pride.

Photo: Richard Joseph

From Scott Monument in Princes Street, Sir Walter's statue looks across the city. The climb to the top is 287 steps, but you get a magnificent view on four sides.

Princes Street forms a valley down the middle of Edinburgh. On one side is old town, from great rock of Edinburgh castle to Holyroodhouse. Other side is new city.

Photos: British Travel Association

At Holyrood Palace tragic Mary, Queen of Scots, lived and ruled during 16th century. Old town between the castle and palace is called the Royal Mile.

Behind the National Gallery looms the great Castle Rock. From castle battlements you get a superb view of the city and the Forth River in the distance.

Photos: British Travel Association

Glasgow is the largest city in Scotland and the second largest in Great Britain.

Biggest Glasgow industry is shipbuilding. John Brown's built Cunard's two *Queens*.

Loch Lomond, 23 miles long, is "Queen of the Scottish Lochs." Trossachs tour takes you between Glasgow and Edinburgh by Loch Lomond, Loch Katrine.

Photos: Richard Joseph; top right, Maurice Greenberg (Black Star); bottom, British Travel Association

Abbotsford is Sir Walter Scott's estate, across from the tweed-milling town of Galashiels, south of Edinburgh. Scott lived in this baronial mansion till 1832.

Loch Lomond steamer heads north from Inversnaid, between bonnie, bonnie banks.

The Forth Bridge, near Edinburgh, a mile long, took seven years to build, in 1880's.

Photos: British Travel Association; bottom left, Alleyne M. Runyon

Scotland

Dancing is an important part of Scottish gatherings, where kilted males compete.

Skirl of bagpipes is a familiar sound. Reed wind instruments' origin is unknown.

If you come by ship direct to Scotland, tender takes you up Clyde to Glasgow.

Bagpipe band celebrates the arrival of *Britannic*. You won't forget eerie sound.

Photos: British Travel Association; Alleyne M. Runyon; bottom, Richard Joseph

CAERNARVON CASTLE WAS KEY FORTRESS IN THE WELSH CAMPAIGNS.

WALES IS LAND OF COAL, CONTRAST

If you read *How Green Was My Valley* by Richard Llewellyn, or saw the picture, you have some idea of this land of twisting roads, craggy mountains, of hard-working, song-loving people. You won't forget the beauty of Welsh choral singing when you've heard it in a country chapel. Song climax is annual Eisteddfod.

Photo: British Travel Association

Wales

Aberystwyth is west coast's big resort, with castle on rock jutting out to sea.

Photos: British Travel Association

Llandudno is a beach town on a peninsula at the northern tip of Wales. Planned a

Elan Valley reservoir at Aberystwyth is in one of many green valleys of Wales.

century ago, and laid out beautifully, it has mountains of Snowdonia as backdrop.

Welsh children turn out in their gayest costumes for Eisteddfod at Llangollen.

Good place for hiking is road from Barmouth to Dolgelley, where curfew rings.

St. David's Cathedral, Pembrokeshire, has none of Salisbury's lofty grace, but its low pitched roofs and square tower are in keeping with its bleak village. On the inside, the austerity changes to elaborate, almost Moorish ornamentation.

Photos: British Travel Association

NORTHERN IRELAND GAVE THE U.S. TEN PRESIDENTS

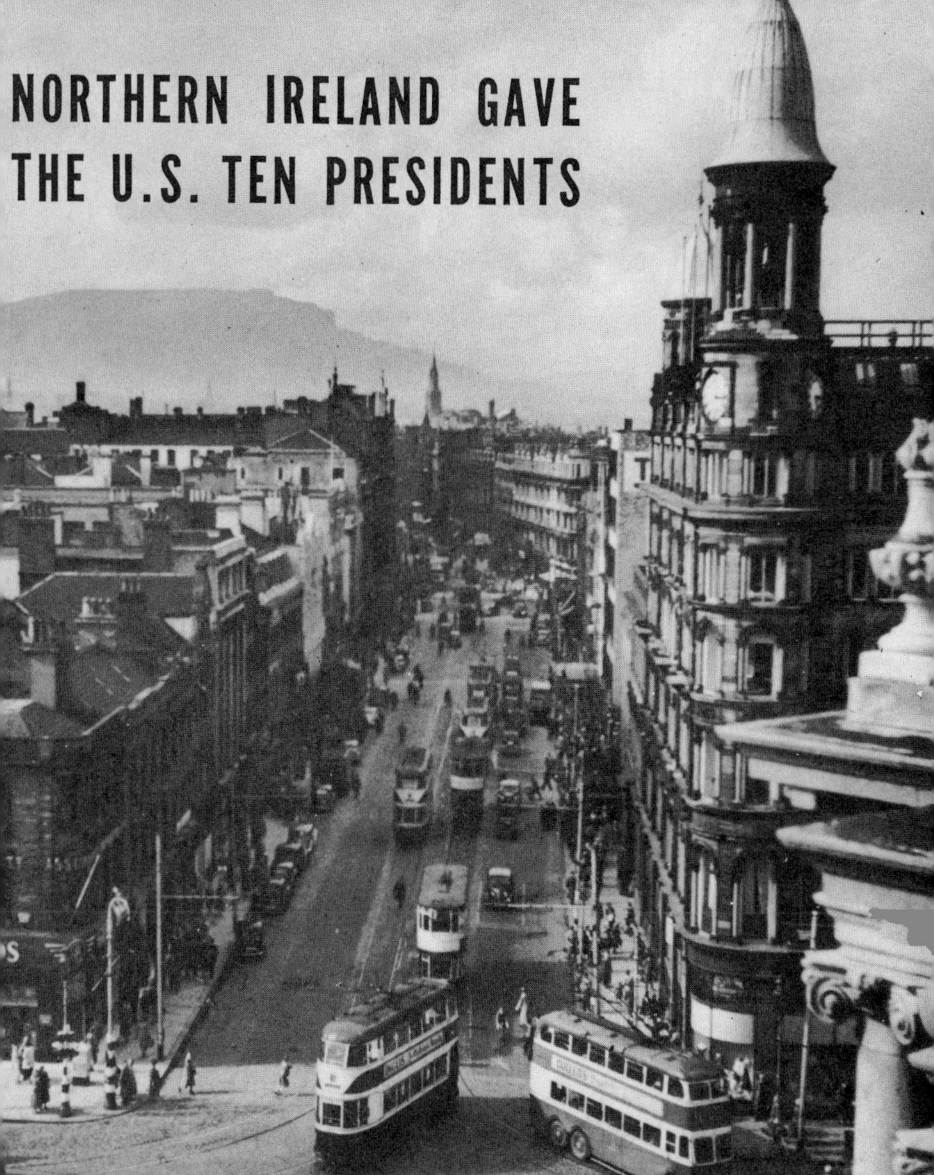

CITY HALL LOOKS DOWN DONEGALL PLACE, BELFAST'S MAIN STREET.

One reason why Northern Ireland will probably seem so familiar to you is that so many Ulster emigrants have come to the United States. Of the 33 men who have been Presidents, from George Washington to Dwight Eisenhower, at least ten are claimed to be of Ulster ancestry. Northern Ireland may be reached by boat or plane from Glasgow to Belfast, direct by plane from London. If you're coming up from Ireland, it's an easy trip by plane, train, bus or driving in your own car.

Photo: British Travel Association

Northern Ireland

Carrickfergus Castle is one of the best preserved Norman castles in the world.

There's wild country, and farmlands with hedges dividing them into tiny tracts.

Northern Ireland Parliament Buildings are situated atop hillside at Stormont.

Stormont Castle houses Prime Minister and certain departments of government.

Fair Head is the most northerly point in County Antrim. Nearby is the interesting Ballygalley Castle Hotel, a part of which dates back as far as the 17th century.

Photos: British Travel Association; top right, Richard Joseph

The Giant's Causeway is the greatest scenic attraction in Northern Ireland. Legend says these great basalt rocks once formed causeway across sea to Scotland.

Photo: British Travel Association

Northern Ireland

Dunluce Castle is near Portrush and Port Stewart which have wonderful beaches.

Londonderry City is 75 miles from Bel fast. This is Shipquay Gate, Guild Hall.

Bangor, County Down, is historic town that has become a favorite sea resort.

Belfast Castle is one of city's many sights: Art Gallery, Museum, University.

Because it has a seacoast of 245 miles and many rivers, lakes and tideways, Northern Ireland has an abundance of boating, and some magnificent fishing.

Photos: British Travel Association; bottom, Richard Joseph

RELAND INVITES YOU TO "COME BACK TO ERIN"

e mentioned the number of emigrants ıo had come from Northern Ireland to e U.S.A., and that's probably even ore true of Ireland itself. As you walk wn the street, you'll often think you cognize someone, because the second, rd and fourth cousins in America look t like the folks back home. You'll d Ireland a peaceful land whose pas-al scenes, green fields and hills, and ft mists will calm your nerves.

Getting to Ireland can be fun. Maybe u'll land at Cobh from your transatlantic steamer, or touch down in your plane at Shannon Airport, busiest center of international air traffic in the world. Gayest trip is from London on the Irish Mail, leaving London at tea time. About 11 p.m. you board a trim little ship at Holyhead, and sleep until you arrive at Dun Laoghaire, a few minutes from Dublin, the next morning. Or you can fly from London to Dublin by Aer Lingus.

All in all, you'll find St. Patrick's Island one of the friendliest nations to visit, even if you don't win a Sweeps!

'CONNELL STREET SHOPPERS SET URBAN PACE UNIQUE IN IRELAND.

ıoto: Fogra Failte

The Custom House, on the northern bank of the River Liffey, between O'Connell Bridge and the sea, was built in 17 from designs by James Gandon, Irelan

ost gifted architect. One of Dublin's nest public buildings, it ranks among the most beautiful in Europe. Burned in 1921, it has been completely restored.

oto: Fogra Failte

Ireland

An Tostal is Ireland's traditional festival, held each Spring. Here is a floral float passing the Presidential Dais reviewing stand at the General Post Of

Royal Dublin Society Horse Show is a high spot of the Dublin social season.

Arus Mhic Diarmuida is the ultra-moc bus terminal of Ireland Transport

Photos: Fogra F

ounty Sligo combines wild seacoast with lling plains, mountains like Benweeskin.

Garravogue River drains Lough Gill into sea. On its south bank is town of Sligo.

unting to hounds is a most popular ort. These are Meath foxhounds, from north of Dublin. Other noted packs are Duhallow hounds, Tipperary foxhounds.

otos: Fogra Failte

Ireland's fertile fields and pastures occupy more than half nation's working people.

Tipperary plays Kilkenny in Hurling, Irish national sport for 3,000 ye.

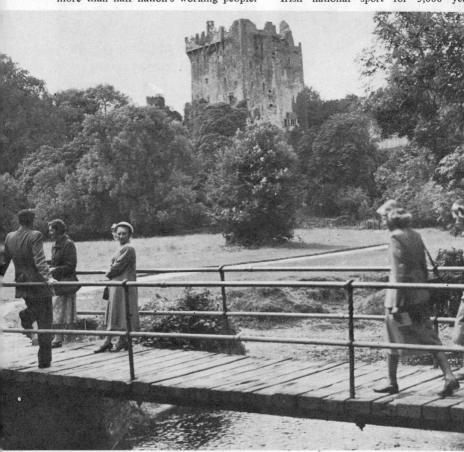

"Lips that touch the Blarney stone will have the gift of gab," according to the Irish myth. Famous stone is at Bları Castle, is bussed by thousands annua

Photo: Fogra Fc

Glandore, fishing village on a small inlet of the Atlantic, in the southern part of County Cork, has a population of 82, is noted for its delightfully mild climate.

Photo: Fogra Failte

This Aran girl lives on Inishmore, one of 3 Aran Islands, 28 mi. west of Galway.

Aran Islanders are rugged; not as prin tive as shown in movie, *Man of Ara*

Glendalough, County Wicklow, means Glen of the Two Lakes. Thackeray called it "sweet, wild and sad even in sunshin Visit the 6th-century St. Kevin Monaste

Photos: Fogra Fa

SCANDINAVIA

S.A.S. plane flies over northern Norway.

Clear-weather views from air are superb.

The Scandinavian countries are a geographical unit, joined by many ties of language, race and religion. And yet the several countries, Norway, Sweden, Finland, Denmark and Iceland, have many differences that make for delightful variety.

The first prehistoric cities of Scandinavia were founded by tall, blond Vikings who were not converted to Christianity until the year 1000. Wonderful relics of their early art are to be found in the museums of Oslo, Stockholm and Copenhagen.

Scandinavia is easily reached by air from the U.S. with good service by Scandinavian Airlines System and Pan American World Airways. Many flights offer free stopover privilege at Iceland. Swedish American Line's *Stockholm* and the luxurious new *Kungsholm* offer service from New York to Copenhagen and Gothenburg in 8 or 9 days. Norwegian America Line's trim *Oslofjord* and *Stavangerfjord* take you direct to Oslo in 9 days. From England, there is service both by sea and by air, and the same applies if you come from France or Benelux area. Fast express trains run to Copenhagen from Paris and other cities on the continent.

Shopping is delightful in Scandinavia for designers and craftsmen take great pride in their work. All the countries maintain permanent exhibits of arts and crafts, where you can examine them at leisure.

As a bookreader, you'll be especially interested in Scandinavian literature and in the many bookshops.

Photos: Scandinavian Airlines System; right, Konstantin Kostich

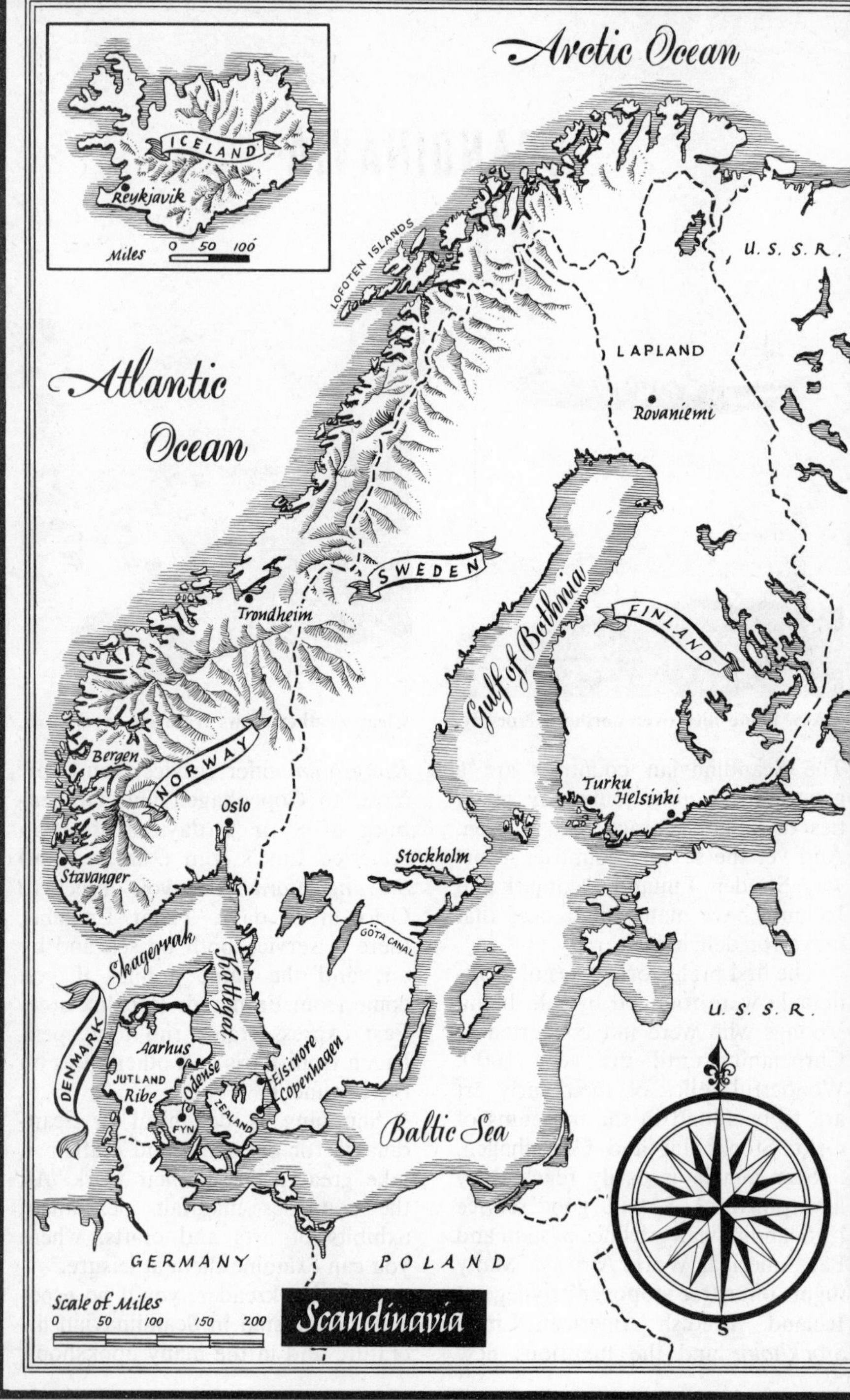

Scandinavia

n Henningsvaer Harbor, Lofoten Islands, nearly 1000 fishing boats moor for week end.

RUGGED NORWAY HAS MIDNIGHT SUN

Norway is a long, rangy country, with terrific distances, but you'll find the magnificent scenery worth the travel. People everywhere are friendly, from the cosmopolitan residents of Oslo to the Lapps of Nordland, "Land of the Midnight Sun." The fjords, deep inlets from sea, are nation's most spectacular sight.

Photo: Robert Capa (Magnum)

Across Oslo harbor, you see the new City Hall, inaugurated in 1950 during the

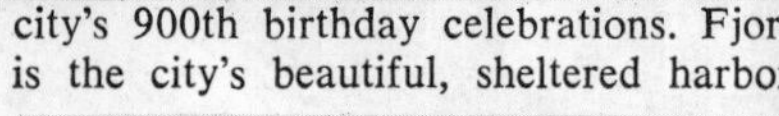
city's 900th birthday celebrations. Fjor is the city's beautiful, sheltered harbo

Statue of Henrik Ibsen, famous for his plays, stands before the National Theater.

Oslo University, founded 1811, has beaut ful buildings. Also visit Nobel Institut

Photos: Norwegian National Travel Offi

Oslo is modern in design, with planned business and residential neighborhoods.

"Karl Johans Gate" is the main business street, from station to Royal Palace.

Oslo's parks are famous. This is flower market, in the city. Holmenkollen, in hills behind town, gives a magnificent view. Bygdoy Museum has the *Kon-Tiki* raft.

Photos: Norwegian National Travel Office

Norway

Geiranger Fjord is noted for the Pulpit, a rock promontory, Bridal Veil Falls.

Trondheim is Norway's 3rd city, seapc and gateway to north. This is marke

Bergen, Norway's 2nd largest city, has miles of docks, old Hanseatic buildings dating from early 16th century when th League dominated the commercial lif

Photos: Norwegian National Travel Offic top right, Burton Holmes (Ewing Galloway

otunheim Mountains, in south central Norway, are popular for hiking. Legend says these majestic mountains, with 8,097 ft. peak, are home of "Jotuns," or giants.

Norwegian children might have stepped out of the pages of *"Leif the Lucky."*

Chair lift at Krokkleiva outside Oslo gives mountain climbing thrill easy way.

Heddel Stav church, Telemark, is one of thirty 700- to 900-year-old timber churches.

Market place at Stavanger: This 8th-century city is one of Norway's oldest.

Photos: Norwegian National Travel Office

Stockholm's many waterways and canals give it the title of "the Venice of the North." At top right is City Hall, most magnificent modern building in Europe

SWEDEN OFFERS A GAY VÄLKOMMEN!

Sweden has everything to attract the tourist: it's the land of smörgåsbord and wonderful things to eat; it shares marvelous scenery and such natural phenomena as the midnight sun with its neighbor, Norway; and happy, vigorous Swedes like visitors, make them welcome

Photo: Swedish National Travel Office

oyal Dramatic Theater saw debuts of reta Garbo, Ingrid Bergman, others.

From gardens of City Hall, you see older area called "City between the Bridges."

npressive Grand Hotel is located at he fashionable resort of Saltsjöbaden in the Stockholm archipelago, about one hour's trip from the center of the city.

'hotos: Swedish Na-
ional Travel Office

Fiddlers of Dalarna Province preserve charming customs and manner of dress.

St. Lucia's Day, December 13, is celebrated by girls wearing candle crowns.

Lapland extends across the northern e of Norway, Sweden, Finland, and nort

Sofia Girls demonstrate their grace and rhythm at Jubilee celebration in Town Hall gardens. Swedes love to keep fit.

Stout fishing boa put out into Balti

Photos: Swedish National Travel Offi

west extremity of USSR. Mount Akka, in Swedish Lapland, is one of the most beautiful mountains in the country, with parts of it covered by eternal snows.

from Karlshamn port. Sport fishing is good.

Regattas in the Stockholm archipelago demonstrate skillful boat-handling of Swedish sailors, "born" with the knowledge.

Sweden

Arsta Railway Bridge, Stockholm, frames the modern Southern General Hospital.

View of Skeppsbron docks shows man boats that go to coastal points, Finlan

The Old City, also called "The City between the Bridges," is the oldest part of

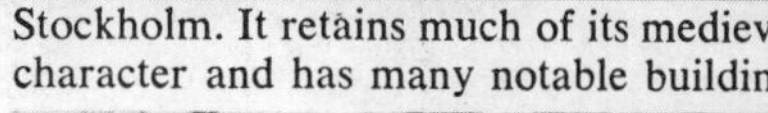

Stockholm. It retains much of its mediev character and has many notable buildin

The Kvikkjokk region of Lapland, with many lakes, rivers, has rich vegetation.

Gota Canal offers charming steamer trip 350 miles, Gothenburg to Stockholm

Photos: Swedish National Trave Office; top left, Uno Kaba bottom right, Konstantin Kostic

THIS IS PARLIAMENT IN HELSINKI, "WHITE CITY OF THE NORTH."

FINLAND IS MODERN AND CORDIAL

Finland is known for its ultra-modern architecture, sunlit nights, beautiful scenery. Its people are blond, blue-eyed, and hospitable. If you want a vacation in an off-the-beaten-track country that offers some of the best facilities for comfort, your answer is Finland, a democratic republic that is ripe for discovery.

Photo: Finnish National Travel Office

Helsinki Stadium, site of 1952 Olympic Games, shows sport-mindedness of Finns.

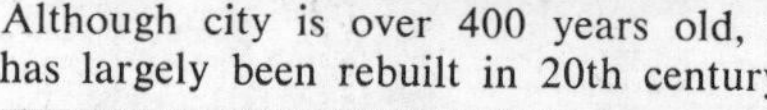

Although city is over 400 years old, i has largely been rebuilt in 20th century

In front of National Theater is statue of Aleksis Kivi, 19th-century novelist.

"Havis Amanda" statue symbolizes "The Maid Helsinki rising from the waters."

Photos: Finnish National Travel Office

Rovaniemi, capital of Finnish Lapland, is just south of the Arctic Circle. It is a winter-sports center and the trading and administrative center of that area.

Pallastunturi Inn, in Finnish Lapland, is good center for winter sports. There's skiing, hiking, hunting, salmon fishing. It's nearly 700 miles north of Helsinki.

Reindeer are frequent sight in Lapland; they pull a narrow sledge called *pulkka.*

Lapp newlyweds show colorful costumes, the men with white reindeer fur *peski.*

Photos: Finnish National Travel Office

Finland

Olavinlinna Castle is in East Finland's lake region at summer spa of Savonlinna.

Aulanko National Park is top resort and recreation area. This is Hotel Aulanko.

The Sauna, famous Finnish steam bath, is fixture of every home and of many hotels

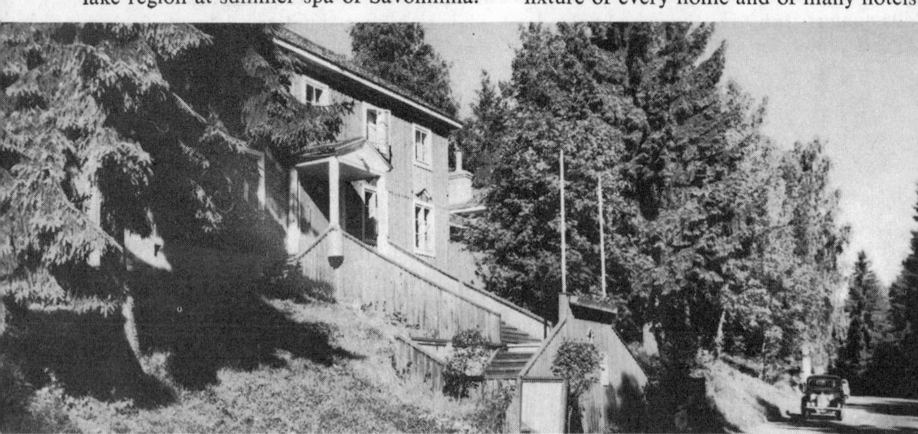

Vehoniemi Tourist Inn is a delightful stopping place in south central Finland. From here you can go by water bus through lake regions to Aulanko Park

Photos: Finnish National Travel Office

COPENHAGEN'S DANISH RENAISSANCE TOWN HALL WAS BUILT IN 1894.

FOR FRIENDLINESS, COME TO DENMARK

Among the predominant characteristics of Denmark are friendliness, flowers and song. The nation consists of the peninsula of Jutland and some 500 islands, including the large ones of Fyn and Zealand, the island that contains the capital city of Copenhagen, often called with good reason "the Paris of Scandinavia."

Photo: Danish National Travel Office

Denmark COPENHAGEN

Gefion Fountain is at beginning of Langelinie, delightful walk beside the sea.

Statue of "The Little Mermaid" is based on one of Andersen's noted fairy tales.

The Tivoli is beautifully landscaped amusement park in the center of town, where you can hear symphony, dance, dine, attend famous pantomime theater.

Photos: Danish National Travel Office

The Banqueting Hall in Christiansborg Castle is used by the King to receive in

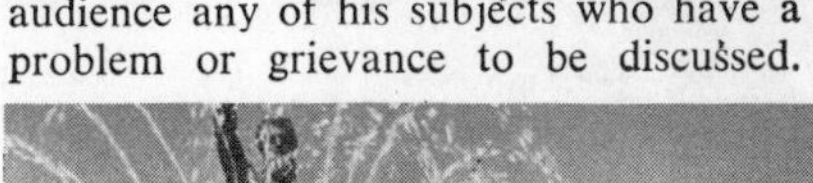

audience any of his subjects who have a problem or grievance to be discussed.

Church of Our Savior has an uncommon winding stairs on *outside* of the spire.

Frederiksborg Palace, in suburb of Copenhagen, now houses Historical Museum.

Photos: Danish National Travel Office

Palace of Amalienborg is the present royal residence, and the Changing of the Guard takes place there at noon daily, with waving flags, fanfare of trumpets.

Photo: Danish National Travel Office

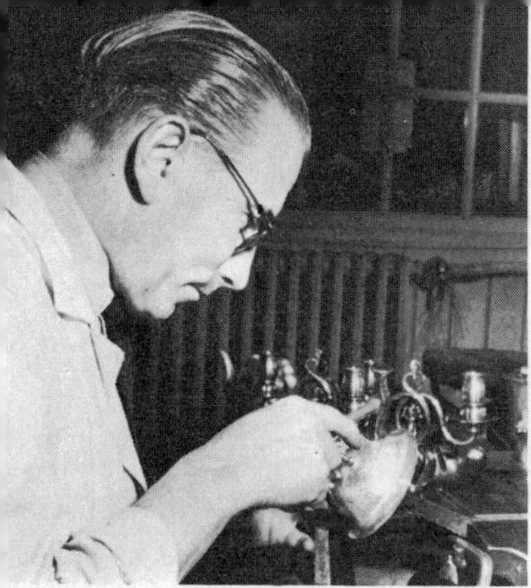

ilver is Denmark's top shopping attrac-ion; Georg Jensen is most famous name.

Tivoli restaurants are good places to try the celebrated Danish smørrebrød.

t going-to-work time and quitting time bicycle avalanche sweeps the streets.

As fresh hauls are brought in, fisher-women clean them at quayside market.

The large sight-seeing motorboats that ly the canals take visitors past many of the most interesting parts of the city. Christiansborg Castle tower is at left.

Photos: Danish National Travel Office; top right, Konstantin Ko-stich; center right, A. Milton Runyon

Denmark

Rosenholm Castle, in charming Jutland setting, is one of beautiful old castles.

Folk dances are performed at open-ai Museum at Lyngby, near Copenhagen

Archways of Christiansborg Castle glow with the lights of a midwinter evening.

Unobtrusive doorway on a Copenhage street opens to this lovely old courtyard

Professor Olsen is one of the master designers of Royal Copenhagen Porcelain.

Hans Christian Andersen's character live on in Royal Copenhagen figurines

Photos: Danish National Travel Office; center, David Grunbaum, A. Milton Runyon; top right, bottom left, Konstantin Kostich

ı this little house in Odense, great
ory teller Andersen lived as a child.

utumn sunshine gives mystic quality to
npressive towers of Rosenborg Castle.

ound Tower at Regensen, built by King
hristian V, now serves as observatory.

Odense, 3rd largest city of Denmark, has cathedral honoring Saint Canute.

Ribe is one of the fairytale towns of Denmark where storks nest on the roofs.

ıotos: Danish National Travel Of-
ce; center left, David Grunbaum

Old town of Randers was important commercial center back in the Middle Ages.

Aarhus, Denmark's second city, has Tov Hall that's ultramodern in architectu

Probably the smallest Town Hall in the world is to be found in Aebeltoft, Jut-

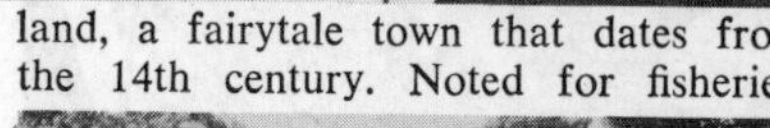

land, a fairytale town that dates fro the 14th century. Noted for fisherie

Late autumn sunshine casts long shadows of strollers in Royal Square, Copenhagen.

The Jelling Runic Stone was erected i year 980 by King Harald the Bluetooth

Photos: Danish National Travel Offic top left, bottom left, David Grunbaur

cient guns guard Kronborg Castle, the sinore Castle" of the play, *Hamlet*.

Children's Day celebration is one of the many expressions of Danish gaiety.

ronborg Castle at Elsinore is the an- ıal setting for the "Hamlet Festival." From heights of the ramparts you can see the not-far-distant coast of Sweden.

ɔvely Danish countryside is best seen ɔwly, traveling by bicycle or car. In small town you may come across peasants and fishermen in charming old costumes.

otos: Konstantin Kostich; center, nish National Travel Office

Reykjavik, capital of Iceland, is chief port of nation, commercial and fishing center. Unique hot-water supply syster built 1945, utilizes natural hot spring

Gullfoss gets its name of "Golden Fall" from double rainbow seen in its spray.

ICELAND IS ONE O NEWER REPUBLIC

The first permanent settlement of Ic land was made in 874. The Althing, general assembly, was established in 93 and is the oldest legislative body the world still in existence. After referendum in 1944, the union with De mark was ended and the new republic w proclaimed.

Average annual temperature at tl capital ranges from 30° in January 52° in July. Only about a quarter the land is habitable, mainly the wes north and east coasts. Iceland is tl westernmost state of Europe, 500 mil northwest of Scotland. It is complete "different," a magic, bewitching lan

Photos: Ewing Galloway; botto Hans Malmben (Black Sta

EUROPE

Because we have reserved southern Europe for the Mediterranean Cruise ection, this part covers France, the three Benelux countries, western Germany, Switzerland and western Austria. To get to this part of the ontinent from the United States, ou are faced with the same happy ilemma: which way to travel? If ou are of the school of thought that believes in stepping at once into the and of your choice, you can do so y boarding one of the foreign-flag arriers in New York. France offers he new *France,* the *Liberté* and *Flandre,* and the services of Air France. The Netherlands boasts the *Nieuw Amsterdam* and the smaller ships of Holland-America line, and KLM, the Royal Dutch Airlines. Switzerland and Belgium have no ships, but Swissair gives service of Swiss punctuality, and Sabena treats ou royally on the way to Belgium.

On the way home, or on the way over, for that matter, you may want o try the superlative service that American lines offer. In ships, we have the great *United States* and proud *America.* And in the air, we rejoice in the dependability of Pan American World Airways and TWA Trans World Airline. Of course, you also have excellent service to the continent by Britain's great Cunard-rs which let you off at Le Havre or Cherbourg. And BOAC connects with all air services.

You travel in comfort on "Blue Train."

When you arrive on the continent, there are travel choices, too. You may want to hire a car, as so many people are now doing. The railroads have many de luxe trains with romantic names, *Golden Arrow, Blue Train, Orient Express.* Busses are becoming increasingly popular, with good services like Europabus being able to take you by more attractive roads, and wait for you while you do your sightseeing. Quickest way to get from city to city on longer hauls is by air, either by one of the services mentioned above, or by British European Airways and Scandinavian Airlines which have very good continental networks.

Now turn the page for a preview, or postview, of your great journey.

Photo: French National Railroads

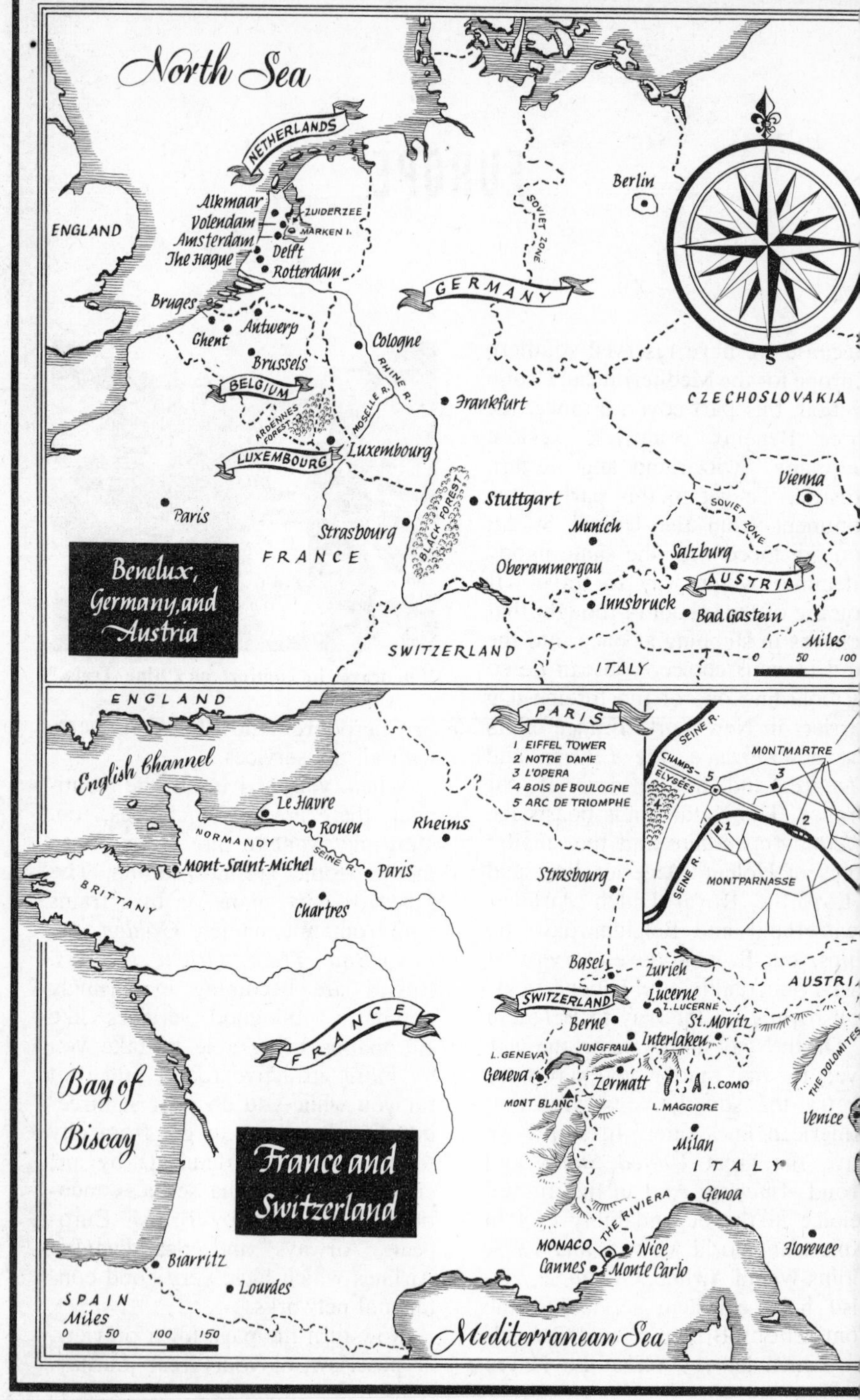
North Sea
NETHERLANDS
ENGLAND
Alkmaar
Volendam
Amsterdam
The Hague
ZUIDERZEE
MARKEN I.
Delft
Rotterdam
Bruges
Ghent
Antwerp
Brussels
BELGIUM
ARDENNES FOREST
LUXEMBOURG
Luxembourg
MOSELLE R.
RHINE R.
Cologne
Frankfurt
GERMANY
SOVIET ZONE
Berlin
CZECHOSLOVAKIA
Paris
Strasbourg
BLACK FOREST
Stuttgart
Munich
Oberammergau
Salzburg
Vienna
SOVIET ZONE
AUSTRIA
Innsbruck
Bad Gastein
FRANCE
SWITZERLAND
ITALY
Miles
0 50 100
S
Benelux, Germany, and Austria
ENGLAND
English Channel
Le Havre
Rouen
Rheims
NORMANDY
SEINE R.
Paris
Mont-Saint-Michel
BRITTANY
Chartres
PARIS
1 EIFFEL TOWER
2 NOTRE DAME
3 L'OPERA
4 BOIS DE BOULOGNE
5 ARC DE TRIOMPHE
SEINE R.
CHAMPS ELYSÉES
MONTMARTRE
MONTPARNASSE
Strasbourg
Basel
Zurich
AUSTRI
SWITZERLAND
Lucerne
L. LUCERNE
Berne
St. Moritz
JUNGFRAU
Interlaken
L. GENEVA
Geneva
Zermatt
L. COMO
MONT BLANC
L. MAGGIORE
THE DOLOMITES
Venice
Milan
ITALY
FRANCE
Bay of Biscay
France and Switzerland
THE RIVIERA
Genoa
MONACO
Nice
Cannes
Monte Carlo
Florence
Biarritz
Lourdes
SPAIN
Miles
0 50 100 150
Mediterranean Sea

AMSTERDAM HAS 1,000 CANALS, MOST GOING DIRECTLY THROUGH CITY.

HOLLAND MEANS WINDMILLS, TULIPS

The Netherlands is a compact country, about one and a half times the size of Massachusetts. Because a quarter of the land is below sea level, as much as 21 feet, it has to be protected by dikes, windmills and electric pumps. Holland has picturesque old towns, villages that cling to old customs, and modern cities.

Photo: Three Lions

Glass-top passenger boat traverses the Amstel River. Dam on this river, from

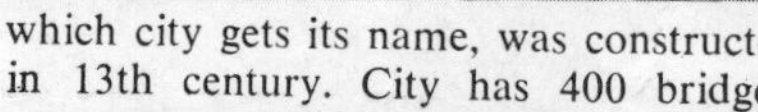

which city gets its name, was constructe in 13th century. City has 400 bridge

Kalverstraat, with its many silversmiths, and Leidschestraat are shopping centers.

Rijksmuseum has fine Dutch and Fler ish paintings, Rembrandt's *Night Watc*

Photos: Netherlands National Tourist Offic bottom left, Netherlands Information Servic

Flower vendor displays her blooms beside Amsterdam's ancient Powder Tower.

Hotel L'Europe has steps at its front door giving easy access to the canal.

Royal Palace, on Dam Square, is not the Queen's home, is used for state affairs.

Amsterdam is a world-famous center for the cutting and polishing of diamonds.

Photos: Netherlands National Tourist Office; top left, Konstantin Kostich

Peace Palace at The Hague, built 1913, now houses the International Court of Justice under the UN. The Hague is one of the most beautiful cities of Europe.

Parliament Buildings: The Hague is not the capital, but is seat of government.

The Royal Family arrives at "Hall of Knights" for the opening of Parliament.

Photos: Burton Holmes (Ewing Galloway); Netherlands National Tourist Office; Netherlands Information Service

Delft, five miles from The Hague, is one of the most typical old Dutch towns.

A center for ceramics, Delft sends its blue china and pottery all over world.

Rotterdam, principal Netherlands port, is rising anew from 1940 devastation.

On the lake at Sneek, northern Holland, many international regattas take place.

Photos: Netherlands National Tourist Office; bottom right, Konstantin Kostich

Netherlands

Scheveningen, fashionable sea resort near The Hague, has annual Music Festival.

In Alkmaar, cheese market comes to life on Friday mornings, May to September.

Kampen is an ancient city with town hall many buildings dating to 14th century

Breda was site of treaty that gave New York and New Jersey colonies to British

Cheeses come to Alkmaar by barge, are unloaded by men with traditional garb.

Photos: Netherlands National Tourist Office; bottom right, Netherlands Information Service

BELGIUM DISPLAYS MANY TREASURES FOR VISITORS

ANTWERP IS RIVALED ONLY BY ROTTERDAM AS TOP EUROPEAN PORT.

Belgium is a tiny country, 175 miles at its greatest length, but it is a tremendous treasure house of Flemish painting and Renaissance architecture. Here, oil painting began at least as early as in Italy. Another of Belgium's great tourist attractions is its forty miles of fine beaches, with resorts like Spa, Ostend and Knokke-LeZoute. Still another magnet is green beauty of Ardennes forest.

Photo: Le Mont (Ewing Galloway)

Fortress-like Steen is one of the few traces left of medieval Antwerp. Parts date back to the 10th century; during 13th century the castle was a prison.

Not all windmills are in Holland. This impressive one is on the way to Ghent.

Fountain of the Nymphs stands in front of Antwerp's late Gothic guild houses.

Photos: Three Lions; bottom left, Pan American World Airways

athedral of Notre Dame, Antwerp's incomparable Gothic structure, was built in 14th and 15th centuries, has 400-ft. spire. Contains several Rubens paintings.

hoto: Ewing Galloway

Center of Brussels is *Grand' Place,* site of original 10th century settlement. Here are situated Town Hall (above), begun in 14th century, and medieval guildhalls

Photo: Pan American World Airways

Arcade Cinquantenaire opens on a park and connects two galleries, one containing military antiquities, the other an art collection with rare ivories, enamels.

Brussels, capital of Belgium, is center of country's banking and commercial life, and one of Europe's richest, most beautiful cities. Town square has flower stalls.

Photos: Ewing Galloway; bottom, Pan American World Airways

Ghent is main city of East Flanders, has 10th century cathedral, old guildhalls.

Bruges (right) is Flemish for bridges; more than 50 cross the canals of this famed medieval town dating from the 7th century. Caxton learned printing here.

Photos: Pan American World Airways; right, Ewing Galloway

The Citadel rises atop a cliff in Dinant on the Meuse, with 13th century church in foreground. This resort town is not[illegible] for copper handicrafts, Montfat grotto[illegible]

The cathedral at Tournai is one of the most notable in Belgium, with Romanesque towers, a Gothic choir. Contains famous paintings by Jordaens, Massys, etc

Photos: Three Lions; bottom Official Belgian Tourist Burea[illegible]

350,000 AMERICANS SEE FRANCE YEARLY

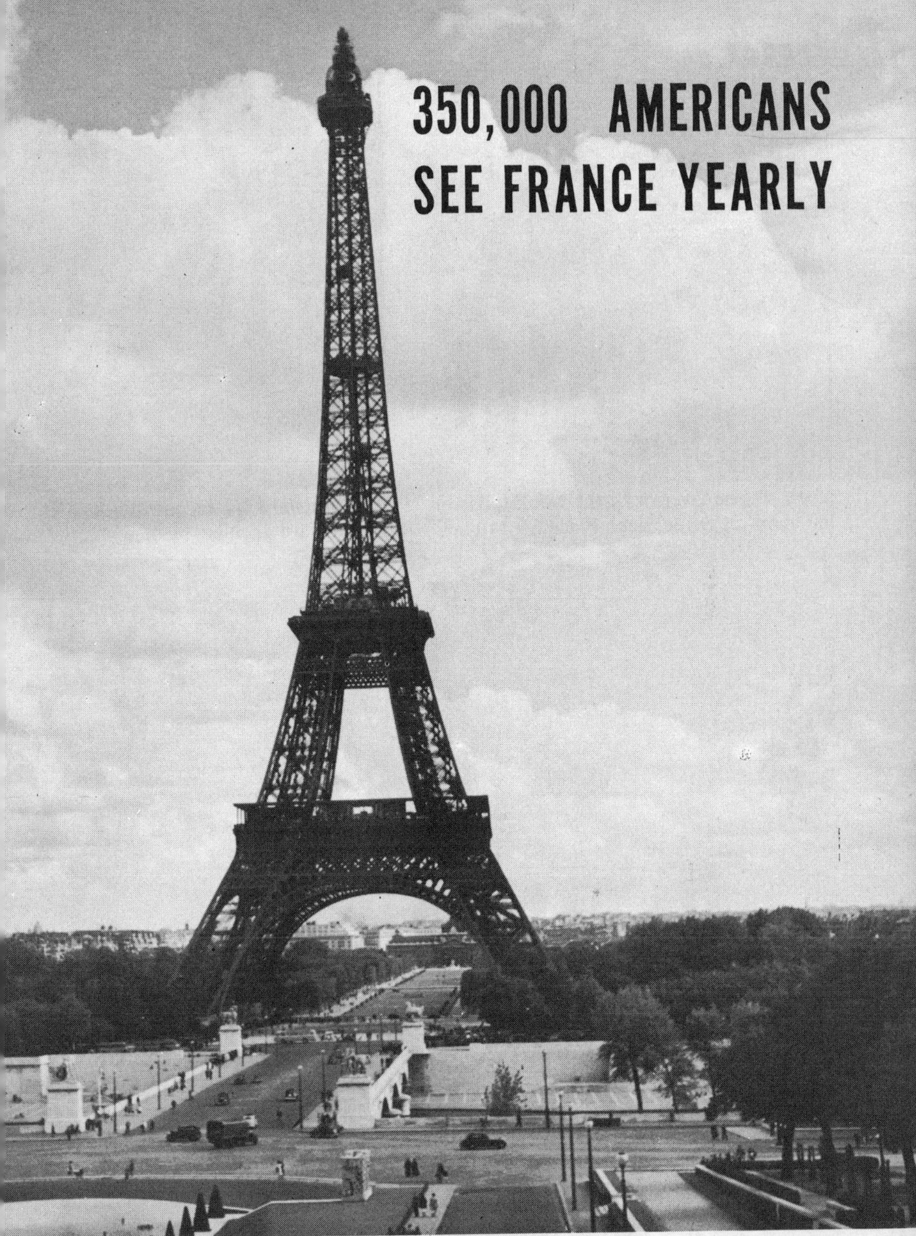

EIFFEL TOWER, TRADEMARK OF PARIS, REACHES 984 FEET INTO SKY.

The one spot that most Americans going abroad head for is Paris, the city that "has everything for everyone." And the whole of France is a land of enormous variety: the quaint towns of Normandy and Brittany, the glorious sun-deck of the Riviera, the magnificent Chateau Country, winter sports in the French Alps. And everywhere, but everywhere, the food makes travelers pigs in clover.

Photo: Konstantin Kostich

Notre Dame overlooks the bookstalls on left bank of Seine, near Place St. Michel.

Fashion show by Jacques Fath: Feminin visitors are thrilled by new "collection.

Cathedral of Notre Dame has impressive location on tiny Île de la Cité in the Seine, the oldest part of Paris. You can climb the tower, see great 13-ton bell.

Photos: A. L. Koolish; top right, Konstantin Kostich; bottom, TWA Trans World Airline

Île St. Louis is next to Île de la Cité; they're like two ships in the Seine, moored by bridges like Pont de la Tournelle (above). It's quiet, lonely here.

The Panthéon is the burial place of the patron saint of Paris, Saint Genevieve.

The Madeleine church is built like a Roman temple, with Corinthian colonnade.

Photos: French Government Tourist Office

Magnificent Opera House is the largest theater in the world, although it has fewer seats than the Châtelet or Milan's La Scala. Façade is lavishly decorated.

Sacré-Coeur, on top of Montmartre, is oriental-looking church of white stone.

Little streets in Montmartre, full of cafés, tiny shops, lead to Sacré-Coeur.

Photos: French Government Tourist Office; bottom left, A. L. Koolish; bottom right, Pan American World Airways

Artist paints in front of tiny 12th century church of St. Julien-le-Pauvre.

Vendôme Column has bronze bas-reliefs made from cannon Napoleon captured.

Arc de Triomphe du Carrousel is reduced copy of the Arch of Septimius Severus in Rome. On top is a bronze chariot group. Building in background is the Louvre.

Photos: French Government Tourist Office

Bois de Boulogne is huge park on west side of Paris, with lakes and ponds, two race tracks—Auteuil and Longchamp lovely drives and fine summer restaurants

Métro is elaborate system of fourteen underground railways, with interchanges.

Les Invalides, founded as home for disabled soldiers, contains Napoleon's tomb

Photos: French Government Tourist Office

The Foreign Legion parades down the tree-lined Champs-Elysées to celebrate July 14th, Bastille Day, or Fête Nationale. At top is the great *Arc de Triomphe.*

Les Halles are the great Paris produce markets, where you wind up a big night at four a.m. for a bowl of onion soup with the farmers and market workers.

The Sorbonne, the University of Paris, was started in 1253 as theological school.

Gardens of the Palais-Royal make quiet park near the fashionable shopping area.

Photos: French Government Tourist Office

Auteuil, in the Bois de Boulogne, has steeplechases, Longchamp has flat racing.

Kiosks for newspapers and magazines are distinctive sight along Paris boulevards.

Palais du Luxembourg, once a royal residence, is noted for beautiful gardens.

Marché aux Puces, or "Flea Market," has art, antiques, bargains for skillful buyers.

Photos: French Government Tourist Office

Arc de Triomphe is the largest triumphal arch in the world, 160 feet high. Ride to top for magnificent view, since avenues radiate from arch in all directions.

Beautiful Sainte-Chapelle was built by St. Louis as shrine for Crown of Thorns.

The Bourse is the Paris stock exchange, housed in building like a Roman temple.

Photos: A. Milton Runyon; bottom right, French Government Tourist Office

Shops line arcaded Rue de Rivoli. Rue de Castiglione leads to Place Vendôme.

Comédie-Française does plays of Molière, other greats, as well as modern drama.

Folies Bergère is probably best known music hall in the world, famous for the elaborateness of its shows, with some three hours of beauty, music and color.

Photos: French Government Tourist Office

posing western façade of great Palace Versailles has 375 windows, many in Hall of Mirrors where World War I treaty was signed. Palace housed 10,000.

½-mile trip to Versailles gardens is popular Sunday outing for Parisians.

Versailles fountains play on certain Sundays, are sometimes lighted at night.

tos: A. Milton Runyon; bottom right, nch Government Tourist Office

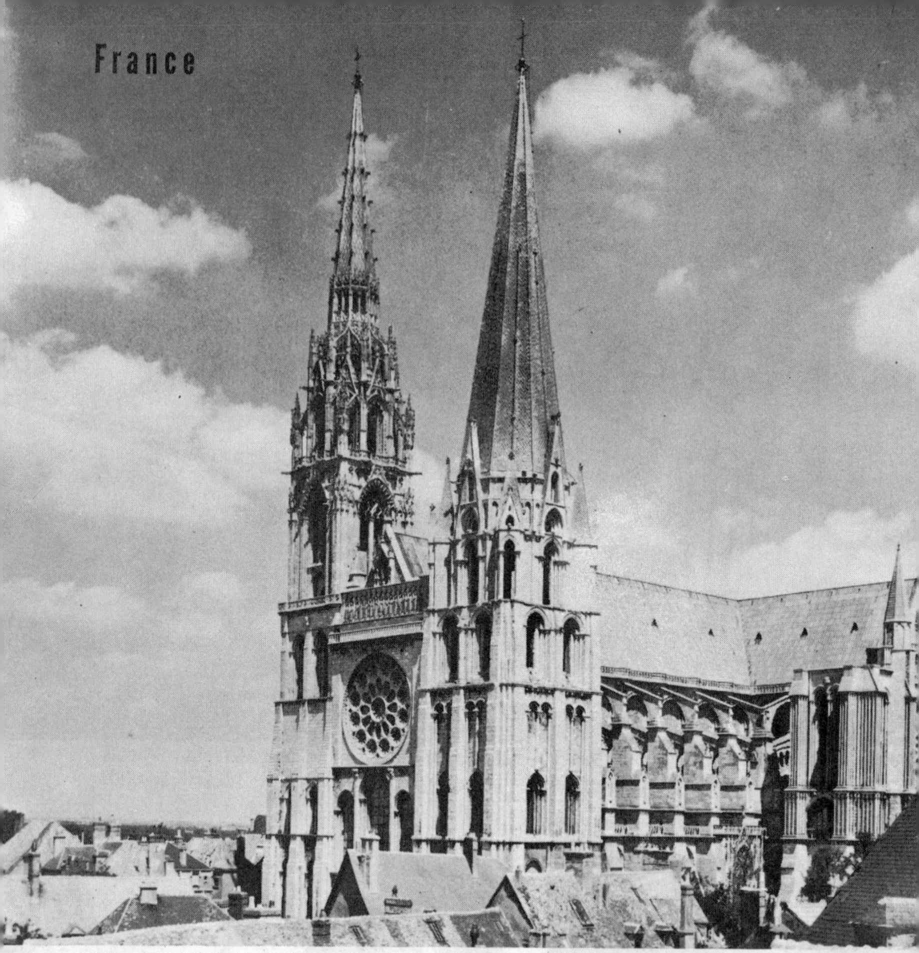

Chartres Cathedral is noted for stained glass, sculpture, and two lofty spires, 375 ft. and 350 ft. Ornate taller one work of gifted artist Jehan de Beu

Fontainebleau, second in interest only to Versailles, has lovely forest nearby.

La Malmaison was scene of literary a artistic salon of Josephine Bonapar

Photos: TWA Trans World Airline; bo tom right, French Government Tourist Offi

tat, 15 miles from Le Havre, is re- with beach flanked by white cliffs.

Port of Le Havre, with 2 big breakwaters, accommodates liners big as *United States.*

fleur, picturesque seaport at mouth of e, has 15th century wooden church.

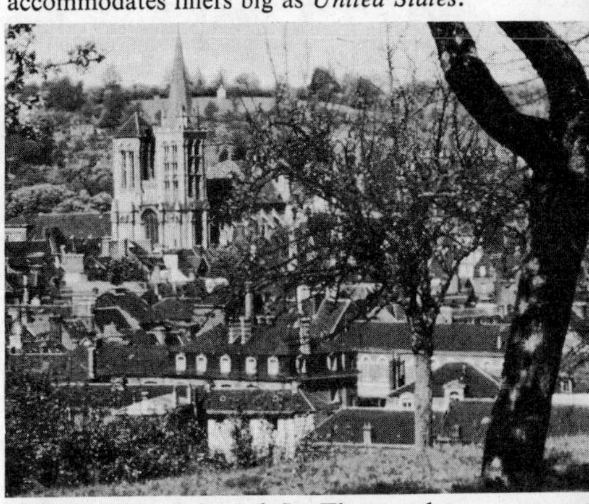

Lisieux, with shrine of St. Theresa, has become an important place of pilgrimage.

uisite lace is made in Chartres, Le , Alençon, treasured everywhere.

Vierville-sur-Mer was "Omaha Beach" of 1944 American landings in Normandy.

os: French Government Tourist e; bottom left, Richard Joseph

Mont-Saint-Michel is the great "citadel in the sea" connected with mainland by mile-long causeway. Abbey, founded 708, is France's greatest tourist me

Saint-Servan (above) is part of resort area that includes Saint-Malo, Paramé.

Novelist Chateaubriand spent his hood in this castle near Saint-M

Photos: Konstantin Kostich; bot
French Government Tourist O

nan, with medieval walls, towers, is pping place on way to Brittany coast.

Douarnenez is near tip of Brittany, picturesque fishing port for lobster, tuna.

atched cottages of Normandy are like ir British cousins, even more homey.

Concarneau fishing boats go out into Bay of Biscay in search of sardines, tuna.

tos: French Govern-
t Tourist Office

France

Rheims Cathedral, begun 1211, century in building, is French national symbol.

Grosse Horloge, Renaissance clock tov is feature of Rouen, port city on Se

Champagne grapes, grown on Île-de-France crest, are processed at Rheims.

Hay wagons, and signs advertis *apéritif* wines, are often seen on roa

Photos: French Government Tou Office; bottom left, Konsta Kostich; bottom right, Richard Jo

nonceaux was the home of Diane de iers, mistress of Henry II. Unique feature is bridge over Cher river, built by Delorme for Catherine de' Medici.

mbord, the great castle of François I, ds in the midst of 13,344 acre park. The roof is remarkable for its pinnacles, sculptured chimneys, spires, and capitals.

umont, with its massive feudal towers, chateau used by Catherine de' Medici.

Church at Saint-Cyr: Balzac and Anatole France lived in this village on Loire.

s: French Govern- Tourist Office

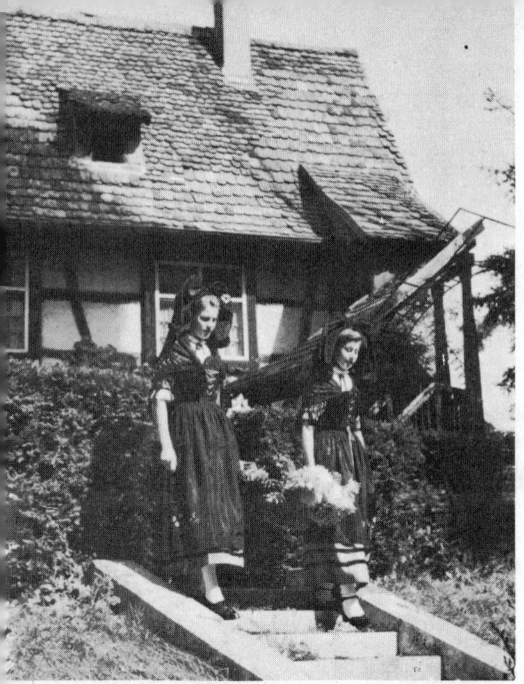

Girls of Alsace still wear long plaits, and the traditional big-bowed costumes.

Strasbourg is capital of Alsace, and of the great artistic centers of Eu

Château de Haut-Koenigsbourg, on high Vosges peak, looks across to Germany.

Colmar, "Little Venice," is lovely t of ancient houses along the River La

Photos: French Go ment Tourist C

amonix is leading summer and winter ort of the French Alps, dominated by

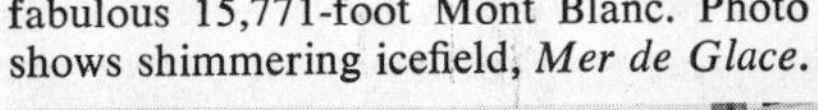

fabulous 15,771-foot Mont Blanc. Photo shows shimmering icefield, *Mer de Glace*.

ble railway carries skiers, tourists to at view from top of Mont Brévent.

La Clusaz is tiny winter sports resort on road between Chamonix, Annecy.

tos: French Govern- t Tourist Office

Biarritz, on Bay of Biscay, is one of France's most fashionable resorts. Its 7-mile beach, mild climate attracted Na leon III, Empress Eugenie, other roya

Basilica at Lourdes ranks next to Rome as leading Catholic place of pilgrimage.

Thousands come annually to be cure grotto where St. Bernadette saw vis

Photos: French Gov ment Tourist C

ies-de-Béarn, with charming homes, health resort just east of Biarritz.

Cauterets, with its hot sulphur springs, is spa and resort of central Pyrenees.

ke of Gaube, near Cauterets, is fine ot for hiking amid scenic splendor.

Basque game of pelote is well attended at the village of Saint-Jean-Pied-de-Port.

uring Middle Ages, Saint-Jean was end much-traveled mountain pass to Spain.

Dances of the Basque country are vigorous, colorful as the costumes of dancers.

otos: French Govern- nt Tourist Office

Cannes is headquarters for the British colony on the Côte d'Azur, and yachting

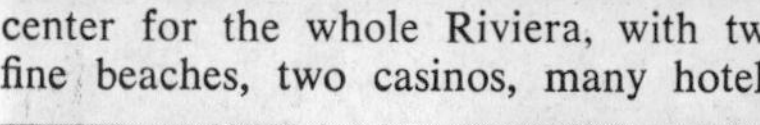

center for the whole Riviera, with tw fine beaches, two casinos, many hotel

St. Jean is an old fishing port at tip of lovely Cap Ferrat, abode of the wealthy.

Walking is a pleasure on Cap Ferrat, f autos are barred from many promenade

Photos: Konstantin Kostich; botto left, French Government Tourist O fice; bottom right, Richard Josep

'uisine at Nice is mixture of Parisian, rovincial and Italian—and wonderful!

Nice, Queen of the Riviera, is a major city as well as most fashionable resort.

lenton is at the very tip of the Riviera, ith the Italian frontier at its edge. Many habitués like it because the Alpes-Maritimes loom right over the beaches.

otos: French Government Tourist 'fice; top left, Richard Joseph

Prince's Palace is guarded, but there's no customs barrier at Monaco frontier.

MONACO IS 370 ACRES OF GAIETY

Next to Vatican City, Monaco is the world's smallest state. It has a population of 20,000, but only about 2,000 are actually citizens or Monégasques. They are not allowed in the Casino, but they don't have to pay taxes because the Casino at Monte Carlo makes sufficient money to finance the whole principality. Monaco has been independent ever since the end of the Napoleonic Wars, in 1815.

Monte Carlo Casino is world famous, not only for its roulette wheels and other intricate forms of gambling, but also for a first-class theater and concert room.

Photos: Pan American World Airways

UNICH IS FAMOUS FOR MARDI GRAS FESTIVITIES, COSTUME BALLS.

OMANTIC GERMANY OMES TO NEW LIFE

West Germany, the German Federal Republic, has much to offer the tourist: its old medieval towns, gray with age, its majestic rivers and idyllic landscapes. While the people are throwing much of their energy into reconstruction, they have time for fun, and Germany now has some of the gayest night life in Europe. Frankfurt is good place for first stop.

to: Robert Copa (Magnum)

Pension Anton Lang at Oberammergau: Passion Play is performed every 10 years.

Oberammergau Play is now presented in modern theater, needs 1250 performers.

Between Passion Plays, the residents of Oberammergau carve religious figures.

Photos: A. L. Koolish; center left and Danube River, German Tourist Information Office; bottom left, TWA Trans World Airline

Germany

Garmisch-Partenkirchen, site of Olymp winter games in 1936, is great ski reso

anube River at Riedlingen (below): fter the Volga, it's continent's longest.

Ehrenfels Castle is 13th century relic, amid terraced vineyards on Rhine river.

Lindau is old town on an island in Lake Constance, with bridges to mainland.

Kehlsteinhaus at Berchtesgaden looks out over the beautiful Salzburg Alps.

Photos: German Tourist Information Office; top, Charles Marschalek

Heidelberg, on Neckar river, is noted for country's most famous university, and for Heidelberg Castle, imposing rui built and rebuilt over past 700 year

Mainz, one of Germany's great historical cities, celebrates Rose Monday Festival.

The Black Forest has modest ski lodge plush resort centers like Baden-Bader

"Trinkhalle" at Baden-Baden is lovel spot to imbibe healthful spring water

Photos: German Tour ist Information Offic

logne at night: majestic cathedral stained only slight damage in the war. Begun in 1248, it was completed in 1880; contains relics of Wise Men of the East.

erlin's main street, Kurfürstendamm, is ain busy with shopping, entertainment. This is view of the restored boulevard as it looks from the Kempinski Hotel.

otos: German Tour- Information Office

AUSTRIA IS LAND OF ALPS, GREEN VALLEYS, AND MUSIC

Austria, the "heart of Europe," is famed for its towering Alps, its meadows and forests and villages, and its wealth of entertainment, climaxed by the Salzburg Music Festival. You'll enjoy seeing t gay Tyrolean costumes, flowered shaw and dirndls. You'll wander in fair tale villages like this one in the Tyr

Kitzbühel is a Tyrolean medieval town that is both winter and summer resort.

Innsbruck's Maria Theresa Street lea toward high peaks of the Eastern Al

Photos: Austrian State Tourist D partment; top, Konstantin Kost

ıe Graben, the "moat," is now principal ɔpping street in great city of Vienna.

ılvedere Palace was built for Prince ıgene who kept the Turks out of Europe.

ienna's Opera House, one of world's nowned, is only one at street level.

otos: Austrian State Tourist Depart- ɪnt; top left, Charles Marschalek; top ht, Pan American World Airways

St. Stephen's Cathedral, consecrated in 1147, has slender 448-foot Gothic spire.

The famous "white horses of Vienna" give performance at Salzburg Festival.

How to climb an ice wall is taught at the High Alpine School at Heiligenblut.

At Salzburg Festival, Hofmannsthal's "Jedermann" is staged on the domplatz.

Church at St. Wolfgang contains Pach altar, world's most valuable wood carvin

Zell am See, because of conjunction air currents, is ideal place for glidin

Peasant festival at Schwaz: This is typical feature of the Austrian scene

Photos: Austrian State Tourist Department bottom left, Pan American World Airway

SWITZERLAND MEANS MOUNTAINS AND WATCHES AND CHOCOLATES

JUNGFRAU'S MIGHTY 13,650-FT. PEAK WAS FIRST CLIMBED IN 1811.

In winter, Switzerland is unquestionably the winter sports capital of the world, and the glistening snow brings bright new beauty to its tremendous mountains. In summer, the sparkling lake resorts are at their best. Throughout the year, the country is one of boundless hospitality with some of the best food and the most comfortable hotels in the world. If you like creature comforts, this is for you!

Photo: A. L. Koolish

This is a typical holiday home in Swiss chalet style, at Villars-sur-Ollon, Vaud.

League of Nations buildings at Genev symbolize Switzerland as great neutral

Calvin Memorial in Geneva's *Promenade des Bastions* hails freedom of religion.

The Lake of Geneva is enlivened by many trim excursion steamers which take you from Geneva, at west end of lake, to Lausanne, Vevey, Montreux, other points.

Photos: Swiss National Travel Office; top right, TWA Trans World Airline

astle of Chillon, near Montreux on Lake eneva, is one of the best preserved medieval castles in Europe—the scene of Byron's poem, "The Prisoner of Chillon."

Iontreux itself is a charming town, hudled between the lake and the Alpine peak of Rochers de Naye, 6,700 feet. This is chief resort area of French Switzerland.

otos: TWA Trans World Airne; bottom, Konstantin Kostich

Switzerland

Open air train takes passengers up the scenic slopes of Rigi, near Lucerne.

Lucerne is gateway to "Land of Willia Tell." This is Hofkirche, founded in 73

Older parts of Lucerne, with charming houses like this, are on right bank of the Reuss. Vacation capital of Switze land, Lucerne has magnificent scener

Photos: TWA Trans World Airlin top left, Swiss National Travel Offi

iew from Jungfraujoch is magnificent. his is the highest point in Europe that is reached by rail—over 11,000 feet. Innumerable summits are seen all around.

utdoor shopping in Lugano: this ancient wn in the south is Italian in character.

Lido Beach at Lugano offers fine food, amidst gorgeous lake and mountain views.

otos: A. L. Koolish; bottom,
iss National Travel Office

The noble Grossmünster church and the Helmhaus museum are cherished land- marks of Zurich, largest city in Switze land, on Lake of Zurich, Limmat rive

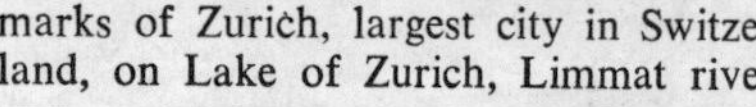

Basel, at French and German borders on Rhine, has market that's open every day.

Basel's new Industries Fair Building ha giant clock with 12-ft. sweep second hand

Photos: Swiss National Travel Offic

ouses of Parliament in Berne, capital ' Switzerland. With its arcades on the

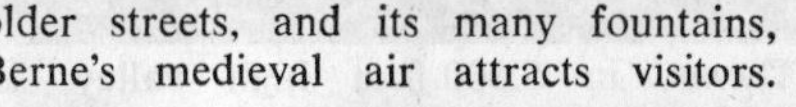

older streets, and its many fountains, Berne's medieval air attracts visitors.

isitors to library of St. Gall's Abbey ıt on slippers to protect ancient floors.

Clock Tower is Berne's traditional landmark and the bear is the city's mascot.

ıotos: Swiss National Travel Of- :e; bottom right, A. L. Koolish

Switzerland

Davos, in 5,000-foot high valley, is first-rank place for skating and skiing.

Sports train of Gornergrat railway a Zermatt climbs toward the Matterhorn

Cresta Toboggan Run, at St. Moritz, is ¾ mile long, with a drop of 500 feet.

Laboratory for Horological Research at Neuchâtel is pride of the watch industry.

Travelers in Zurich candy shop stock u on the world-famous Swiss chocolate.

Photos: Swiss National Travel Offic

THE MEDITERRANEAN

. Constellation gets to Rome fast.

t people are anxious to visit the dle of Western civilization" that Mediterranean area represents, such seats of early culture and ious development as Rome, ens, Venice, Jerusalem and other ent cities.

here are many pleasant ways to to the Mediterranean. Four of major airlines fly directly to ne from New York: TWA, Air nce, Pan American, Alitalia, Italian airline. And of course ne is one of the major terminals nes from northern Europe, Brit-European, Scandinavian, KLM, sair. And air connections are l for other points, Portugal, n, Greece, Israel and all around 2,400 mile length of the Mediter-an Sea.

y ship, there are also splendid ibilities. Two of the finest of erican ships are the *Independ-* and *Constitution* of the Ameri-Export Lines. They call at Gi-tar, Cannes and Genoa on way to les. And the same line has three smaller ships, "The Aces," *Excalibur, Excambion* and *Exeter,* which circle around the Mediterranean, calling at a number of ports. Italian Line ships are headed by the luxurious *Cristo-foro Colombo.* A number of other services offer variety for all different tastes and purses.

However you go, you'll find the Mediterranean area warm and sunny. The climate has become so famous that other regions around the world often advertise their "Mediterranean-like climate." And you are always surrounded by history: from the days of the Phoenicians, through glories of Carthage, Greece and Rome, down to present day importance as great shipping lane between ports of Europe, Asia.

Gibraltar is seen from "Independence."

: TWA Trans World Airline;
n, American Export Lines

The Mediterranean
ENGLAND
Atlantic Ocean
FRANCE
GERMANY
POLAND
CZECHOSLOVAKIA
AUSTRIA
HUNGARY
RUMANIA
YUGOSLAVIA
BULGARIA
GREECE
TURKEY
ITALY
SPAIN
PORTUGAL
MOROCCO
ALGERIA
TUNISIA
LIBYA
SYRIA
LEBANON
ISRAEL
SUEZ CANAL
L. MAGGIORE
L. COMO
DOLOMITES
Milan
Genoa
Venice
Florence
Belgrade
Coimbra
Lisbon
Segovia
Madrid
Toledo
Seville
Granada
Málaga
Barcelona
Rome
Naples
Pompeii
Capri
Sorrento
Taormina
Palermo
SICILY
MT. ETNA
Syracuse
ADRIATIC SEA
Dubrovnik
Istanbul
Black Sea
Ankara
Athens
Algiers
Tunis
Casablanca
Beirut
Mediterranean Sea
Miles
0 100 200 300
ROME
VATICAN CITY
ST. PETER'S
TIBER R.
COLOSSEUM
1 Mile
SYRIA
Haifa
Tel Aviv
Jerusalem
ISRAEL
JORDAN
EGYPT
MILES
0 50

ORTUGAL INVITES YOU O ITS SUNNY COAST

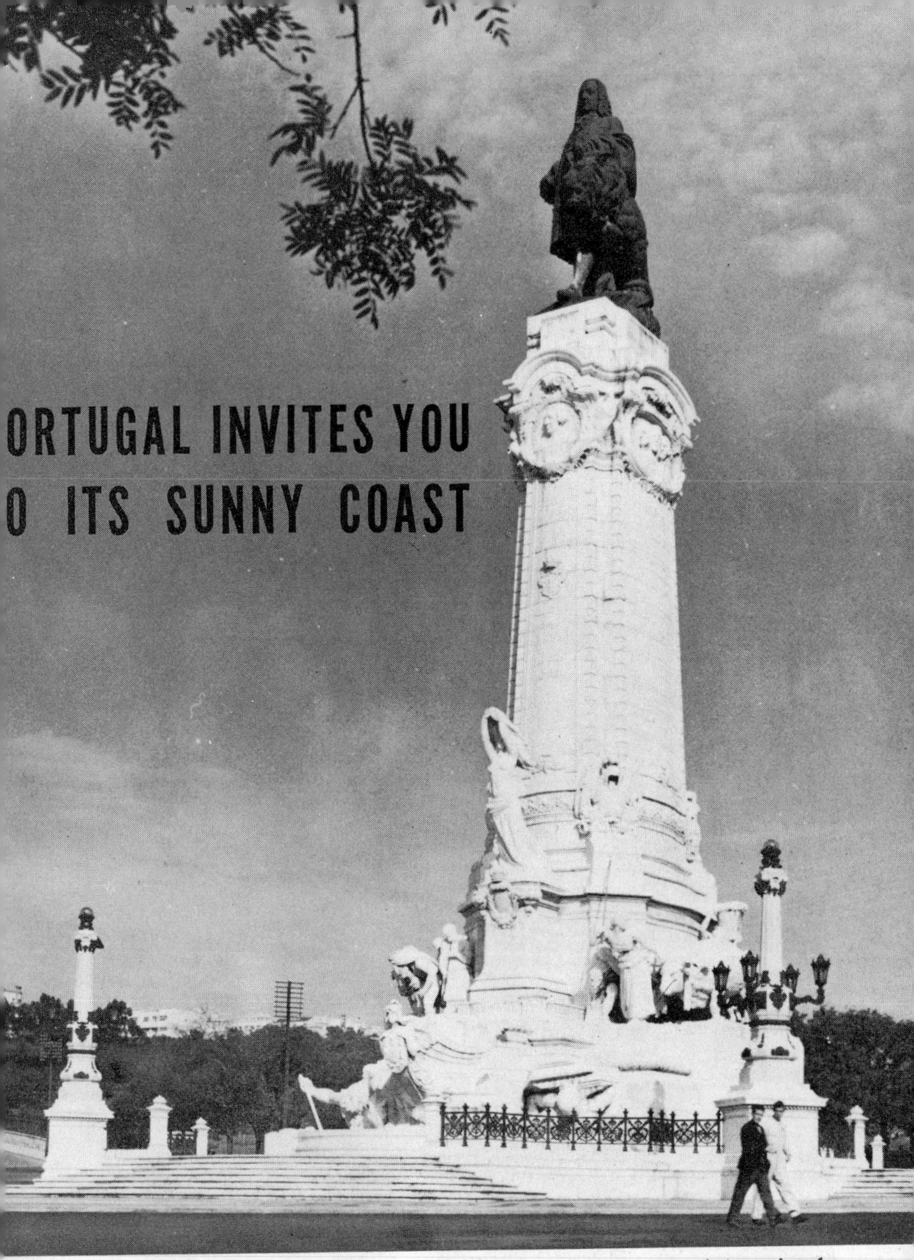

rtugal offers much charm for visitors io want to get off beaten pathways. Its ncipal cities have modern hotels and ere are "tourist inns" in the smaller ices. Main playland of the country is ong the coast, the Portuguese Riviera, th resorts like Estoril and Cascais. Lisbon is one of the great international capitals of the world, with a "different" atmosphere that stems from its glamorous past when Portugal ruled half the New World. Monument above is in memory of the Marques de Pombal who rebuilt Lisbon after the 1755 earthquake.

oto: TWA Trans World Airline

Rossio Square is geographical center of Lisbon. It has flower market, statue of Peter the 4th, and is flanked by nationa theater and the central railroad statio

Castle of St. George was site of famous battle that repulsed the Moors in 1147.

Alfama district, crowded and colorfu is clustered about 12th century cathedra

Photos: Ewing Galloway; bot tom, TWA Trans World Airlir

tra, 14 miles northwest of Lisbon, has Palace of Pena perched high on a hill above the town, most fascinating of the country's magnificent old royal palaces.

hing is major occupation in the many bors of Portugal. These gaily painted boats are at Lisbon. Some fishermen use nets that are floated out from the shore.

tos: TWA Trans World Airline

Portugal

Basilica of Shrine of Our Lady at Fátima attracts almost as many as Lourdes.

Coimbra is Portugal's university city. Velha" is a 12th century Roman edi

Estoril is fabulous seaside resort, just 15 miles from Lisbon, with magnificent beach, flower gardens, casino, fine ho bridle paths by the sea and up into h

Oporto, second city of Portugal, is famous for port wine. This is cathedral.

Nazaré is typical fishing village wh men wear bright plaids and stocking c

Photos: Casa de Portugal; top center, TWA Trans World Ai

deira, Portuguese island 625 miles to thwest of Lisbon, is known as "Pearl of the Atlantic." S.S. *Independence* is shown in beautiful harbor of Funchal.

ood-sled transportation indicates the mitiveness of life on Madeira island.

Santa Maria is one of the 9 main Azores islands, 1200 miles to west of Lisbon.

tos: Deane Dickason (Ewing Galloway); tom left, Burton Holmes (Ewing Galloway); tom right, TWA Trans World Airline.

SPAIN IS LAND OF GREAT TRADITIONS

Spanish civilization dates back to the stone age. The Basques may be descended from Cro-Magnon man whose art has been found in caves at Altamira. The history of Spain is long and involved, but it reached a great climax after Columbus' discovery of America sparked enormous expansion of the empire which came include almost all of the Americas a around the world to the Philippines. T Spain of today is a land of color, mu and gaiety, with many reminders of p glories. Madrid (Plaza Mayor above) Spain's capital and geographical cent

Photo: Spanish State Tourist Off

astellana Hilton Hotel is newest and ost luxurious in the gay city of Madrid.

Madrid's newer sections with spacious streets contrast with the old quarters.

ith over a million population, Madrid as subway, other modern transportation.

Calle de Alcalá is one of several wide tree-lined boulevards in modern Madrid.

otos: Spanish State Tourist Office;
left, Hilton Hotels International

Prado Museum is one of world's greatest, with works of Velázquez, other masters.

Even in busy Madrid, one can see fa carts lumbering slowly along to mark

Puerta del Sol, once one of gates of old ramparts of Madrid leveled 4 centuries ago, has undergone a recent face-lifti and become principal square of the ci

Throne Room is one of many impressive parlors in the sumptuous Royal Palace.

Palace, built on the site of old alcaz houses many of Spain's treasures of a

Photos: Spanish State Tourist Office; top left, T Trans World Airline; top right, Charles Marsch

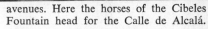

utstanding feature of Madrid is the :eat number of broad squares and noble avenues. Here the horses of the Cibeles Fountain head for the Calle de Alcalá.

Rose gardens are a feature of beautiful :etiro Park, with its lovely trees, lake.

Concert at Retiro Park is at other end of entertainment scale from 2 bull rings.

notos: Spanish :ate Tourist Office

San Juan de los Reyes, in Toledo, was built by Ferdinand and Isabella.

Santo Tomé church houses the painting b El Greco, *The Burial of Count Orga*

Toledo's greatest glory is its splendid cathedral, a combination of five styles.

Steep cobbled streets of Toledo remin one of Moorish towns of North Africa

Photos: TWA Trans World Air line; bottom right, Richard Josep

mposing walls of Toledo include the isagra Gate (above) and the Mudejar

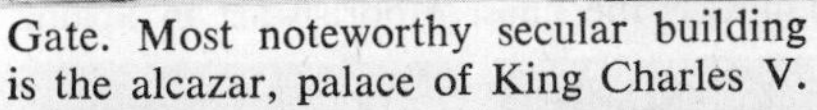

Gate. Most noteworthy secular building is the alcazar, palace of King Charles V.

Many-turreted alcazar, in Segovia, was ite of crowning of Queen Isabella I.

Lofty Roman aqueduct, with 170 arches, is still used to supply water to Segovia.

hotos: TWA Trans World Air-ne; bottom, Richard Joseph

Granada's Alhambra, home of Moorish kings, is the finest Moorish art in Spain.

Grapes, for home use, and olives for ex port, are Spain's main industrial crops

Granada gypsies perform a gay dance for tourists before one of their houses

Málaga, noted for sweet Malaga wine, is famed winter resort on the Mediterranean.

It is one of the oldest cities of Spain, said to have been founded by Phoenicians.

Photos: Virginia Black; Richard Joseph; Pan American World Airways; Spanish State Tourist Office

alon Arabe shows exquisite decorations of the alcazar, Moorish palace in Seville.

Lofty Giralda Tower, over 300 feet high, is part of beautiful cathedral of Seville.

Typical Majorcan dress is worn by this woman climbing a "street" in Pollensa.

Spanish mantillas come into their own at the Seville Fair which follows Holy Week.

Photos: Spanish State Tourist Office; top right, Pan American World Airways

Fight over design prevented completion of Barcelona's Church of the Holy Family.

Costa Brava (rugged coast) is section between the French Riviera and Barcelona

Battle-scarred gates lead to Valencia, Spain's third city, near Mediterranean.

Photos: Pan American World Airways; bottom left, Spanish State Tourist Office

llfight at El Espinar, near Barcelona, elow) is one of 500 a year in Spain.

Spain is noted for its many fiestas at different seasons, this one at Santander.

Santander is surrounded by the Picos de Europa, mountains that rise to 8800 feet.

Santiago de Compostela, at Spain's northwest tip, is a pilgrim city of world renown.

Photos: Spanish State Tourist Office

Spain

Mountain village of Valldemosa is on the Spanish island of Majorca, in Balearics.

Country homes in Majorca feature co chimney corner seats by the kitchen fi

Canary Islands are Spanish possessio off northwest Africa. This is Santa Cru

Old houses at Sóller, on Majorca, are reflected in waters on the picturesque harbor. The town is surrounded by oran trees; its port ships oranges and win

Photos: Ewing Galloway; top right a center right, Spanish State Tourist Offi

TUNISIA IS SITE OF ANCIENT CARTHAGE

700,000 people lived in Carthage before the time of Christ; now it's a desolate plain. When you visit Tunisia, in North Africa, you'll feel that ancient history peers over your 20th century shoulder.

Tunis is capital of Tunisia and a mecca or tourists looking for the unusual.

Old Moslem quarter of Tunis is a maze of crooked streets, extensive bazaars.

the tree-lined square which runs from thedral to port are many sidewalk cafés.

Newly excavated ruins of Carthage baths bring back memories of high school Latin.

otos: TWA Trans World Airline

ALGERIA IS FRANCE IN AFRICA

Whereas Tunisia and Morocco are Pr
tectorates, Algeria has a much closer lin
being an actual Department. In Algie
the capital, you might imagine that y
were in slower-moving version of Pa

Algiers is chief Mediterranean port of French North Africa. It stretches along the bay for ten miles, its white hou
gleaming brilliantly in the strong s

Famous "Ouled-Naïl" dancers perform at tiny Bou-Saâda, 125 miles from Algiers.

Dancers take their name from Ouled-N
mountains, on edge of the Sahara des

Photos: TWA Trans World
line; bottom, Richard Jo

thedral on Place Malakoff is one of many impressive buildings in Algiers.

nmam-Meskoutine is noted spa with springs in the Constantine mountains.

mmel Gorge from above: Atlas moun-s cut off desert interior from the sea.

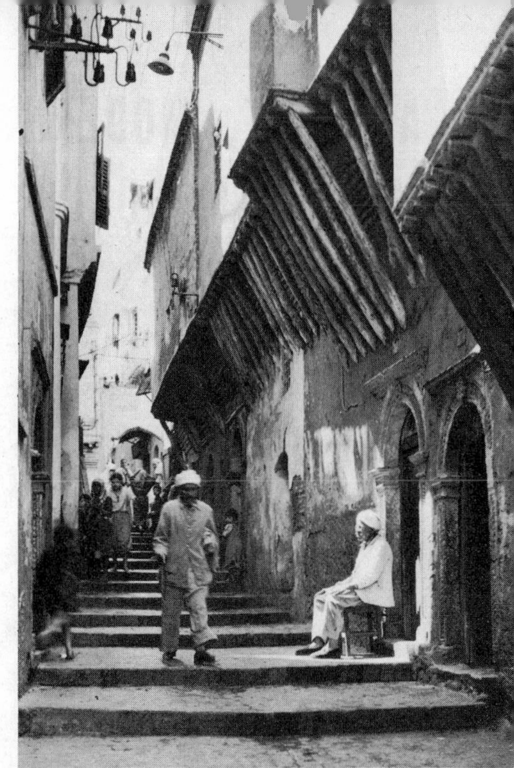

Casbah section of old Algiers has real labyrinth of narrow terraced streets.

Roman ruins at Djemila include arch of triumph, a forum, 3rd century temple.

tos: TWA Trans World Airline

ANCIENT, MODERN MIX IN MOROCCO

Morocco extends along the Atlantic a Mediterranean at northwest corner Africa. It's divided into French Moroc Spanish Morocco, and the Internatio Zone of Tangier, across from Gibralt

Casablanca, the largest city of French Morocco, was scene of history-making conference between President Roosev and Prime Minister Churchill in 19

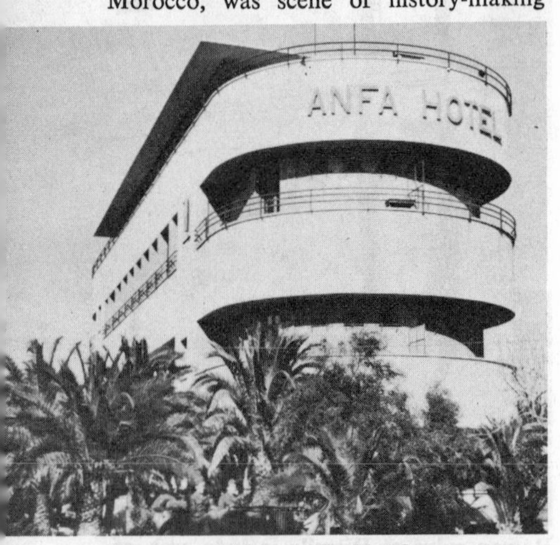

Modern-looking Anfa Hotel, on a green bluff outside the city, was meeting site.

Modern Casablanca forms a semicir around old city. This is the Post Offi

Photos: United Press; bottom left, Ac bottom right, Windrow-Phelps (Black S

IE COLOSSEUM IS BEST KNOWN SYMBOL OF MIGHT OF ANCIENT ROME.

UNNY ITALY IS A ARADISE ON EARTH

The surrounding sea and the protecting Alps give Italy a wonderfully balanced climate in both winter and summer. The scenery has great variety: lovely beaches, beautiful lake resorts, magnificent Alps and Apennines and Dolomites. Lovers of culture, history find incomparable wealth in Italian art and archeology.

ɔto: TWA Trans World Airline

The Colosseum had room for 50,000. Cross commemorates the early Christian martyrs who died in the amphitheat victims of lions, sport of early Roma

orum Romanum was the center of economic, political and religious life of ancient Rome. This is site of Castor's Temple and temple of the vestal virgins.

The Tiber River winds through Rome much as the Seine through Paris, the Thames through London. This is San Angelo bridge, with dome of St. Peter'

Vatican Library is one of world's most beautiful. Contains over half a million books, and many rare manuscripts lik 4th century Codex Vaticanus of Bibl

Photos: Konstantin Kostich; bo tom, Italian State Tourist Offi

St. Peter's, covering an area of 163,728 square feet, is largest, most majestic of Christian churches. Colonnades are by Bernini; great dome by Michelangelo.

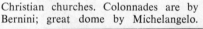

Papal Fountain has insignia of the Chigi, same shape as crown worn by Pope Pius.

Swiss Guards have served at the Holy See as attendants of the Pope since 1505.

Photos: TWA Trans World Airline; bottom left, Copyright, Herbert List (Magnum); bottom right, Italian State Tourist Office

Castel Sant'Angelo, approached by the celebrated Sant'Angelo bridge over the Tiber, was built at command of Emperor Hadrian as mausoleum for Roman rulers.

Formal gardens of Castel Gandolfo: This is country residence of the Pope, south of Rome on the Appian Way, and by the Lateran treaty now part of Vatican City.

Photos: TWA Trans World Airline; bottom, Konstantin Kostich

Claudian Aqueduct, with its series of superb arches, was built in year 52 A.D.

Villa d'Este, with fountains, terraced gardens, is beauty spot at nearby Tivoli.

Appian Way is the old highway to Rome from the south, lined with cypress trees.

Tivoli, viewed from Villa d'Este: town is noted for waterfalls, Hadrian's villa.

Photos: Konstantin Kostich; top left, TWA Trans World Airline

Florence was "cradle of the Italian Renaissance." Uffizi Palace, in background, has one of world's richest collections of paintings and 1,500,000 volume library.

Photo: Konstantin Kostich

Ponte Vecchio, across the Arno, contains many tiny shops. Gallery across top, that connected Uffizi Palace (tower at left) with Pitti Palace, was partly destroyed.

Beautiful Boboli gardens are on grounds of Pitti Palace, once residence of the great Medici family, Florentine statesmen, rulers, and patrons of the arts.

Photos: TWA Trans World Airline; bottom, Italian State Tourist Office

The mystic quality of Venice expresses itself in this photo of gondolas before San Marco square, with Santa Maria della Salute seen through early evening haze.

Venice is intricate network of canals, big and small, with countless bridges.

Bridge of Sighs was passage for prisoners from Ducal Palace to airless cells.

Photos: A. Milton Runyon; bottom left, Richard Joseph

[R]ialto Bridge over the Grand Canal has [t]wo rows of shops, twelve on each side.

[C]a' d'Oro, the Golden House, is splendid [h]ome of 15th century Venetian patriarch.

Cathedral of San Marco, dedicated in 830 to patron saint of Venice, is most ornate.

Grand Canal, 2 miles long, is the chief artery of Venice, winding in an S-curve from the Piazza San Marco to the railroad station. Width averages 228 feet.

Photos: Richard Joseph; top right, Konstantin Kostich; center left, Italian State Tourist Office

At top of cable railway at Ortisei, you can have refreshments while enjoying the

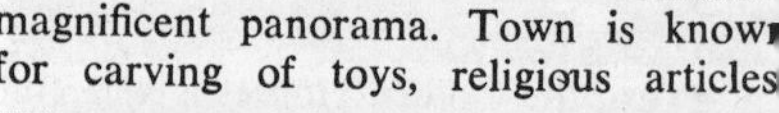
magnificent panorama. Town is known for carving of toys, religious articles

Wild flowers add to beauty of Dolomites near principal resort, Cortina d'Ampezzo.

Dolomite Alps of northern Italy are known for vivid sunrise, sunset colors.

Photos: Konstantin Kostich; bottom, Italian State Tourist Office

driving through Dolomites, you often ne on wayside shrines on roads that reach almost 9,000 feet. Highest peak is Marmolada, towering up 10,964 feet.

tina d'Ampezzo is both a summer and ter resort, in center of Dolomites, one of Europe's finest mountain areas. Brenner Pass is 45 miles to northwest.

o: Konstantin Kostich; bot- Italian State Tourist Office

Milan cathedral is elaborately decorated with over 100 pinnacles, 3,000 statues. An elevator takes you to the roof wh you can see white marble figures close

Photo: Konstantin Kos

site Milan cathedral is the Galleria io Emanuele where all Milan meets.

Castello Sforzesco was once a barracks, now interesting archeological museum.

, chief industrial center of Italy, world's grandest railroad station.

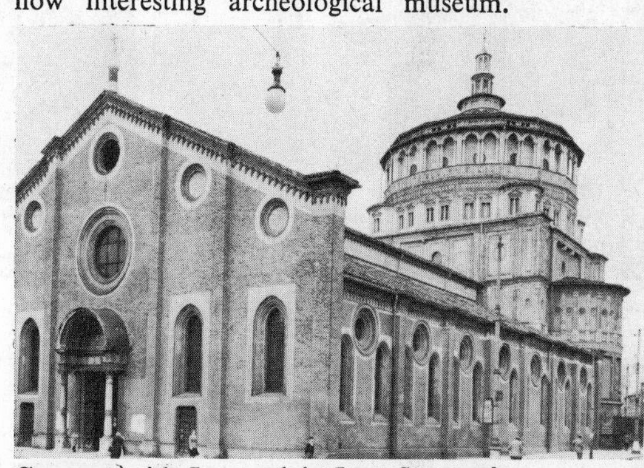

Convent with Leonardo's *Last Supper* is next to Santa Maria delle Grazie church.

ala Opera House, with its red and auditorium, is world's most noted.

Leonardo da Vinci—painter, sculptor, architect and engineer—faces La Scala.

A. Milton Runyon; top right, right, TWA Trans World bottom, Charles Marschalek

Bellagio is on tip of promontory that divides beautiful Lake Como into its two southern arms. This popular re has many villas, gardens, ancient chu

Lake Como, Italy's 3rd largest, is in Lombardy, 25 miles to north of Milan.

Lake steamers call at resorts of C Bellagio, Lecco, Tremezzo, and ot

Photos: Italian State Touris fice; bottom, Konstantin K

Garda has wonderfully clear blue s, many lovely white villages. This is Riva, at northwest extremity of the lake, with palace built by the Venetians.

Maggiore contains famous Borro- Islands. This is view from Isola Bella, site of 1934 conference at which Germany denounced the Versailles treaty.

Konstantin Kostich; Charles Marschalek

Genoa, port city at center of the Italian Riviera, rises from waterfront to height of over 1,000 feet in surrounding Municipal palace has letters of Colu

Maritime Station at Genoa is home port of Italian Line ships and port of call of many others. Genoa rivals Mars as chief seaport of the Mediterra

Photos: Konstantin Kostich; tom, Italian State Tourist

ly

edral at Orvieto is noted for its ning façade, miracle of fine carving.

12th century church of St. Francis of i is monument to his gentle spirit.

Pisa's graceful Leaning Tower is 180 ft. high, and 14 ft. out of perpendicular.

ci is resort on Gulf of Spezia, one rgest, safest Mediterranean harbors.

Nearby is a 12th century Pisan castle, which is now used as marine observatory.

s: Konstantin Kostich; center
Italian State Tourist Office

Greatest spectacle in Naples is lovely view across the bay to no-longer-smoking Vesuvius. Many parts of the city have grown up into the surrounding hil are reached by funiculars. Neap are famous for songs like *Santa*

Photo: TWA Trans World

aruso was hissed at his debut at San arlo Opera House. Though he was often urged to return after he made his fame international, he would never come back.

astel dell'Ovo (Castle of the Egg) is n its own tiny island opposite the Via 'arthenope where the principal hotels of Naples are located. The medieval castle was begun by the Norman King William I, completed and modified by his successors.

notos: Italian State Tourist Office;
ottom, TWA Trans World Airline

Umberto I Square is the center of lovely Capri.

Marina Piccola looks out to great Faraglioni rocks.

CAPRI ATTRACTS VISITORS WITH BA

Photos: TWA Trans World Airline; top left, Italian State Tourist Office

.OVELY VIEWS.

Visitors arrive at Capri by small steamers from Naples, a distance of 20 miles.

Blue Grotto gets its name from dazzling blue light produced by the bright sun.

Funicular railway links Marina Grande with town of Capri, 456 feet higher up.

Photos: TWA Trans World Airline

Pompeii was buried by the eruption of Vesuvius in 79 A.D. This is the Forum.

Temple of Apollo is one of ruins fo by excavations that were begun in 1

Lava-paved streets of Pompeii were used by chariots of city's 20,000 residents.

Well-preserved homes are chief source information about ancient domestic li

Photos: TWA Trans World Airli top right, Konstantin Kostich; b tom, Italian State Tourist Off

orrento is charmingly situated amid range and lemon groves on mountainous peninsula south of Bay of Naples. *Come Back to Sorrento* is more than a song.

ost dramatic road in Italy is the one om Sorrento to Amalfi, along rugged coast and over the hills that rise to a 4,734 foot height in Monte Sant'Angelo.

otos: Konstantin Kostich

From Taormina, you can see Sicily's Mt. Etna, highest active volcano in Europe.

Sicily is known as "Island of the Sun" and brightness penetrates narrow alleys

Greek Theater of Syracuse is largest most beautiful of all the Hellenic ruins

Palermo at night: With over 500,000 inhabitants, it is one of Italy's largest and most aristocratic cities. Buildings rang from Norman-Arab to 20th centur

Photos: Italian State Tourist Of fice; top right, Richard Josep

EMPLE OF JUPITER DATES FROM DAYS OF ROMAN RULE IN ATHENS.

HE MAJESTY OF REECE LIVES ON

Whether or not you've read the works of Plato and Aristotle, you'll want to know something of the great civilization that reached its peak more than four centuries before Christ. A visit to the Acropolis time-machines you back through the centuries. And you'll find modern Athens a bright and busy city of 1¼ million.

oto: Konstantin Kostich

Academy of Athens, University of Athens and National Library are proud buildings

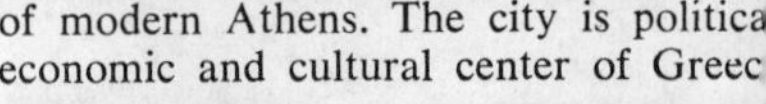
of modern Athens. The city is politica economic and cultural center of Greec

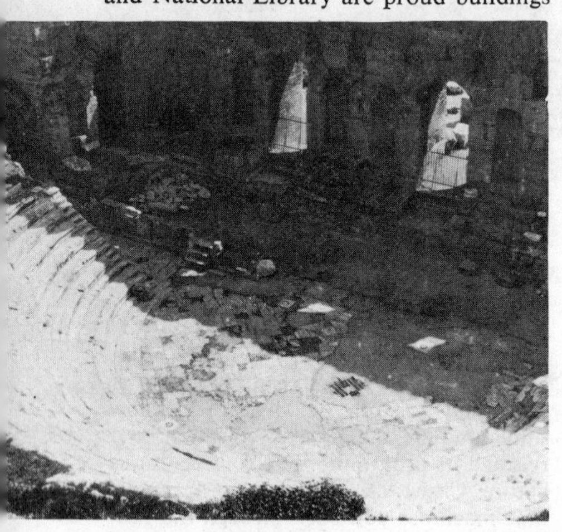

Your imagination can place thousands of listeners in the vast Temple of Music.

Palace guard reminds you that in 1946 plebiscite called for return of monarc

Photos: Royal Greek Embassy Inf mation Service; bottom left, S. Booth; bottom right, Richard Jos

e **Acropolis** rises proudly on 180-foot
above the Attic plain. The Parthenon and many large buildings were built in Golden Age of Pericles, 2400 years ago.

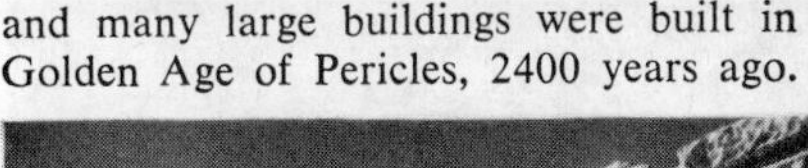

turesque **Corfu,** second largest of the
nian islands, was Homer's "Scheria."

The Caryatids have carried Erechtheum roof on their heads about 24 centuries.

tos: Royal Greek Embassy Informa-
Service; bottom right, Three Lions

YUGOSLAVIA OFFERS SCENIC ADVENTURE

Yugoslavia is now a member of Europ
Travel Commission and is inviting to
ists to enjoy its good food and sup
scenery of places like Dubrovnik and
Dalmatian Island of Rab in the Adria

Parliament in Belgrade: Strategic site of capital makes it "key to Balkans."

Budva is port city on Adriatic, with Orthodox Eastern cathedral, built 14

Dubrovnik, walled city on south coast, was called Arragosa, the root of *argosy*.

Jajce is medieval town on Vrbas riv with ruined castle and lovely waterf

Photos: Konstantin Kost

ome of Rock mosque is on site of temple where Jesus turned out money changers.

AST AND PRESENT EET IN ISRAEL

Modern Israel has much to offer visitors who are politically and socially aware of the ferment of our times. And as the ancient "Land of the Bible" it attracts pilgrims to Jerusalem, the River Jordan, Nazareth, Tiberias on the Sea of Galilee, and Mount Zion. New roads, hotels make it easy to visit old and new Israel.

ıto: Pan American World Airways

Israel

Sunset over Jerusalem: View shows the great no man's land between the old city and the new. On left is King David hotel Buildings at right are in Arab sector

Haifa, seen from Mt. Carmel, is principal seaport of Israel and industrial center.

The Sea of Galilee is associated wit many events of New Testament histor

Photos: Robert Capa (Magnum); bo tom, Israel National Tourist Cent

ypical of modern architecture of Israel YMCA building near Jerusalem's walls.

Street vendor's shop looks archaic, but he has modern convenience of telephone.

rom Mount of Olives you see whole of erusalem spread out before you, and much of it seems as it might have been 2000 years ago, behind the ancient wall.

he carpenter shop at Nazareth is place hat attracts many pilgrims to Israel.

Tel Aviv from the air: Largest city and commercial hub, with 300,000 population.

hotos: Israel National Tourist Center; top ft, Pan American World Airways; top right, ichard Joseph; bottom left, S. A. Booth

SIRKECI SQUARE IN ISTANBUL IS THE BUSY CENTER OF A BUSY CITY

TURKEY IS LINK BETWEEN EAST, WEST

Mention of Istanbul or the Golden Hor probably puts you in mind of a thrill by Eric Ambler or a movie of Humphre Bogart's. Turkey is an ancient land th used to join Europe, Africa and Asia i its empire. Istanbul, once Constantin ple, is partly in Europe, partly Asi It is terminus of famous Orient Expres

Photo: Turkish Information Offi

nkara is centrally located modern city, ›w the fast-growing capital of Turkey.

These old Roman ruins are near Smyrna, port long known for its export of figs.

osporus Strait connects the Sea of armara and the Black Sea, separating European and Asian Turkey. The tower is part of Rumeli Hisar fortifications.

rom dock near the Yeni (New) Mosque, erry boats leave for Bosporus crossing.

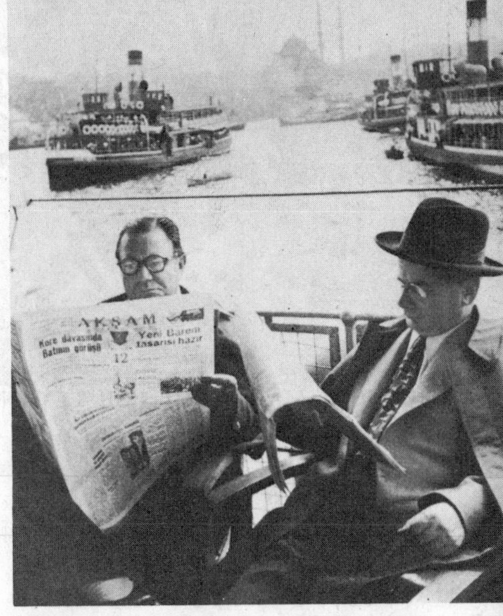

International commuters read the news on daily trip between Europe and Asia.

notos: Turkish Information Office

BEIRUT, MAIN PORT FOR LEVANT STATES, IS CAPITAL OF LEBANO

LEBANON HAS ANCIENT LURE

Lebanon is a tiny country, just 120 mi long and 35 wide, proclaimed an inc pendent nation in 1941. Beirut, the ca ital, was a flourishing Phoenician c some 3000 years ago. Today it is tra and transportation center for both O ental and Western Worlds, the gatew for travelers to Jordan and to Isra

Photo: Deane Dickason (Ewing Gallowa

ROUND-THE-WORLD CRUISE

"President Cleveland" at Hong Kong.

BOAC Jet-Prop Britannia Flies Pacific.

A Round-the-World Cruise is the most glamorous of voyages: it is the sort of trip that's offered as the grand prize in a contest, the kind that wealthy travelers with plenty of time take aboard a luxury liner like the *Caronia,* or that more and more people are now making by air, or a combination of air and sea. Each year a few lucky souls embark on conducted tours around the world, taking about 3 months, and costing some $5,000 and up apiece.

On the less expensive side, you can go all the way around the world on the American President liners, *President Polk* and *President Monroe,* in about 14 weeks, at fares as low as $2,000 each. There are special sightseeing arrangements in most ports. By air, Pan American routes that cover 83 countries and colonies make it possible to plan an itinerary that will reach your interests in almost any part of the globe. And all sorts of ship-and-air combinations are possible: by way of Pan American, TWA, Northwest Orient Airlines, and such ship lines as American Export, Matson Line, American President, and the several British lines that cover points in India and Africa.

Should South Africa be interesting to you, Farrell Line ships will take you directly to Capetown. And for a quick return, Pan American has through-plane service.

BOAC now speeds travelers to the Pacific in jet-prop Britannias, from New York and San Francisco westward to Honolulu, Tokyo and Hong Kong.

Photos: American President Lines and British Overseas Airways Corporation

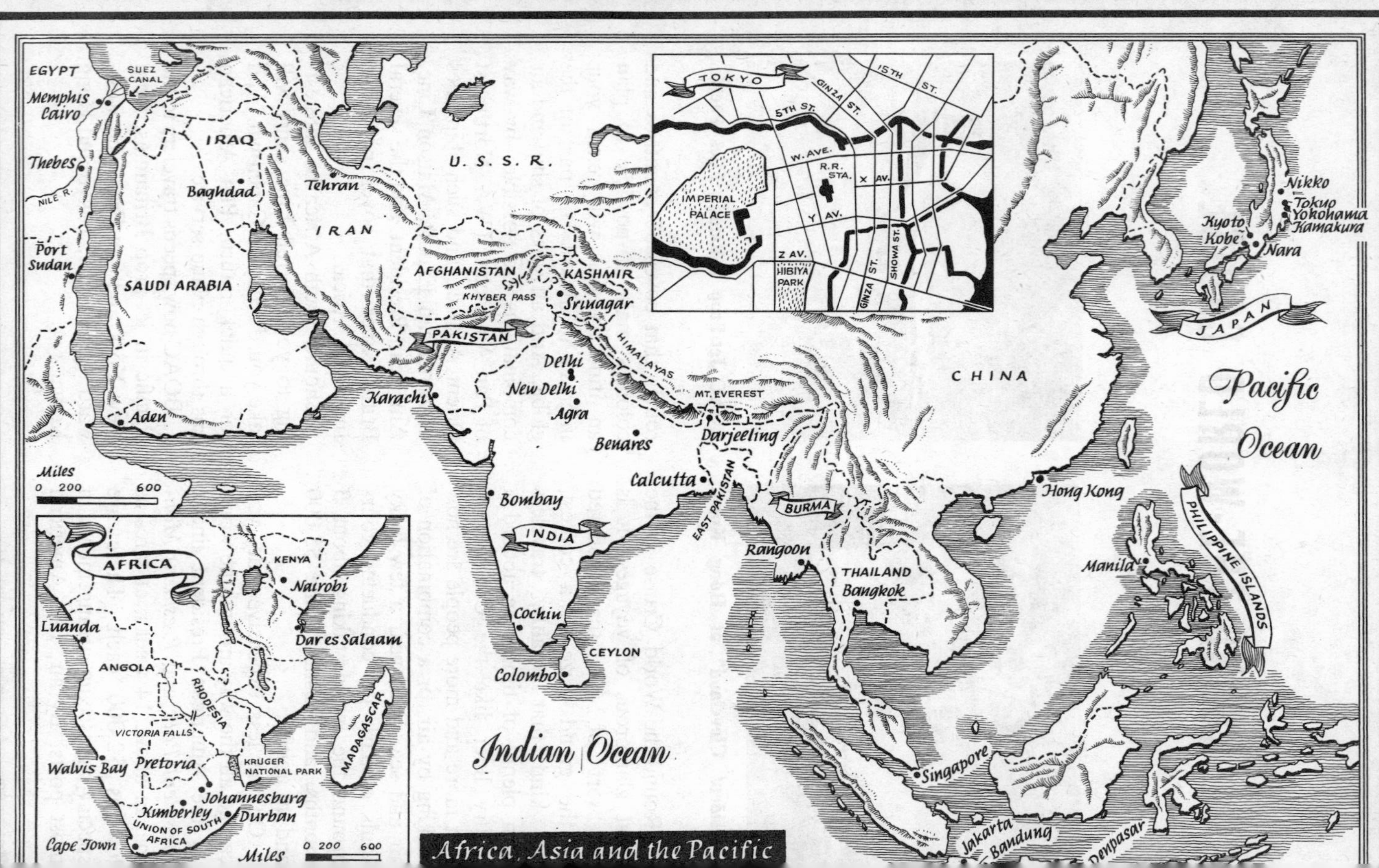

Africa, Asia and the Pacific

NEARLY 50,000 CLIMB PERFECT CONE OF FUJIYAMA EVERY SUMMER.

JAPAN IS LAND OF EXQUISITE BEAUTY

The four islands of Japan offer scenery of every conceivable type: forests, lakes, mountains, swift rivers, hot springs, and miles of rice paddies. The charming gardens feature foliage rather than blooms. The cities offer Western comforts, but are filled with gaudy color. Buddhist temples, Shinto shrines are everywhere.

Photo: Japan Travel Bureau

Tokyo, capital of Japan, is on the shore of the Bay of Tokyo; it is traversed by

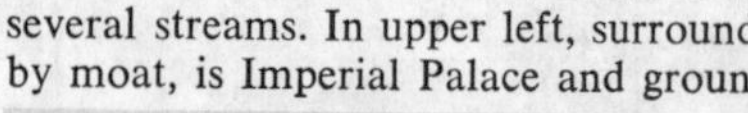

several streams. In upper left, surround by moat, is Imperial Palace and groun

Ginza Street, brilliantly lit at night, is Tokyo's fashionable shopping district.

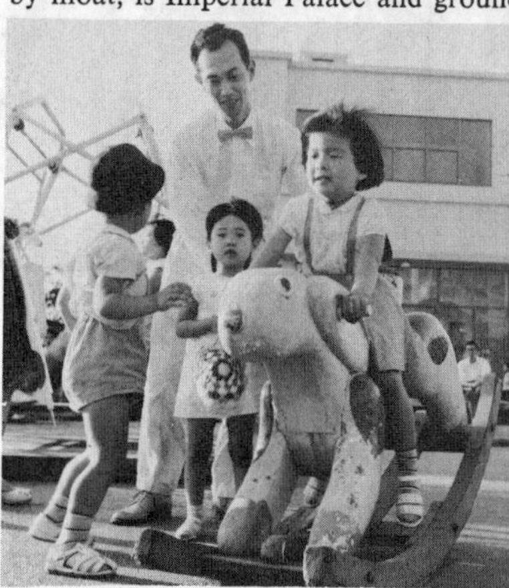

Tokyo department stores have roof play grounds to keep children happy and busy

Photos: Japan Travel Bureau bottom left, Ewing Galloway bottom right, Peggy Mann

chiman Shinto Shrine, at Kamakura, s built 1063, features long stairway.

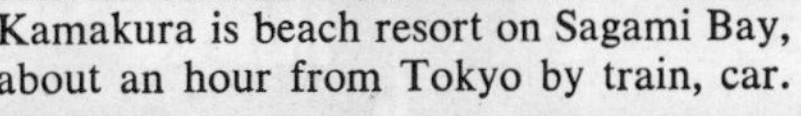

Kamakura is beach resort on Sagami Bay, about an hour from Tokyo by train, car.

eat bronze Buddha of Kamakura stands ft. high and dates from the year 1252.

The Kabuki-za in Tokyo is the best-known theater where classical drama is done.

tos: Ewing Galloway; bot-
, Japan Travel Bureau

Stepping stones in Heian Shrine's garden are set crooked, so devils will fall off.

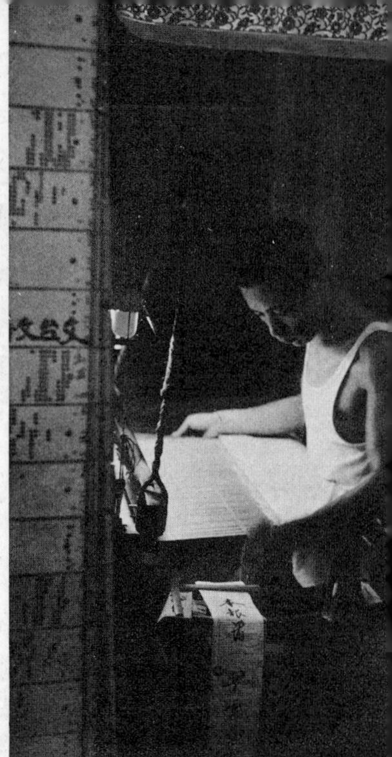

A Kyoto craftsman weaves the fascinati patterns of lovely Japanese silk scarve

Kyoto has some 3,000 Buddhist temples and Shinto shrines. One of most beautiful is Heian shrine, originally built in 7 This is one of Kyoto's several festiv

Photos: Ewing Galloway; Pe Mann; Japan Travel Bure

Nikko, about 90 miles north of Tokyo, is ummer resort in the Japanese Alps. It has 141,000-acre Nikko National Park. This is Shinto ceremony at Ieyasu Tomb.

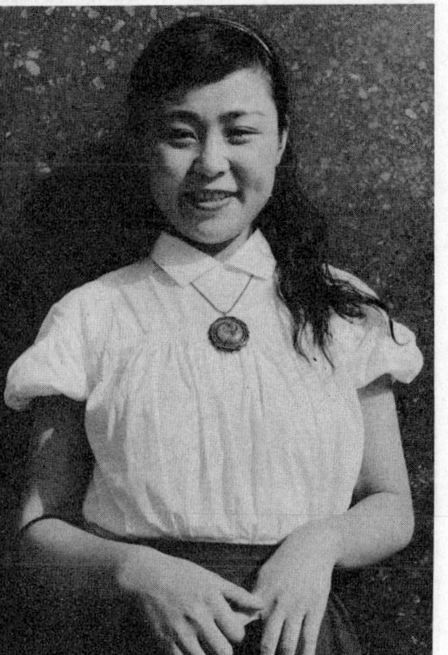

apanese girl guide: Customs of the land re explained in a charming, gay manner.

Nara's great 13-foot bell is in world's largest wooden building, Daibutsu-Den.

hotos: Ewing Galloway; bot-
m left, Peggy Mann; right,
n American World Airways

HONG KONG IS BUSIEST PORT OF FAR EAS

Typical of the British Crown Colony of Hong Kong are streets so steep that they have to be terraced into steps. 28,000 British soldiers guard 2 million people.

From top of Victoria Peak you get vi of tall buildings of Hong Kong and harbor beyond. The cable railway t up 1800-foot peak is a tourist favori

White pagoda is on estate of Aw Boon Haw, fabulous owner of "Tiger Balm."

Fishing junks tie up at port of Aberdee on either side of island from Hong Kon

Photos: Pan American World Airwa

ong Kong is one of the world's few free rts, where all goods are without duty. Many Chinese articles are made here by factories moved from Shanghai, Canton.

oto: Henri Cartier-Bresson (Magnum)

THERE ARE 7,000 PHILIPPINE ISLANDS

The Republic of the Philippines, given full independence on July 4, 1946, has some 7,110 islands, with over 4,500 of the smaller ones still unnamed. Discovered by Magellan in 1521, the Philippines for more than 300 years were part of Spain's vast empire, were ceded to the U.S. in 1898. Today, the new democracy has up-to-date facilities for tourists, welcomes them to its friendly, charming resorts.

Legaspi Landing, Manila Hotel: Dama by war, the hotel is now fully resto

Escolta Boulevard is one of the shopping streets of Manila, Philippines' big city.

Photos: Ewing Galloway

ce terraces on Luzon (below) date back
00 years, are still cultivated today.

University of Manila, badly bombed in war, has world's largest sun dial in garden.

Malacañan Palace in Manila is official residence of President of the Philippines.

Photos: Ewing Galloway; bottom right, Fenno Jacobs (Three Lions)

Temple of Dawn, in Bangkok, called *Wat Arun,* has 245-foot tower which gives a magnificent view of city from the to It is surrounded by four smaller tower

CLASSICAL DANCING IS ONE OF THE GLORIES OF SIAM'S HERITAG

THAILAND IS A NATION OF TEMPLES

There are few more entrancing sights i the world than the many temples of Sian the country that's been known officiall as Thailand since 1949. Bangkok, capit city, has many canals. Houses are ofte of teakwood, roofed with red tile. It i colorful city of almost a million peopl

Photos: TWA Trans World Ai line; bottom, Richard Josep

at Phra Keo ("wat" means monastery or nple) is the most famous and wonderful of all. It has the great Emerald Buddha, wrought from a single piece of jaspar.

at Benchamaborpitr (Temple of the fth Sovereign) is built of Italian marble, Chinese tile, a combination of old Thai style with foreign materials, new methods.

tos: TWA Trans World Airline

JAKARTA, JAVA, IS INDONESIA CAPITAL

The Republic of Indonesia achieved independence as recently as August 1945. The island of Java, fourth larg of the Indonesia group, is most import industrially, culturally, and political

Bandung is favorite vacation spot, 75 miles southeast of Jakarta, and with much

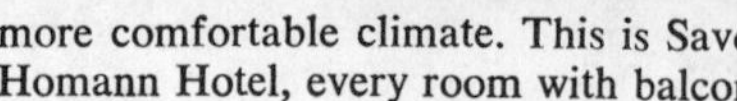

more comfortable climate. This is Sav Homann Hotel, every room with balco

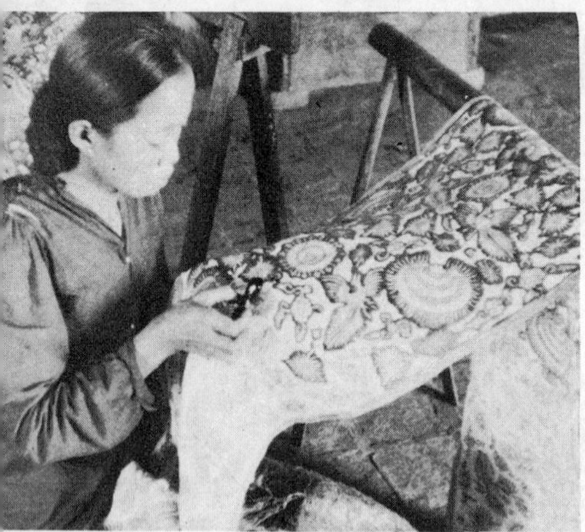

Java is noted for colorful and intricate batik, producing magnificent designs.

Native "taxis" wait for travelers co ing from Jakarta's Tugu railway static

Photos: Deane Dickason (Ewing Ga loway); bottom left, Richard Josep bottom right, Owen (Black Sto

ALI IS SYMBOL OF HE FAR-AWAY

you were asked to name the most tic, far-away-from-it-all place you ld think of, you might very well say li"—the Indonesian island of batik, cing girls, and good leisurely living.

Weaving is occupation of many Balinese women; they do colorful batik dye work.

king batik designs are used on the tumes used for the ceremonial dances.

Bali's predominant religion is Hinduism which spread to island in 7th century.

men of Denpasar demonstrate the ce of carriage for which Balinese are known. Many go in for ritual dancing, wearing colorful costumes headdresses.

os: Richard Joseph

SUMATRA HAS MANY MOUNTAIN LAKES, LARGEST BEING LAKE TOB

SUMATRA COMPLETES INDONESIAN PICTURE

Sumatra is the second largest island Indonesia. Java, Bali and Sumatra are most important parts of the Indon group in terms of cultural developm There are major oil fields in Suma and coal mines. The important cities the island are Palembang, Medan, Pad

Photo: Republic of nesia Information C

ANGOON MEANS "END OF STRIFE"

Originally a fishing village, Rangoon was won by King Alaungpaya, given its name to signalize his victory, and developed as the capital of Burma. Badly hit in World War II, it's now re-building.

he Independence Monument, Rangoon: urma achieved independence in 1948.

Shwe Dagon Pagoda, 2 miles from center of Rangoon, is Buddha's greatest shrine.

owntown Rangoon is dominated by the ıle Pagoda which enshrines a Hair of Buddha and other Relics from India. At the right is the City Hall of Rangoon.

otos: Consulate of the Union of Burma; ttom, Bob Lauback (Black Star)

Singapore has regular taxis, but a more original way of getting about is in one of these "trishaws"—three-wheeled b cycles powered by sun-hatted driver

ANDERSON BRIDGE CROSSES SINGAPORE RIVER BY THE POST OFFIC

SINGAPORE IS GATE TO THE FAR EAST

The British Colony of Singapore is th main port of call on route from Europ to the Far East, midway between Ind and China. Its famous Raffles Hotel ha long been a symbol of the romance o world trade, and the Singapore sling symbol of relaxation after work or pla

Photos: Horace Bristol (Black Star); bo tom, Deane Dickason (Ewing Gallowa

reat Southern Hotel, Chinese-operated, s casement windows for maximum ventilation in the hot months. Beside hotel at left is Palace Theater, also Chinese.

ltan Mohammed Mosque is on North ridge Road, near Arab Street. One of the most beautiful sights in Singapore is the botanical garden with its monkey-jungle.

otos: Deane Dickason (Ewing lloway); bottom, Ewing Galloway

Clock-tower lighthouse is landmark in busy downtown Colombo, surrounded by a great variety of vehicles: native c carts, jinrickshas, modern motor ca

PANORAMIC VIEW SHOWS HARBOR OF COLOMBO, CEYLON'S CAPITA

MUCH OF WORLD'S TEA COMES FROM CEYLON

Since 1948 Ceylon has been a domini of the British Commonwealth. The capi city of Colombo has had many chang since World War I and is now one of t world's cleanest and most modern citi Ceylon raises rice, coconuts, rubber, te

Photos: Deane Dickason (Ew Galloway); bottom, Ewing Gallow

lden Buddha in temple at Colombo: tside of town about 6 miles is the Temple of Kelaniya, very sacred because of a visit made to this spot by the Buddha.

e Perahera is an annual pageant held Kandy during the month of August.

Mount Lavinia Hotel, overlooking ocean, is only eight miles outside of Colombo.

tos: TWA Trans World Airline; Embassy ;eylon; Deane Dickason (Ewing Galloway)

INDIA IS LAND OF MYRIAD WONDERS

The Republic of India (a sovereign sta since January 1950) boasts the famo Taj Mahal, sacred Ganges River, the gre cities of Bombay, Calcutta, New Del and the fabulous pink city of Jaipu

The 20 ornate Jain temples in Calcutta are one of the city's great sights. Jainism is an offshoot of Hinduism, one belief b ing that it's wrong to kill, even insec

Photo: TWA Trans World Airl

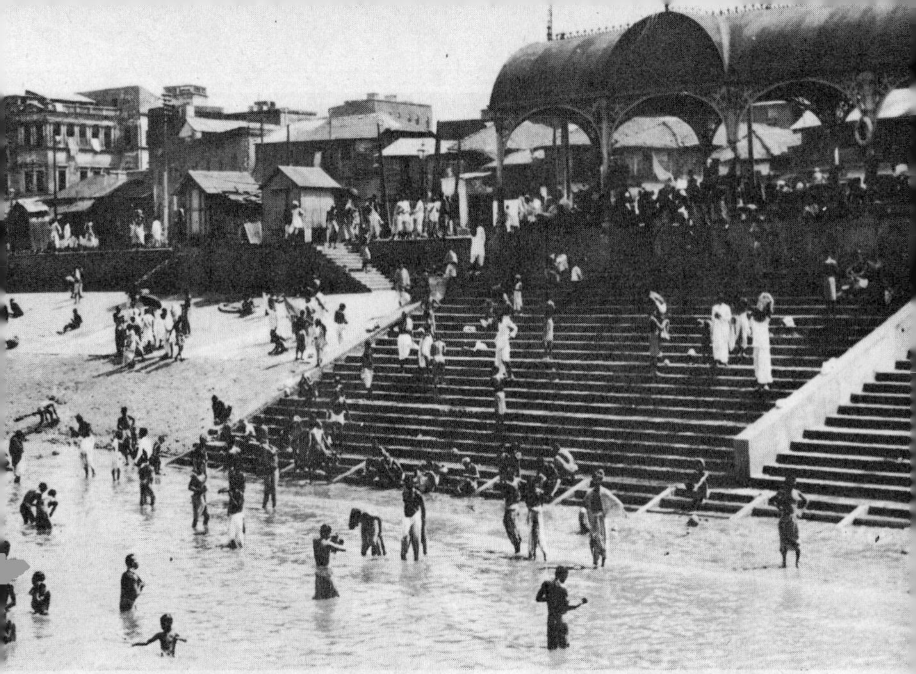

e Holy Ghat is bathing place in the oghly River (one of the many mouths of the Ganges) in Calcutta. Native "bum" boats provide transportation on river.

lcutta's parks and gardens—Botanical, ological, Eden—have much of interest.

Belur Temple, eight miles from Calcutta, is center of Shri Ramakrishna Mission.

tos: Alice Schalek (Three Lions); Richard ph; Government of India Tourist Office

The Taj Mahal, made entirely of white marble, is a world famed masterpiece. It was built 1630–48, at Agra, by Sh Jehan as memorial to his beloved w

Panch Mahal is one of ornate buildings at fabulous deserted city of Fatehpur Sikri, about 20 miles from Agra. C was abandoned because of lack of wat

Photos: Deane Dickason (Ew Galloway); bottom, Richard Jos

ew Delhi, seat of the government of the epublic of India, is a magnificent city. Picturesque old buildings mingle with modern ones. This is President's house.

roup of round-the-world tourists finds lephant ride the oddest transportation.

Ten thousand Moslems pray before great Mosque of Delhi on a Friday morning.

ikh taxi drivers of Calcutta don't look ike their New York or Chicago brethren.

Jantar Mantar is early 18th-century observatory constructed by a Rajput King.

hotos: Richard Joseph; top, Deane Dickason Ewing Galloway); center right, Ewing Galloway

View of the Himalayas (which in Sanskrit means "abode of snow") from Sandakphu. Conquest of Everest and Annapurna h: drawn world interest in this great rang

The Bathing Ghats and temples on bank of the Ganges River are visited by tens of thousands each year. Hindus come t the sacred river as Moslems go to Mecca

Photos: Ewing Gallowa

ALE OF KASHMIR
S A GARDEN SPOT

Kashmir is one of the loveliest countries of the East, traversed by lofty ranges of the Himalayas, with lakes, rivers, forests. It is noted for its rich agriculture and its manufactures, especially Cashmeres.

rinagar, capital of Kashmir, on the helum River, is known as "Venice of the East," intersected with canals and waterways, with boats as transportation.

)al Lake, on outskirts of Srinagar, has everal Moghul Gardens, visited by boat.

A shikara, a sort of Kashmiri gondola, takes you about in canalled Srinagar.

'hotos: Schalek (Three Lions); bottom left, . Berko (Black Star); right, Black Star

Hyderabad, one of main cities of Western Pakistan, has its own style of air-conditioning: wind scoops on most of th buildings take in air, force it downwar

PAKISTAN IS DIVIDED INTO TWO REGIONS

Pakistan, once a province of India, was made an independent state in 1947, as a homeland for Indian Moslems. The two parts of the nation are separated by 900 miles of Indian territory. The larger part is West Pakistan, with Karachi as its capital. East Pakistan, one-sixth as large, has as its regional capital, Dacca.

Balconies are characteristic of houses in Karach While auto traffic grows, the victorias still thriv

Photos: Deane Dickason (Ewin Galloway); bottom, Camera Cl

Iuman-headed Sphinx guards 3 Pyramids f Giza. At left is Pyramid of Khafra.

Near Great Pyramid, Kamal el-Malakh made his discovery of the Cheops bark.

'Look, no hands!" say camel-mounted ıomads, eager for a piaster or two.

hotos: TWA Trans World Airne, bottom, Richard Joseph

EGYPT IS ANCIENT LAND OF THE NILE

The origin of Egypt's hoary culture is not revealed even in the many writings that have come down to us in all sorts of early forms. Some findings of the Ancient Kingdom date as far back as 3400 B.C., and the greatest creative period was from about 1580 to 945 B.C. Today you can ride in air-conditioned trains, stay in comfort at the Semiramis Hotel on the Nile (which has taken the place of burned-down Shepheard's), or at Mena House in shadow of pyramids.

The great Citadel in Cairo was built about 1179 by Saladin. It contains the

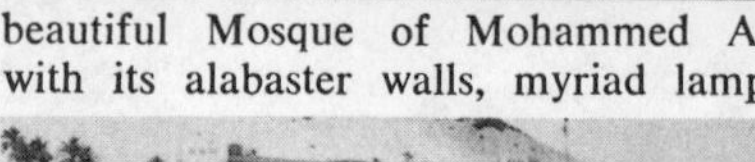

beautiful Mosque of Mohammed Al with its alabaster walls, myriad lamp

Cairo bazaars offer brass goods, marble and alabaster, gold and silver inlays.

Nile boat is shown opposite Catarac hotel at Aswan, site of irrigation dam

Photos: TWA Trans World Airline; bot tom right, Egyptian State Tourist Offic

gyptian women of Luxor, the ancient ty of Thebes, use their heads to help

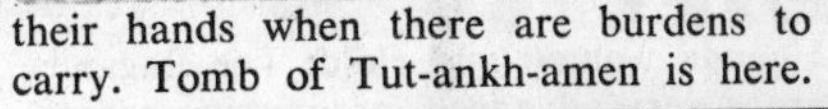

their hands when there are burdens to carry. Tomb of Tut-ankh-amen is here.

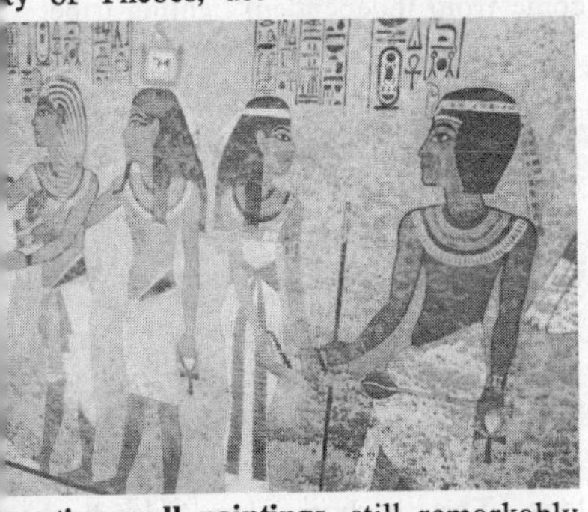

gyptian wall paintings, still remarkably right, decorate wall of King Tut's tomb.

labaster Sphinx is one of sights at 1emphis, capital of the Old Kingdom.

Temple of Luxor, built 1400 B.C., has huge pillars over fifty feet in height.

hotos: Henri Cartier-Bresson (Magnum); center eft, TWA Trans World Airline; bottom left, S. A. ooth; bottom right, Egyptian State Tourist Office

ADVENTURE CALLS IN BRITISH EAST AFRICA

Whether your name is Hemingway Smith, you'll find East Africa a land great variety, abundant wild life, amazi flora. It has the highest mountain (Ki manjaro) and the largest lake (Victor on the continent. British East Africa co sists of the Colony and Protectorate Kenya, Protectorates of Uganda, Zan bar, Trust Territory of Tanganyika.

Uganda woman and child: The Baganda are a very advanced, progressive people.

Newly initiated Masai warriors: The come from independent fighting tribe.

Dar es Salaam, meaning "Haven of Peace," is the capital of Tanganyika Territory. This harbor, almost landlocke handles over half of territory's export

Two full-maned lions seek the shade of a tree on Serengeti Plains, Tanganyika.

Arab dhows have traded with the Eas African coast for at least ten centuries

Photos: East Africa Railways & Harbours top right, lower left, Tanganyika Publi Relations Dept., bottom right, Len Youn

Elephants and other big game abound in the Amboseli Game Reserve lying below Africa's highest mountain—the snow-capped dome of Kilimanjaro, 19,340 ft.

Mt. Kenya is 17,056 ft. high. Some of Kenya tribes think it residence of gods.

Kilindini harbor on Mombasa Island is the gateway to both Kenya and Uganda.

Photos: Len Young; bottom right, East Africa Railways & Harbours

VICTORIA FALLS SURPASSES NIAGARA IN BOTH WIDTH AND HEIGHT.

DAVID LIVINGSTONE EXPLORED RHODESIA

British influence in Northern and Southern Rhodesia owes much to Livingstone and to Cecil Rhodes. Southern Rhodesia is in new Central African Federation which also includes Northern Rhodesia and Nyasaland. Victoria Falls, greatest natural feature of area, is on border between Northern and Southern Rhodesia.

Photo: Pan American World Airways

SOUTH AFRICA IS LAND OF CONTRASTS

Union of South Africa, British dominion of 13 million people, has busy cities of Johannesburg, Cape Town and Durban, fabulous gold mines, the great Kruger National Park, endless stretches of veld.

Johannesburg's busy Commissioner Street shows mushroom growth of gold center.

Drakensberg mountains tower above tourist hostel in Natal National Park.

Pretoria is the Union's administrative capital, though the legislature convenes at Cape Town. Winston Churchill escaped from prison here during Boer War, 1899.

Photos: Pan American World Airways

Union of South Africa

Durban is magnificently located on Natal Bay of the Indian Ocean. Marine Parade

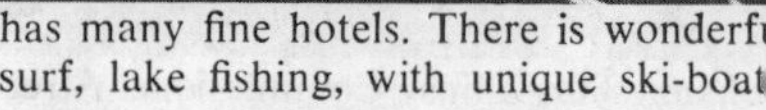

has many fine hotels. There is wonderf surf, lake fishing, with unique ski-boat

Visit to Kruger National Park is thrilling. You stay in thatched cottages, cook meals outdoors if you like. You driv right by lions, zebras, leopards, hippo

Photos: South Africa Tourist Corporation; Pa American World Airways; South African Railway

imberley diamond mine reached 1,200 et as open mine; shafts were carried to 4,000 feet. This mine was abandoned in 1915, but area is still diamond center.

Durban, you see Zulus in gay costume nd headdress drawing rickshas in street.

All these diamonds came from one day's output of Wesselton, Dutoitspan mines.

otos: Pan American World Airways; bot-m right, South African Tourist Corporation

Union of South Africa

Cape Town, legislative capital of the Union, has many impressive buildings. Flower Market is in front of City Ha with Table Mountain in backgroun

Aerial cableway to top of Table Mountain, 3,500 feet, gives view of both Atlantic and Indian Oceans. Cape Tov has lovely harbor, is compared to Napl

Photos: Pan Am-
ican World Airw

BERMUDA AND THE CARIBBEAN

The many islands, large and small, off the southeast coast of the United States have become most popular for both winter and summer vacations, because they give you "a trip abroad" with minimum time and with any sort of expenditure you wish to make.

There are dozens of cruises through the Caribbean, especially from December through March, many of them by transatlantic liners put on the job of earning dollars for their owners during the time when travel to the European ports is slack. Taking such a ship is a good way to "try out" a trip abroad and see how it appeals to you. Many of the cruises offer lavish entertainment, planned shore excursions.

There are also regularly scheduled trips throughout the year by such attractive vessels as Furness' *Queen of Bermuda* and new *Ocean Monarch*. They make frequent trips to Bermuda, with longer cruises from time to time. Easter and Christmas cruises are especially popular.

By air, almost any point in the West Indies is reached in a few hours. Pan American, BOAC, Eastern Airlines and others provide a network of air routes that will take you any particular place, or a combination of places, quickly and

"Ocean Monarch" docks at St. George's.

pleasantly. Bermuda is served by Pan American, BOAC and Colonial. The flight takes 3 to 4 hours, depending upon equipment and winds.

Variety is certainly offered by the enchanting isles of the West Indies. If you want gaiety, bustle and lots of entertainment, choose Havana, San Juan, or Kingston. For quietude in the dignity of British colonial atmosphere, you'll like Nassau and Bermuda and Montego Bay. For the real "far, far away from it all" effect, you'll want one of the Virgin Islands, or the barely discovered Antigua or St. Lucia.

One of the best things to do is to make a sort of survey trip the first time, by cruise ship or by air, and "sample" several places on one trip. Cruise itineraries and air excursions often enable you to visit several of the islands at no greater cost than visiting one. Then you can pick the spot you like the best for next time.

Photo: Furness Bermuda Line

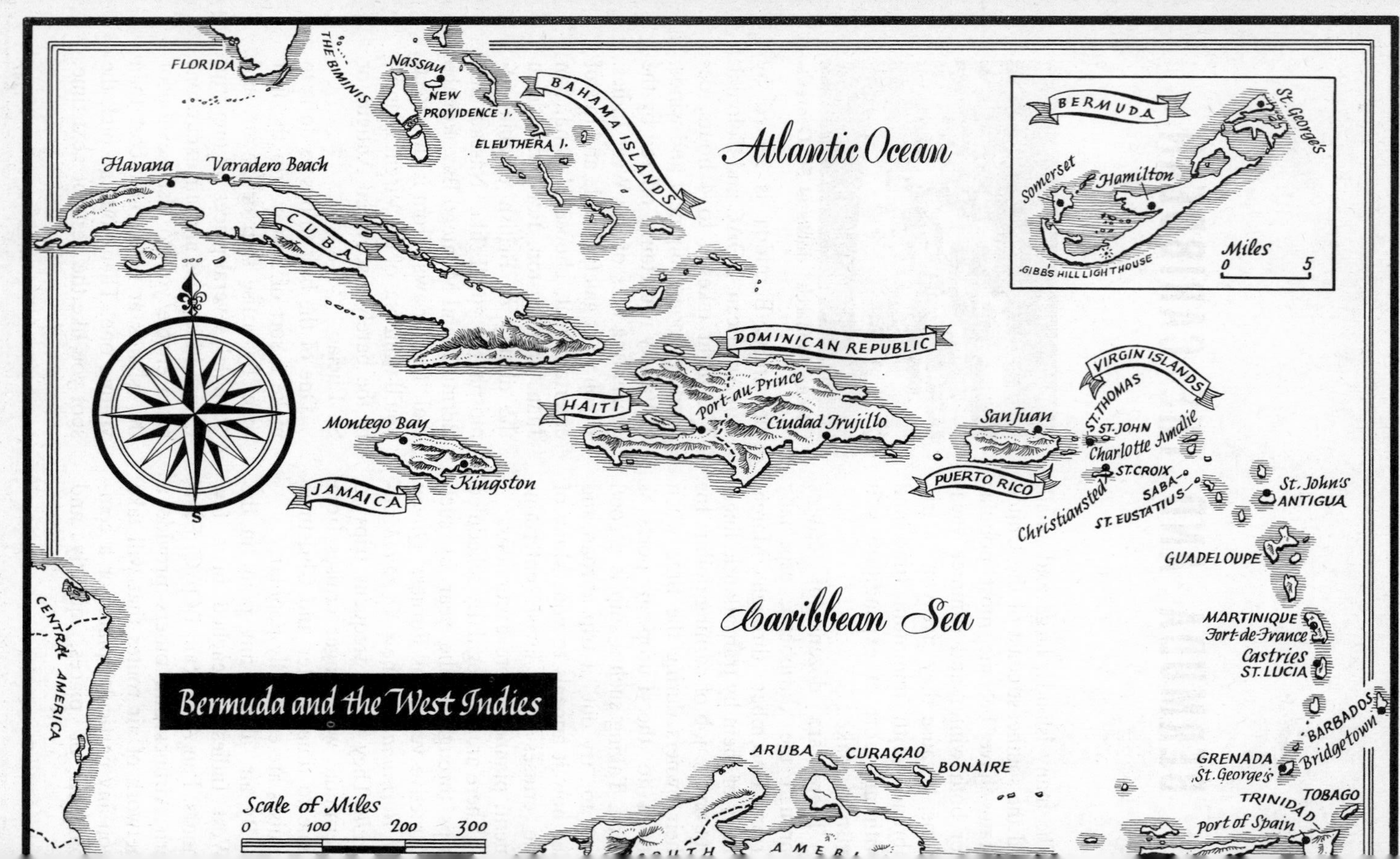
Bermuda and the West Indies
Atlantic Ocean
Caribbean Sea
FLORIDA
THE BIMINIS
Nassau
NEW PROVIDENCE I.
ELEUTHERA I.
BAHAMA ISLANDS
Havana
Varadero Beach
CUBA
DOMINICAN REPUBLIC
HAITI
Port-au-Prince
Ciudad Trujillo
Montego Bay
Kingston
JAMAICA
San Juan
PUERTO RICO
VIRGIN ISLANDS
ST. THOMAS
ST. JOHN
Charlotte Amalie
ST. CROIX
Christiansted
SABA
ST. EUSTATIUS
St. John's
ANTIGUA
GUADELOUPE
MARTINIQUE
Fort-de-France
Castries
ST. LUCIA
BARBADOS
Bridgetown
GRENADA
St. George's
TRINIDAD
TOBAGO
Port of Spain
ARUBA
CURAÇAO
BONAIRE
CENTRAL AMERICA
SOUTH AMER
BERMUDA
St. George's
Somerset
Hamilton
GIBBS HILL LIGHTHOUSE
Miles
0
5
Scale of Miles
0
100
200
300
S

ARAWAY COTTAGE COLONY, WARWICK PARISH, IS ONE OF NEWEST.

OVELY BERMUDA AS PEACE, QUIET

"Tranquil and contenting" were Mark Twain's words for Bermuda, and thousands of visitors have found it so, even when horses and carriages have given way to motorbikes and small English autos. Gulf Stream protection prevents extremes of temperature. Easter lilies, oleander combine with pink sands and blue-green sea waters for real beauty.

to: Bermuda News Bureau

Hamilton Harbor is the home of Royal Bermuda Yacht Club, famous for racing of 14 ft. dinghies carrying 400 feet canvas. Ferries run across busy har'

Surreys and drays have largely been replaced by Austins and Morris Minors.

Bicycles and Velos—bikes with motors front wheel—are favorite transportati

Photos: Bermuda News Bure
bottom left, Lester L. Bc

lds of Easter lilies are a lovely sight in spring. They're shipped everywhere.

Bermuda homes are built of native stone, in white, or in pastel pink, blue, purple.

ape Bay has one of the many secluded aches. The sands, eroded from coral rock, are often pink in color. The water sparkles in brilliant greens and blues.

tos: Bermuda News Bureau;
right, Lester L. Baker

Par-le-Ville Gardens, on Queen Street next to library, make a pleasant place to rest after a trip to Hamilton's m shops where you get fine British wool

Front Street, Hamilton, usually bustling, is very peaceful when shops are closed.

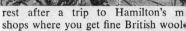

Crystal Caves, Leamington Caves c stalactites and stalagmites, and souven

SWIZZLE INN IS FAVORITE STOP.

WORLD'S TINIEST DRAW BRID

Photos: Bermuda News Bure
two at bottom, Richard Jos

nuda Cathedral stands at a high t, is one of islands' many churches.

The Devil's Hole, a natural aquarium, is place where you can fish without hooks.

's Hill Light House affords a view its top of many of the 150 islands.

This "Moon Gate" is one of several, an odd design said to be copied from China.

QUEEN OF BERMUDA DOCKS RIGHT AT FRONT STREET, HAMILTON

s: Bermuda News Bureau; top center left, A. Milton Runyon

Jai Alai, one of the world's fastest games, is the most popular sport in Havana.

Morro Castle, fort at the entrance to Havana ha
was built in the late 16th century as a protection ag

Float of the Queen of Carnival takes place of honor in festival held each year.

CUBA HAS GAY DAYS AND NIGH

Cuba has always been one of the r
popular islands for U. S. visitors an
fascinating capital, Havana, is the p
that most of them go. It's just a short
from Miami by plane or boat, and you
go direct from New York or Chic
Practically every cruise ship anchors ir
harbor overnight. You can shop for
fume, alligator bags, cigars; there's
National Casino, Oriental Park, som
most exotic night life outside of Pari

Photos: Morro Castle by A. L. Koo
others by Cuban Tourist Commi

A **street vendor** of straw hats and handbags displays his inexpensive souvenirs.

:neers. There's another Morro Castle at Santiago
uba, and still another at San Juan, Puerto Rico.

d rhumbas are a feature of night
which offer most exotic night life.

The National Casino is the "Monte Carlo of America" with all games of chance.

: Cuban Tourist Commission

San Francisco dock, in Havana harbor, is where the tender lands you from your ship anchored in the roadstead. It's ju short walk to Sloppy Joe's, Two Brot

The National Capitol dominates center of the metropolis, founded by Velasquez.

Nacional de Cuba is most famous h in the capital. New pool offers lush liv

Photos: A. L. Koolish; bottom left, C Tourist Commission; right, Kirkeby H

Cristobal, known as the Columbus ıedral, is over two hundred years old.

The Arts Building, recently opened, is representative of the present-day Havana.

eo de Marti (formerly "The Prado") s from the center of Havana to the sea wall. Treelined, it reminds you of the Champs-Elysées, with its sidewalk cafés.

:os: A. Milton Runyon; top right, Cuban Tourist ·mission; bottom, Pan American World Airways

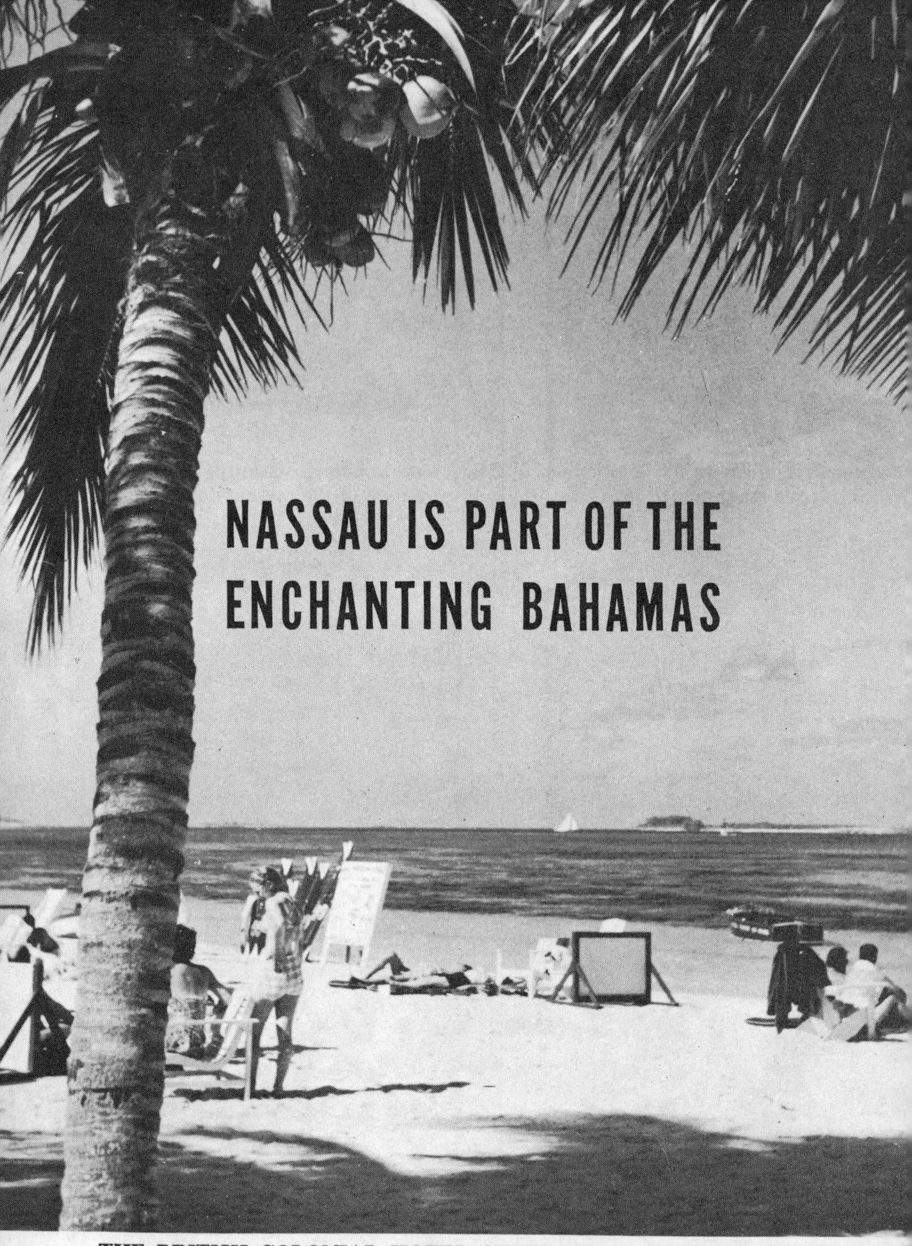

NASSAU IS PART OF THE ENCHANTING BAHAMAS

THE BRITISH COLONIAL HOTEL OFFERS TWO BEACHES, WATER-SKII

Nassau is less than an hour away from Miami by Pan American or BOAC, and the latter offers a 4½-hour direct flight from New York. You'll find it probably the most dignified of the British islands, peaceful, bucolic. The beaches are magnificent, and the climate almost alw warm and sunny. The Bahamas are of the world's great sportfishing grou abounding in tuna, sailfish, barrac bonito, wahoo, dolphin. And the Street shops offer treasures from abr

Photo: A. Milton Ru

he Straw Market, in Rawson Square, can buy straw hats, bags, table mats

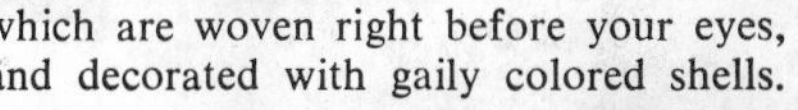

which are woven right before your eyes, and decorated with gaily colored shells.

ist Church was designated as the hedral by Queen Victoria in 1861.

The British Colonial is Nassau's second largest hotel, with two beaches, pool.

os: Nassau Development Board; om right, A. Milton Runyon

Paradise Beach is as famous as Waikiki. Surf temperature averages 70°, even in winter. Palm trees and sun-shelters to its charm. Note cruise ships at anc

Prince George Dock is the place you get boat for short trip to Paradise Beach.

Horse and carriage await visitors Royal Victoria Hotel's tropical gard

Photos: Nassau Develop Board — Frederic M

al Victoria Hotel's new garden pool urrounded by luxuriant trees, plants.

Bay Street is famed for shops offering British textiles, gloves, leather goods.

een's Staircase is 65-step man-made yon, carved out of the solid coral rock.

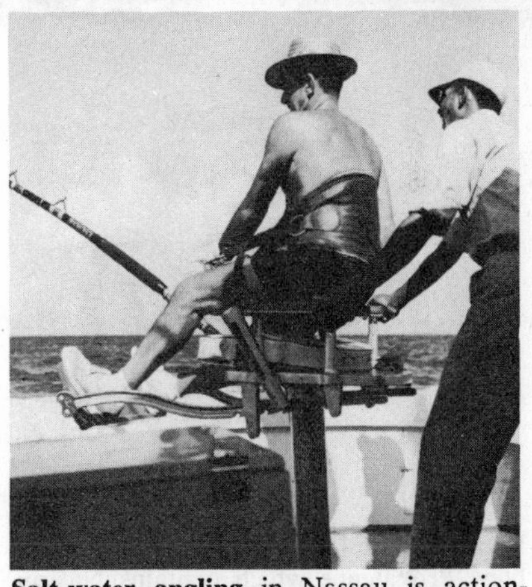

Salt-water angling in Nassau is action-packed, for big game fisherman, amateur.

is octagonal building was once a jail; 1879 it was converted into a library.

Fort Montagu Beach Hotel, seen from Fort Montagu, is Nassau's third largest.

os: Nassau
elopment Board

Eleuthera is a large Bahama island east of New Providence which contains Nassau.

Governor's Harbor has miles of beac and town with name of French Le

Walker Cay is one of 700 Bahama islets. Columbus made his first landfall on one.

Bimini is the Bahama island closes the U.S., noted for its big game fish

Photos: N
Development B

UMMER NEVER
AVES JAMAICA

gest British island in the West ies, Jamaica offers beautiful moun- scenery, lovely beaches and good 'round climate. Daytime tem- atures are in the upper 70's all , and trade winds make for cool ts.

amaica has five different resort as: The first is the capital city of gston and suburban St. Andrews. the eastern tip is Port Antonio and northeast coast. Central Jamaica Ocho Rios. Further west is Man- ille, its mountains and the south st. And on the northwest coast is famous Montego Bay.

amaica is 2½ hours from Miami air, 6 hours from New York, and gston harbor is a port of call for ny cruise ships. Part of the Greater tilles, Jamaica is 140 miles long, miles at its greatest width. It is 90 es south of Cuba. Some of its untains are as high as 7,000 feet.

aican woman plaits hat from ng leaves of the light jipijapa palm.

Noel Coward, English author and playwright, makes his island home at "Blue Harbour."

tos: Jamaica Tourist
de Development Board

Native markets in Kingston offer fresh tropical fruits; shops have English goods.

With razor sharp machete, this cutte about to start on a field of sugar c

Flame blowers provide entertainmen night for visitors at Hotel Casa Bla

WATER SKIIERS SKIM PAST TOWER ISLE, JAMAICA'S $2,000,000 RESO

Photos: Jamaica Tourist Trade Development Bo center right, Gerald Murison, bottom, Pierre Ch

rt Charles, 1656, and Palisadoes airport on long peninsula that encloses harbor.

The south coast has many lakes where fishing is fun, and even washing clothes!

ctor's Cave beach at Montego Bay is of the finest in the entire Caribbean. as fine white coral sand and sea water so clear that a boat floating on its surface seems to be floating in mid-air! Bathing is a constant delight, with no rough surf.

os: Jamaica Tourist
e Development Board

From near Berrydale, on the northeast coast, a 2½ mile sinuously curving stretch of gentle rapids on the Rio Grande is t route of the unique sport of river-rafting

Montego Bay, with fashionable Sunset Lodge and Casa Blanca Hotel, is today the Cannes of Jamaica, even though on 35 years ago it was just a fishing villag

Photos: Vilma F. Bergane; bottom, J maica Tourist Trade Development Boa

HAITI IS A MAGIC ISLAND"

› appreciate Haiti, you'll want to ıow something of its strange history, Toussaint L'Ouverture, of Dessa-ıes, of Henri Christophe, Haiti's ack Napoleon who built the fabu-ıus *Citadelle*. Read John Vander-ok's *Black Majesty*, or William Sea-ook's *The Magic Island*, or Kenneth ›berts' novel of Haiti, *Lydia Bailey*.

Haiti is one of the two Negro re-ıblics in the world, the other be-g Liberia. The official language is ·ench, but most people speak a ·ench patois called Creole.

Haiti is 4 hours by air from Mi-ıi. Panama Line ships call there.

biquitous small boys, usually less ell dressed, pose for your photos.

ıt Centre d'Art, in Port-au-Prince, ee work of many Haitian painters.

The Citadelle was built by Henri Christophe to stop French invasion that never came.

'hotos: Pan American World ıirways, top left, Jerry Hardy

TRUJILLO PEACE MONUMENT IS AT SANTIAGO DE LOS CABALLEROS

THE DOMINICAN REPUBLIC COMBINES OLD AND NEW

Founded 1496 by Bartholomew Columbus, Ciudad Trujillo (formerly Santo Domingo) is the oldest permanent European settlement in the New World. Dominican Republic occupies eastern part of Hispaniola Island, Haiti western

Photo: Dominican Republic Information Center

"SWITZERLAND F THE AMERICAS" —PUERTO RICO

Part of the United States, yet distinctly foreign in its atmosphere, 100-mile-long Puerto Rico offers mountain scenery to rival the French and Swiss Alps, beautiful beaches, and a pleasant climate. The winter temperature averages 74.5° and the summer 80°, a difference of only 5.5°. San Juan is only about 3 hours by air from New York by Pan American or Eastern. Delta-C&S flies daily from New Orleans via Cuba, Haiti and Dominican Republic.

abulous Caribe Hilton, with its New Garden Wing, Is Located Right on the Ocean.

'hoto: Hilton Hotels International

Porta Coeli, "gate of heaven," one of the oldest churches in the western hemisphere.

Flower market offers a profusion of exotic blooms from tropical gardens.

Luquillo Beach is a mile-long crescent, fringed with palms, near El Yunque forest.

University of Puerto Rico has many students and professors from U.S.A.

Photos: Hamilton Wright

El Morro, built in 1539 with ship ballast, guards entrance to San Juan harbor.

Caribe Hilton's distinctive feature is that its 300 rooms have private balconies.

Condado Beach Hotel has been newly renovated, and a new mountain resort, El Barranquitas, has just opened. Best known country club is the Berwind, Rio Piedras.

Native net fisherman demonstrates possibilities for the sportsman. Puerto Rican waters are fished for white and blue marlin, sailfish, Allison tuna, many others.

Photos, Hamilton Wright; top right, Richard Joseph

Fiesta Santiago, celebrated for over 300 years by the villagers of Loíza Aldea, produces weird faces in coconut mask Pageantry and parades last two week

Hotel Montemar at Aguadilla offers cooling breezes, spectacular views from terrace high above the Atlantic. Here newlywe need pay only for one instead of for tw

Photos: Hamilton Wrig

'apoleon's Empress Josephine was born Trois-Ilets, and a marble statue of her rises in the center of the Savannah or public park in city of Fort-de-France.

MARTINIQUE IS 'POMPEII OF THE WEST INDIES"

On May 8, 1902 Mont Pelée blew up with a roar and wiped out the whole 40,000 population of St. Pierre, with just one survivor, a prisoner in an underground dungeon. Martinique is one of the two main French islands in the lesser Antilles, the other being Guadeloupe. 50 miles long by 19 wide, Martinique is very beautiful and a good place for relaxing because there's no night life. By plane it's 4½ hours from San Juan, Puerto Rico; by ship from New York, 8 days.

›to: Pan American World Airways

Important influence of Roman Catholic Church has helped control communists.

Native net-thrower fishermen in Ville-Fontaine show tourists how net is made

Colorful costumes indicate native gaiet also shown in dancing at *Select Tang*

Lido Hotel, four miles from Fort-de-France, is place for bathing and loafing.

Vieux Moulin, Chez Etienne, L'Aube de Manoir offer good French cuisi

Photos: Pan Am-ican World Airw

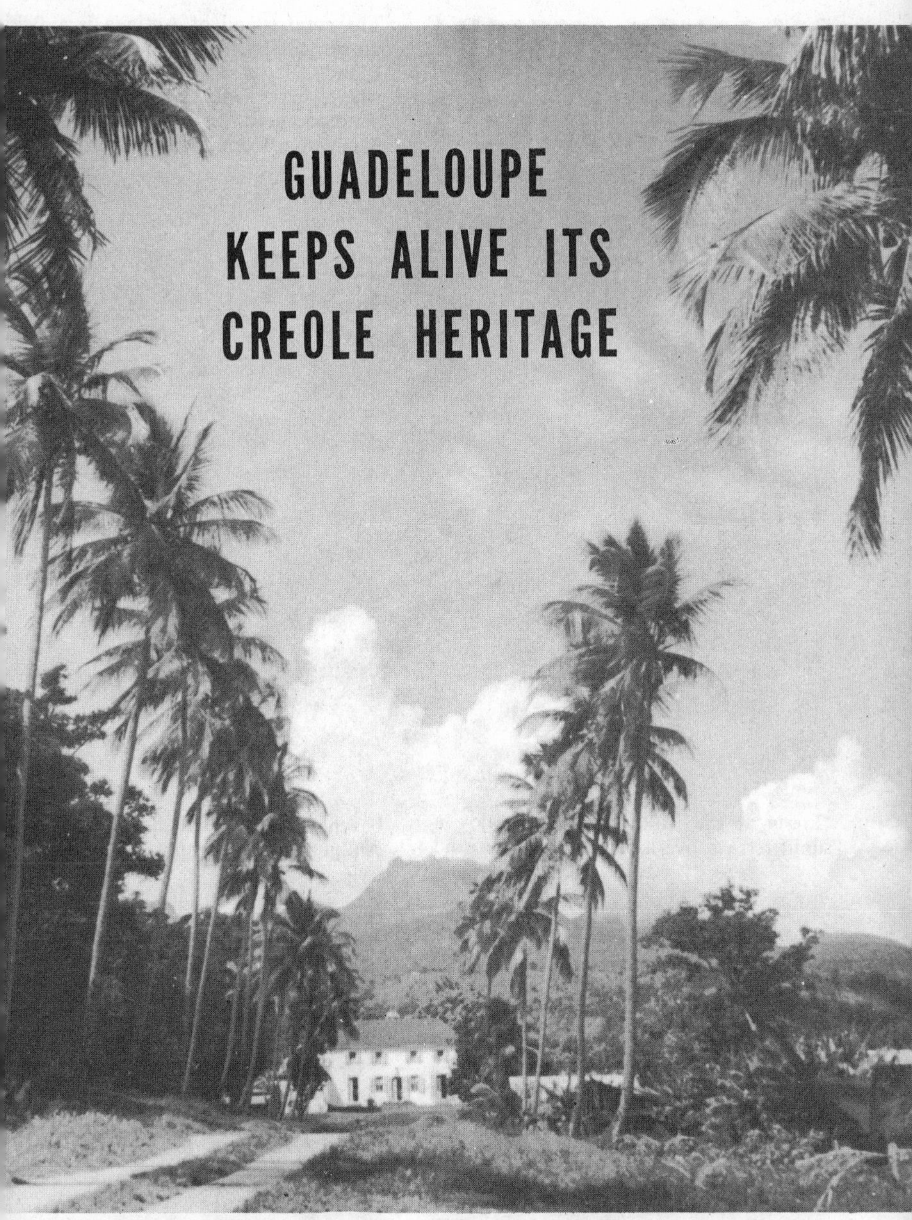

GUADELOUPE KEEPS ALIVE ITS CREOLE HERITAGE

out 80 miles north of Martinique, the er French possession of Guadeloupe one of those "get-away-from-it-all" ces where accommodations are far m luxurious, but the climate is ideal, nery superb, and natives interesting.

Pointe-à-Pitre is the principal city and port. The official capital is Basse-Terre, about forty miles away. A jeepable track leads to the base of the extinct volcano, La Soufrière, a good stiff climb. People keep alive gay Creole customs.

to: French Govern-
t Tourist Office

DISCOVER ANTIGUA FOR FRIENDLINESS

The coral island of Antigua is a British crown colony, capital of the Leeward Islands. It is a quiet, friendly place where every visitor is treated as an honored guest. St. John's is only 3 hours' flying time from San Juan, Puerto Rico.

Guests at the Mill Reef Club enjoy a sunlit terrace overlooking the white sand beaches and clear blue-green wate Antigua has swimming, tennis and gol

Old winches like this were used to haul Lord Nelson's ships onto beach for repair.

Fishing boats may be chartered; wate near reefs are perfect for spear-fishin

Photos: Pan Am ican World Airw

EX-DANISH VIRGIN ISLANDS ARE TRANQUIL, CHARMING

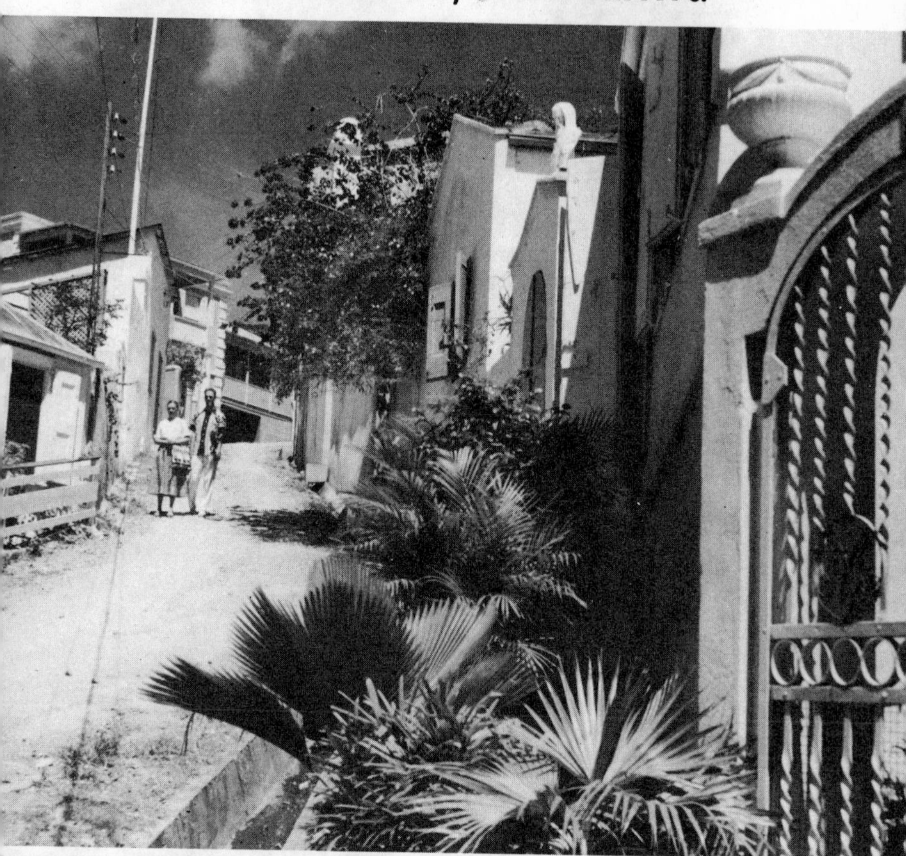

ILLSIDE STREETS OF CHARLOTTE AMALIE HAVE FLOWERING VINES.

ırchased from Denmark in 1917, for .5,000,000, the three main American rgin Islands of St. Thomas, St. Croix ıd St. John are still unspoiled by too ıny tourists. Since they have free-port ıtus, it is possible to buy many wonder- ı things at a fraction of their U.S. prices. ost visitors come for the wonderful cli- ıte, with an average mean temperature 79° F., the bucolic atmosphere, the de- ht of being "abroad" and yet still on me territory.

St. Thomas is 80 miles east of Puerto Rico, 25 minutes by air. The entire plane trip from New York, via Eastern or Pan American takes about 6½ hours. Cruise ships frequently call at Charlotte Amalie, the port of St. Thomas.

St. Thomas is most highly developed island, with the new Virgin Isle and many fine hotels. St. Croix is the largest, most agricultural, with small but good hotels. St. John has most rugged primitiveness, limited but very delightful guest houses.

ıto: Pan Amer- ı World Airways

Distinctive tower features Bluebeard's Castle Hotel, setting for many legends.

Virgin Isle Hotel is newest, luxurious. Swimming pool overlooks hills, harbor.

From the terrace of Bluebeard's Cas Hotel, you look out over the whole tov

Photos: Pan American World Airways; top le A. Milton Runyon; bottom left, Virgin Isle Ho

Charlotte Amalie. On far side is the
ench village, called Cha-Cha Town, whose people are descendants of the early French settlers. Shrine of St. Anne is here.

Cruise ship "Mauretania" stays in harbor, ferries passengers to dock by motorboat.

Steep streets of Charlotte Amalie ofte require steps from one level to anothe

Three youngsters grin for the tourist-photographer in hope of U.S. pennies.

Magen's Bay beach is on Atlantic side c St. Thomas; Morning Star on Caribbea

Christiansted on northeast (above) and Frederiksted on the west are the two principal towns on St. Croix.

This old Danish sugar m is St. Croix Island landmar

Photos: A. Milton Runyon; bottc row, Pan American World Airwc

TRINIDAD IS THE CAPITAL OF CALYPSO

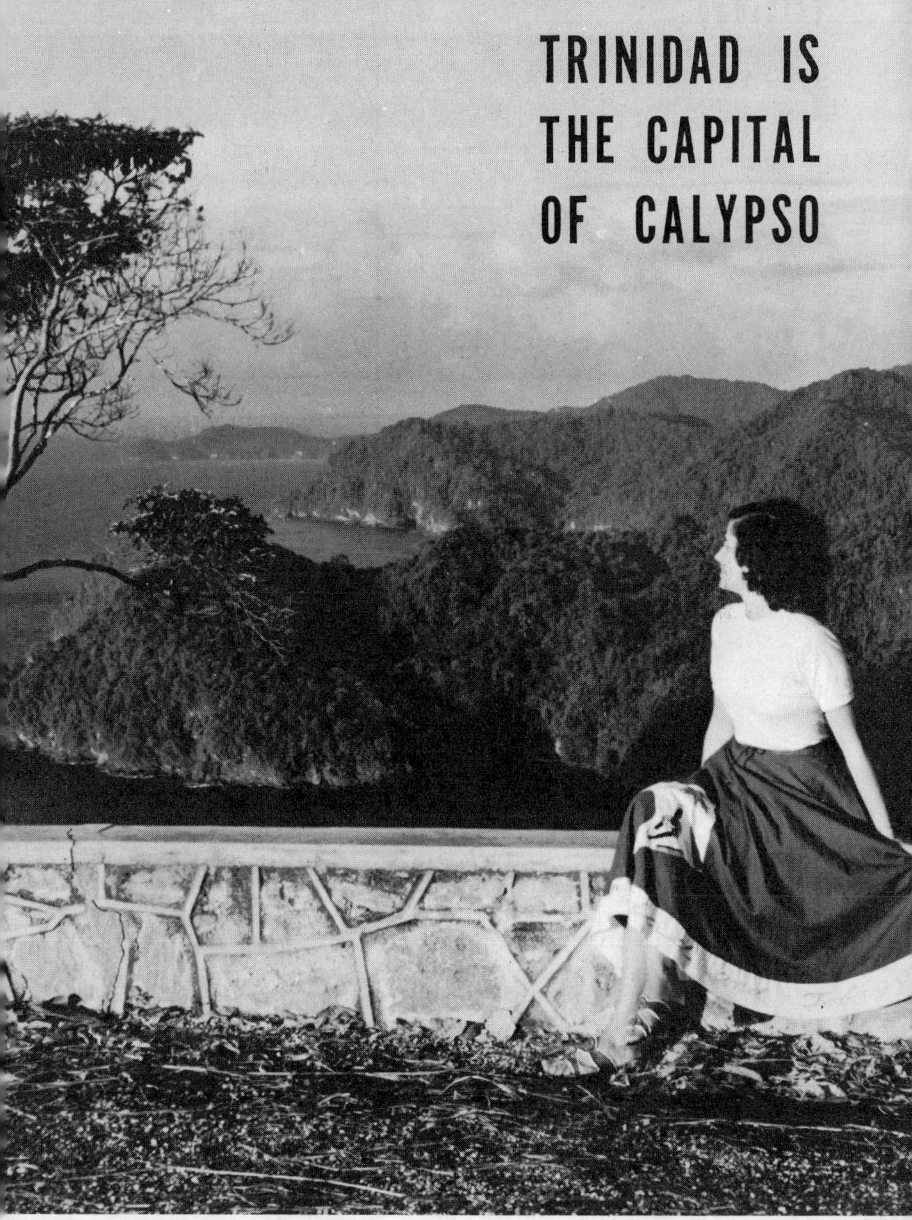

N DRIVE "OVER THE SADDLE" TO MARACAS BAY YOU PAUSE HERE.

ost colorful and polyglot of all the est Indies islands, Trinidad is home of lypso, the satirical and haunting folk ngs. As you walk through the streets of e capital, Port of Spain, you're likely to encounter East Indians, Hindus, British, Spanish, French, Chinese, Africans, Americans. There are Moslem mosques, Hindu temples, bazaars. Port of Spain is 9 hours' flying time from New York.

to: Trinidad and ago Tourist Board

Beautiful Maracas Bay, on North Coast, is reached by drive from Port of Spain that winds through bamboo groves, ba yan trees, coffee and cocoa plantatio

Donkey cart loaded with coconuts is the Trinidad version of sidewalk "milk bar."

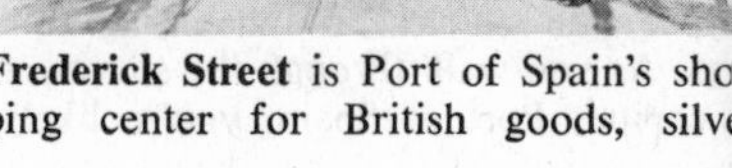

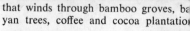

Frederick Street is Port of Spain's sho ping center for British goods, silv

Photos: A. Milton Runyon; bottom ro Trinidad and Tobago Tourist Boc

ch Lake (Asphalt) is supposed to be 5 feet deep. You can walk on surface.

A Sikh, one of many East Indians living in Trinidad, stands before a mosque.

e local "steel bands" consist of steel ums of varying tones beaten to Calypso rhythm. The effect is surprisingly good. January is month of Calypso competition.

ueen's Park Hotel, center of social e, is located on 200-acre Savannah.

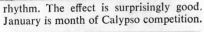

Trinidad's fertile soil yields sugar cane, cacao, coffee, citrus fruits, coconuts.

otos: Trinidad and bago Tourist Board

TOBAGO IS UNSPOILED

Believed to be the spot where Robinsc Crusoe was shipwrecked, Tobago is littl known place whose visitors would like preserve its charm for themselves alon

Aquatic Club beach has cabanas thatched with palm leaves and wonderful beach. It's at Pigeon Point, Man of War Bay. Wit sea goggles you may look at marine lif

Exotic birds of paradise are found only in Tobago and in New Guinea. They're shy, hard to find, but it's an unforgettable experience to see them on this tiny isle.

Tobago is a land of leisure and quie beauty that you have often longed fo There are four main hotels and one gues house, an indication of the privacy here

Photos: Trinidad ar Tobago Tourist Boar

ILLEMSTAD, BISECTED BY ST. ANNA BAY, HAS PONTOON BRIDGE.

IL BRINGS RICHES O DUTCH INDIES

The Netherlands West Indies consist of two widely separated units: the islands of Curaçao, Aruba and Bonaire, off the coast of Venezuela, and 500 miles away in the Lesser Antilles, the islands of Saba, St. Eustatius and southern half of St. Martin (the other half being French). A non-stop flight from New York brings you to Curaçao in just over 8 hours.

oto: Netherlands West
ies Tourist Committee

Bird's-eye view of Willemstad shows t
halves, joined by "Queen Emma" brid

CURAÇAO MIGHT BE HOLLAND AT SEA

Peter Stuyvesant became governor of Curaçao in 1643 and moved to New Amsterdam, now New York, in 1647. For 17 years he was Director General of the New Netherlands and Netherlands West Indies. Formerly a colony, this territory became in 1922 an integral part of the kingdom of the Netherlands. At first glance it looks like a slice of Holland, tidy and well scrubbed, moved out into the Atlantic 40 miles north of Venezuela. But you soon notice the West Indies influence. The buildings come in pastel, and sometimes more violent tints to soften the glare.

Passengers on cruise steamer get vi
of pontoon bridge as it swings to si

Photos: Netherlands W
Indies Tourist Committ

iscadera Bay Club, foremost resort, has atural swimming pool with sea water.

Everything but liquor and tobacco is imported at 3.3% duty; it's almost free port.

loating market forms daily on older side f town, with schooners from many ports.

Foodstuffs are peddled right from the decks. Many merchants are Venezuelan.

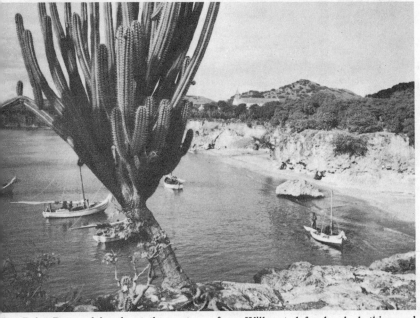

'est Point Bay and beach, at the westn tip of Curaçao, is a popular drive from Willemstad for lunch, bathing and fishing. Aloes cactus flourishes here.

otos: Netherlands West dies Tourist Committee

BARBADOS IS A TROPICAL BRITAIN

Said to have been originally discove
by the Portuguese and named "Los B
bados" because of the bearded fig tr
Barbados was claimed by the British
1605, settled by them beginning in 16
and has been under the British flag e
since—something quite unusual in
history of a Caribbean island. M
easterly of the West Indies, Barbado
1¼ hours by airplane from Port of Sp

Sam Lord's Castle, at St. Philip, is now operated as a residential club, one of several on Barbados, and there are go
small hotels. Life is simple, leisure

Photos: Barbc
Publicity Commi

Excellent roads criss-cross Barbados Island, with its very English landscape.

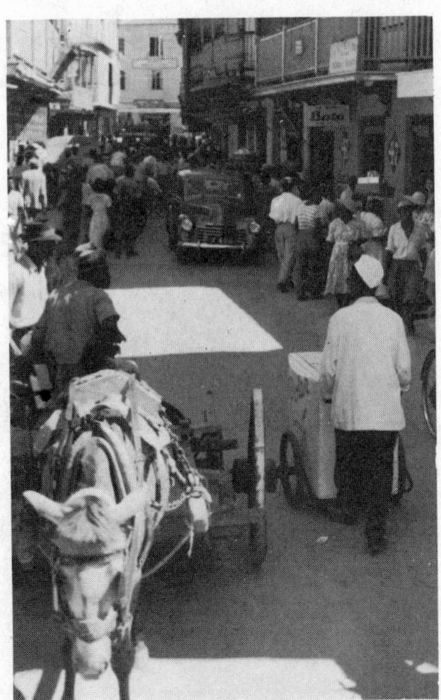

Swan Street, Bridgetown, is filled with carts, cyclists, autos, and pedestrians.

The Savannah, big oblong of grass, is used for polo matches, race meetings. At races the police band plays; the little horses bear colors raced for generations.

Photos: Barbados Publicity Committee

GRENADA IS "THE SPICE ISLAND"

Most southerly of the Windward Islan
Grenada is famous for its nutmeg, clo
and for some of the most beautiful wh
sand beaches in the world. It has Gra
Étang, spectacular volcanic lake 1740
above sea level. Grenada is just 50 m
utes' flying time from Port of Spa

Morne Rouge Beach Club, St. George's, has excellent beach, dining and dancing.

Another fine spot to swim, or dream,
Grand Anse, with two miles of white san

Guests of the Santa Maria Hotel enjoy tea on veranda overlooking picturesque

St. George's. Its red-roofed houses ar
pale pink and green, its atmosphere quie

Photos: Pan Ame
ican World Airwa

arenage Bay is a calm harbor for fish-g boats and cargo schooners. One section of St. George's is on the bay, another on the sea, connected by tunnel.

oto: Pan Amer-an World Airways

ST. LUCIA WAS PORT FOR CLIPPER SHIPS

Directly in the path of the trade wir
on route of the sailing clippers of o
St. Lucia is largest of Windward Islan
Castries has sheltered harbor, one
finest in the West Indies and long
important coaling station. Landmarks a
mineral springs near Soufrière and cor
of the Twin Pitons Peaks. Castries
just 2 hours by air from Port of Spa

Hotel Antoine is high on a hill overlooking the city of Castries, its harbor and background of chocolate drop hi
Pigeon Island Beach Club is charmi

Photo: Pan Am
ican World Airw

CANADA

CANADIAN PACIFIC'S "THE CANADIAN" CROSSES MISSISSIPPI RIVER.

Because many parts of the United States are hot in the summer, nearby Canada has become a favorite vacation ground, offering cool lakes, rivers, beautiful mountains. And in winter, snow for sports is abundant in the Laurentians and Canadian Rockies.

One of Canada's many advantages is its excellent transportation. Canadian Pacific and Canadian National cover it with great railroad networks. There are Great Lakes steamers and St. Lawrence River steamers. Trans-Canada Air Lines will take you across Canada, or abroad. And because the highways are excellent, and less likely to be crowded, many tourists prefer to travel by car, especially on such a scenic drive as the one around the Gaspé Peninsula between Maine and the St. Lawrence. Another excellent idea is to make your trip abroad by way of the St. Lawrence River. You embark either at Montreal or Quebec on a white Canadian Pacific liner and travel nearly a thousand miles in the quiet river waters before you get to the open ocean, and you can get a very good idea of Canada on the way. On the west coast, Canada is the gateway to Alaska, via the 1000-mile "inside passage" route from Victoria and Vancouver up Georgia Strait, Queen Charlotte Strait to Prince Rupert, Juneau and Skagway.

In visiting Canada you will meet the warm friendship of good neighbors. You cross the border without fuss, you need no passport, suffer no restrictions. You'll be amazed at the industrial developments in many places, but you'll enjoy some of the world's great resorts and national parks covering 29,000 square miles.

Photo: Canadian Pacific Railway

Canada
Scale of Miles
0 100 200 500
Arctic Ocean
Pacific Ocean
Atlantic Ocean
ALASKA
YUKON R.
YUKON
NORTHWEST TERRITORIES
BRITISH COLUMBIA
ROCKY MOUNTAINS
ALBERTA
SASKATCHEWAN
MANITOBA
ONTARIO
QUEBEC
NEWFOUNDLAND
NEW BRUNSWICK
NOVA SCOTIA
PRINCE EDWARD IS.
UNITED STATES
Juneau
Ketchikan
VANCOUVER IS.
Victoria
Vancouver
Seattle
JASPER PARK
Lake Louise
Banff
Calgary
GLACIER NATIONAL PARK
Regina
Winnipeg
Kenora
Churchill
Hudson Bay
S
THE GREAT LAKES
MUSKOKA LAKES
Toronto
Niagara Falls
Ottawa
Montreal
ST. LAWRENCE R.
Quebec
LAURENTIAN MTS.
SAGUENAY R.
Tadoussac
GASPE PEN.
Percé
Charlottetown
Saint John
St. Andrews-by-the-Sea
Bay of Fundy
Grand Pré
Halifax
Gander
St. John's
MONTREAL
ST. DENIS
ST. LAWRENCE
ROCKLAND AV.
UNIVERSITY OF MONTREAL
MT. ROYAL PARK
CÔTE DES NIEGES
SHERBROOKE
ST. CATHERINE
NOTRE DAME
ST. JAMES
ST. LAWRENCE RIVER

ATEAU FRONTENAC HOTEL IS LIKE A MEDIEVAL FRENCH CASTLE.

JEBEC HAS CHARM F THE OLD WORLD

Discovered by Jacques Cartier in 1534 and settled by the French under Champlain early in the 17th century, Quebec hasn't lost its Old World flavor. Hand looms, outdoor bake ovens, spinning wheels are still in daily use. Although French is spoken throughout the province, most people also speak English.

o: Canadian
fic Railway

Calèches haul tourists up and down the hills as the driver tells of historic spots.

Rue Sous-le-Cap, in Lower Town, is s to be narrowest street in North Ameri

Quebec is deeply religious city, with Sisters of the Good Shepherd, and many shrines.

St. Louis Gate is one of several rema ing from old fortifications of early da

Hooked rugs, made during long winters, are good buys; so are carved wood figures.

Curling is kind of bowling played wi heavy stones slid along ice toward a ma

Photos: Canadian Pacific Railw top left, Canadian National Railw

Chateau Frontenac's toboggan slide takes you at mile-a-minute speed from near top of Citadel hill down to Dufferin Terrace with spectacular view of St. Lawrence.

Photo: Canadian Pacific Railway

Ste. Anne de Beaupré, a few miles east of Quebec City, is most famous shrine of the New World. The great Basilica burned in 1922, but has been built anew.

Scala Sancta, sacred stairway at Ste. Anne, is worn by the knees of worshipers.

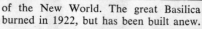

Montmorency Falls, between Quebec and Ste. Anne, are even higher than Niagara.

Photos: Canadian Government Travel Bureau; top, Canadian Pacific Railway

und Lake Inn, Weir, is one of many orts of Quebec and the Laurentians. Laurentides Park and Mt. Tremblant Park have 1500 lakes and cascading streams.

aple sugar camps in the Laurentians ther their annual harvest each spring.

Many a rural Quebec family still goes to Mass on Sunday in a horse-drawn buggy.

usky races are one of Canada's many inter sports: Scandinavian-type skiing in the east, the dashing Alpine kind in western Rockies; skating, hockey, curling.

otos: Canadian National Railways; center left d bottom, Canadian Pacific Railway; cen- right, Canadian Government Travel Bureau

River steamer of Canada Steamship Lines passes Manoir Richelieu, at Murray Bay.

Bonaventure Island, off end of Gasp peninsula, is a sanctuary for gannet

Old Habitant houses like this one on I of Orleans have been lived in 200 yea

Percé Rock is the high point of tour around Gaspé peninsula. It's the pierced rock that Cartier first saw beside th shore, a great stone buffeted by sea

Photos: Canada Steamship Lines; Canadi National Railways; Canadian Pacific Rai way; Office Provincial de Publicité, Queb

Mount Royal, towering above the great ity of Montreal, second largest French-speaking city in the world, has a lookout that gives magnificent view of the city.

)pen sightseeing trolley cars are unique vay to take in Montreal's historic points.

Bonsecours Market is the place where the habitant farmers sell their own produce.

'hotos: Canadian National Railways; ottom right, Canadian Pacific Railway

Brother André's first chapel in Montreal.

St. Joseph's Oratory draws stream of pilgrims every day.

St. Catherine Street is one c the main shopping center

The fame of McGill University has gone around the world, especially for its medicine. Some think ice hockey was invente at McGill. Now skiing has taken ove

Montreal is the world's largest grain-shipping port, transshipment point for Great Lakes. Its extensive docks are bus when St. Lawrence is not ice-blocke

Photos: Canadi Pacific Railw

rand Pré was home of ongfellow's *Evangeline*.

Evangeline's Memorial is in a park full of flowers, memories.

Chester Inlet is quiet spot on the south shore.

ort Royal Habitation was first perma-ent white settlement north of the Gulf.

From Dingwall, Cape Breton Island, boats fish most fertile waters for swordfish, tuna.

Old shipmodeler at Plympton works on craft that brings back exciting memories.

Ox cart plods through village of Shag Harbour, known for its lobster, fisheries.

Photos: Canadian Pacific Railway; top right, Canadian National Railways; center right, Canadian Government Travel Bureau

St. Andrews-by-the-Sea is world-famous resort.

Antique-hunting, fishing, golf, are attractions at St. Andrews.

Country around Greeno Church looks Scottis

Famous "Reversing Falls" at St. John are due to tremendous tides in Bay of Fundy. As tide rises, the falls run uphill, i land from the sea, then they revers

Fundy National Park rises above tide-worn cliffs. It has sea and fresh-water swimming and fishing, including th heated salt-water swimming pool picture

Photos: Canadian Pacific Railway; bo tom, Canadian Government Travel Bure

Nine to thirty miles off Canada's coast, Prince Edward Island is reached by ferry.

Articles of Confederation, making Canada a Dominion, were drawn at Charlottetown.

The crack clipper ship, *Marco Polo,* was wrecked off Cavendish. The beach, now part of the Prince Edward Island National Park, is best-known resort on the Island.

Photos: Canadian National Railways; bottom, Canadian Government Travel Bureau

Gander Airport is main North American terminal for air services to all parts of

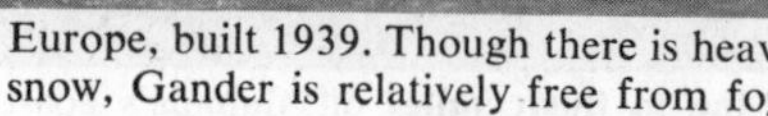
Europe, built 1939. Though there is heav snow, Gander is relatively free from fog

Lumbering is important Newfoundland industry; there are plants for woodworking.

At Cabot Tower, St. John's, Marconi received first wireless across the Atlantic

Fishing (cod, salmon, herring, lobster) on the Grand Banks and Labrador coast is the chief occupation. Newfoundland joined Confederation on March 31, 1949

Photos: Canadian National Railways top, Canadian Government Travel Bureau

Ottawa, whose Parliament buildings on bank of Ottawa River are shown in this airview, was chosen capital by Queen Victoria, became seat of Dominion in 1867.

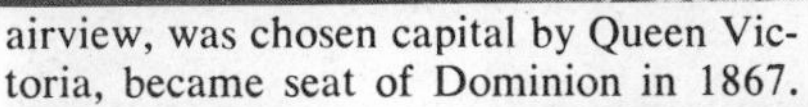

Fort Henry, overlooking Kingston harbor, built in 1812, is now history museum.

Ship passes through the Long Soo Canal. In background you see Long Soo Rapids.

Peace Tower is the dominating feature of Parliament buildings, rebuilt after fire.

Photos: Canadian Pacific Railway; center and bottom left, Canadian Government Travel Bureau

This is one of lakes in the Haliburton district, near Algonquin Provincial Park.

Best vantage point for the widest-angle view of Niagara Falls in the attractive

Toronto, on Lake Ontario, is Canada's second city, business center of flourishing Ontario industry. Since 1912, Canadian National Exposition has been held here.

Photos: Herbert Ford; top right, Canadian Pacific Railway; bottom, Canadian Government Travel Bureau

top-floor big-windowed dining room of the General Brock Hotel. You can watch the *Maid-of-the-Mist* take honeymooners for an exciting close-up near the falls.

Queen Elizabeth Way is excellent highway running from Niagara Falls to Toronto.

Steamer "Sagamo" plies Muskoka Lakes, forest-resort region north of Toronto.

Photos: Canadian Government Travel Bureau; bottom right, Herbert Ford

Fishermen at this lodge go after large and smallmouth bass, northern pike, and trout.

Fishermen's village is near Kenora, Lake of the Woods, 120 miles east of Winnipeg.

This angler's paradise is near border west Ontario; others are more remote

Fish grow big in Ontario's 750,000 lakes and ponds, and its many lively streams

Sampling the fresh-caught trout sizzling over campfire is one of real delights.

Photos: A. L. Koolish

innipeg, capital of Manitoba, is midway tween Atlantic and Pacific. It is dis-

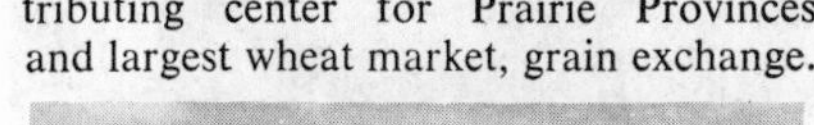

tributing center for Prairie Provinces and largest wheat market, grain exchange.

orld's largest privately owned railway rds are Canadian Pacific's at Winnipeg.

A self-propelled combine harvests barley in the vicinity of St. François Xavier.

ding Mountain National Park, 100 miles rth of Winnipeg, has hotels, cabins.

At Churchill, on Hudson Bay, grain is loaded for trip through Hudson Strait.

otos: Canadian National Railways; cen-, Canadian Pacific Railway; bottom ft, Canadian Government Travel Bureau

Regina, capital of Saskatchewan, is the first training center for famous Royal Canadian Mounted Police recruits. Above is Hotel Saskatchewan. City has many parks.

Prince Albert National Park and eight provincial parks in Saskatchewan provide many miles of forests, lakes, rivers. This is air view of Waskesiu and Lake Waskesiu.

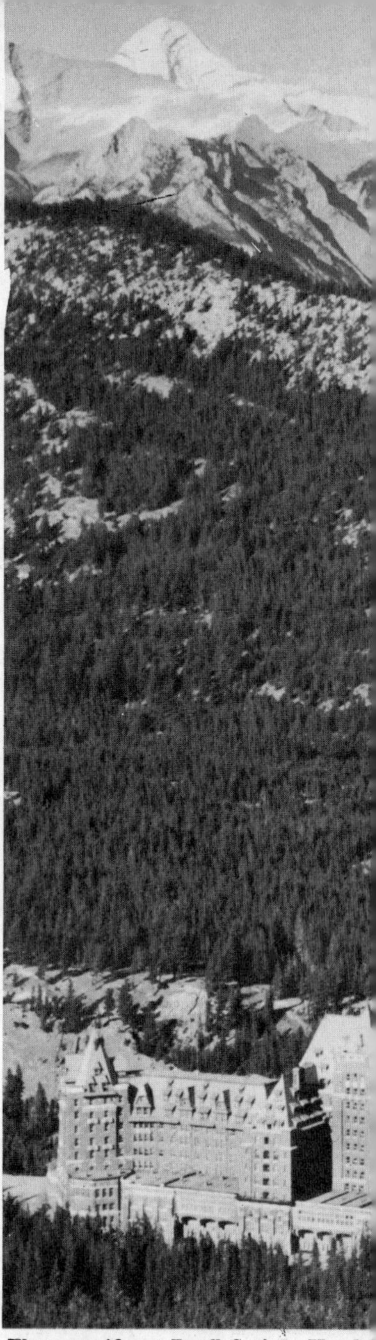

The magnificent Banff Springs Hotel a most spectacular setting overlook the Bow River Valley. It's right in Rockies, at an altitude of 4,538 f

Photos: Canadian Pacific Railway; bot left, Canadian Government Travel Bu

is surrounded by several peaks over
0 feet high. Banff is in southern part
Banff National Park, 65 miles west
Calgary, and is famous as both summer and winter resort, with hot sulphur springs, museum, zoological garden, wild-animal paddock. For 64 years the Indian Days celebrations have been held here.

The Canadian Rockies are North American center of Alpine skiing, with snow 20 feet deep and powder fast. The peaks the Rockies provide a majestic backdr

Behind the Banff ski lift you see peak of Mount Rundle, with Bow River Valley.

Along the Banff-Lake Louise highw you stop to feed Rocky Mountain she

Photos: Canadian Pacific Railway; bott right, Canadian Government Travel Bure

Indian Days, with their contests, climax with awards at the Hotel.

Chieftains parade in all their finery: Crees, Saracees, Blackfeet, and Stonys.

ff **School of Fine Arts,** an extension he University of Alberta, has held summer courses at Banff for twenty years. Students have beautiful scenes to paint.

s: Canadian
ic Railway

Lake Louise, near Banff—sapphire blue in color and surrounded by perpetually snow-capped peaks—has been called beautiful single scene in North Am

Six Glaciers Tea House looks out on Lake Louise and 11,365-foot Mount Victoria.

Trail Riders' packtrain crosses sha Pipestone River on way to base c

Photos: Car Pacific R

oeing is probably best way to enjoy beauty of Lake Louise and the giddy summits around it, in their ever-changing panorama. You may see bighorn sheep.

): Canadian
ic Railway.

Steamer "Princess Elizabeth" pulls into pier at Nanaimo, Vancouver Island. Such steamers ply daily between Victoria, V couver and Inside Passage to Ala

Founded in 1843 by Hudson's Bay Company as a fur trading post, Victoria is now capital of British Columbia. Emp Hotel is attractive; roses bloom all y

Lumber, pulp are important. Logs are dumped at Chemainus, Vancouver Island.

Thunderbird Park is one of severa Victoria; others are Beacon Hill, Go

Photos: Canadian Government Travel Bu center and left, Canadian Pacific Rai bottom right, Canadian National Rai

MEXICO AND CENTRAL AMERICA

t as Canada is a handy "foreign" ationland on the north, so are xico and Central America on the th—and especially so for the dents of the border states of ifornia, Arizona, New Mexico, cas and other states near enough travel by car. The well-paved er-American Highway leads from redo, Texas, through Monterrey Mexico City, a comfortable 3-day of 764 miles. If you're coming m the East, you could cross the der at Brownsville and join the in highway at Ciudad Victoria. om California and Arizona, a oular auto trip south is through Mexican state of Sonora which recently been hard-topping its ds and preparing for North ierican visitors. From Nogales, t south of Tucson, Arizona, you id for Hermosillo and Guaymas. the Gulf of California is the fish- mecca of Puerto Peñasco.

Air travel takes you speedily to xico City and other Central ierican points. Pan American has ietwork of routes serving all the ncipal points. American Airlines s Dallas as take-off point for xico City. Guest Airways, Braniff d others cover different points.

The United Fruit steamers call at atemala, Honduras and Panama nal ports. Standard Fruit Line

Basket vendor waits beside a Taxco road.

and others offer service by passenger-carrying freighters. Panama Line sails from New York to canal ports. By railroad, you can go from New York to Mexico City in three days and three nights, from St. Louis in two days and two nights. And if you wish, you can go all the way on down to Guatemala City by rail.

Whichever way you come, you're sure to find real Latin hospitality in the "My house is yours" tradition.

o: A. L. Koolish

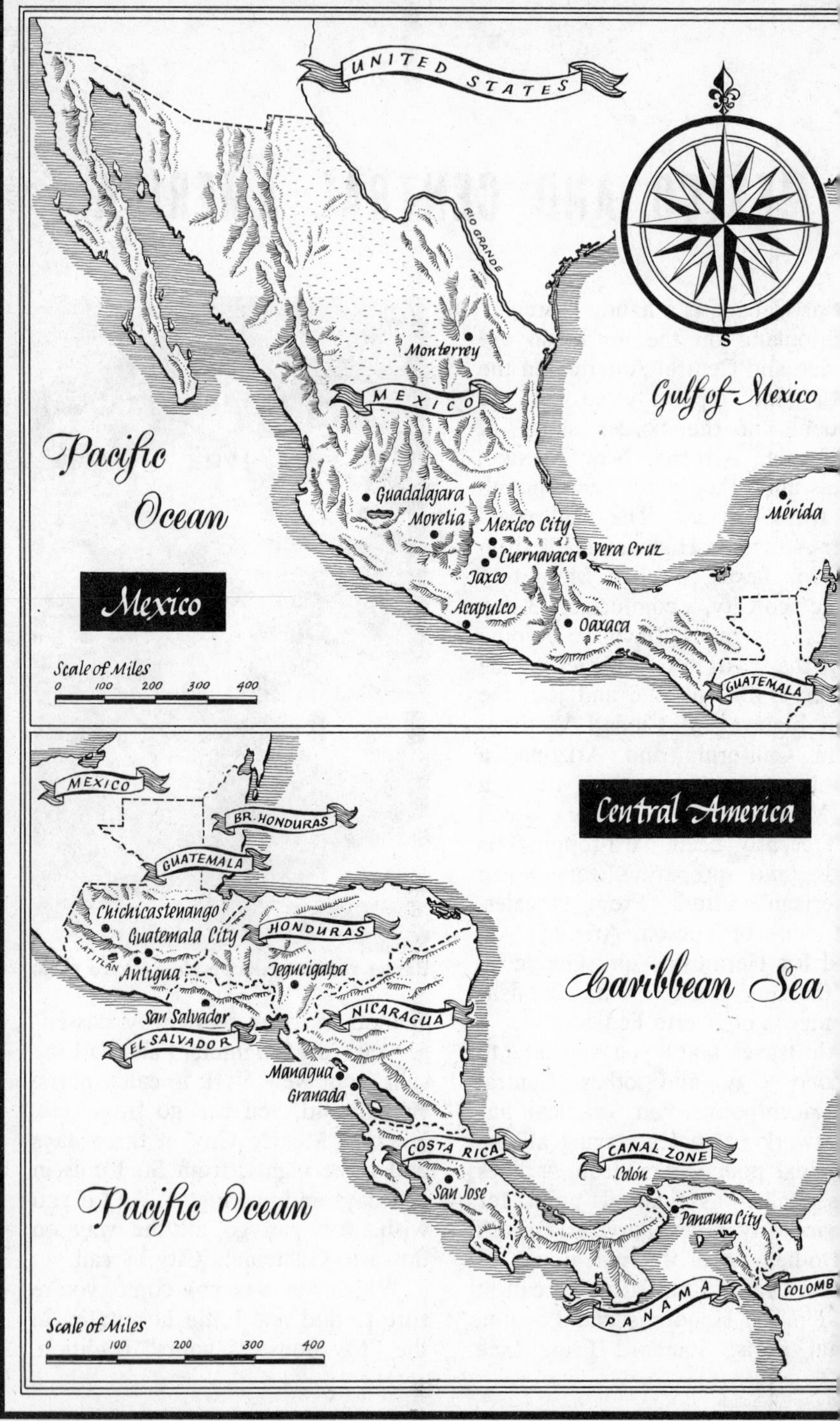

UNITED STATES
RIO GRANDE
S
Monterrey
MEXICO
Gulf of Mexico
Pacific
Ocean
Guadalajara
Morelia
Mexico City
Cuernavaca
Vera Cruz
Mérida
Jaxco
Mexico
Acapulco
Oaxaca
Scale of Miles
0
100
200
300
400
GUATEMALA
MEXICO
BR. HONDURAS
Central America
GUATEMALA
Chichicastenango
Guatemala City
HONDURAS
LATITLAN
Antigua
Tegucigalpa
Caribbean Sea
San Salvador
NICARAGUA
EL SALVADOR
Managua
Granada
COSTA RICA
CANAL ZONE
Colón
San José
Pacific Ocean
Panama City
PANAMA
COLOMB
Scale of Miles
0
100
200
300
400

OLD SPAIN LIVES IN MODERN MEXICO

IS GATE OPENS ON VERSAILLES-LIKE CHAPULTEPEC CASTLE, PARK.

velers from the U.S. are spending re than 180 million dollars a year in xico, land of the ancient Aztecs, ere the charm of Old Spain lives on in a magnificent modern setting. By air, Mexico City is 8 hours from Los Angeles, 3¼ hours from Brownsville, Texas. Or go by train, bus, ship, automobile.

to: A. L. Koolish

The Zócalo, old Mexico City square, is setting for the great cathedral, Church of the Asunción de María Santísima. foundation is on stones of Aztec tem

Dressed for the Fiesta: There are many festivals, some local, some nation-wide.

Benito Juárez, memorial above, was leader who instituted the Reform La

Photos: Ewing Galloway; bottom left, A. L. K ish; bottom right, Pan American World Air

ace of Fine Arts is center of art and sic, with National Theater, murals.

el Reforma has 25 skyline suites king out over the nearby mountains.

dern business section is at crossing Avenida Juárez, Paseo de la Reforma.

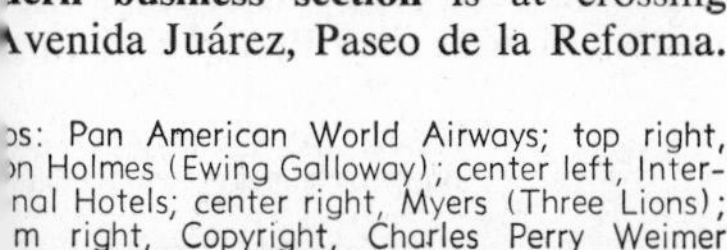

os: Pan American World Airways; top right, on Holmes (Ewing Galloway); center left, Internal Hotels; center right, Myers (Three Lions); m right, Copyright, Charles Perry Weimer

The National Palace, with offices of the President, flanks east side of the Zócalo.

Paseo de la Reforma leads from center of Mexico City to Chapultepec Castle.

From fashionable symphony of Chávez to strolling players, Mexico is musical.

Temple of Quetzalcoatl, the wind god of the ancient Toltec civilization which preceded the Aztecs, is 29 miles f Mexico City, at San Juan Teotihua

The great Pyramid of the Sun is also at San Juan Teotihuacán. Once used as altar and observatory, it is 217 feet h has bigger base than Pyramid of Che

Photos: A. L. Koolish; bo Burton Holmes (Ewing Gallo

za de Toros: Mexico City's bull ring largest bullfighting arena in world.

Pre-fight ceremonies and parade have a fascinating array of color and costume.

dfight begins with grand entry of all bull's antagonists: Three toreros,

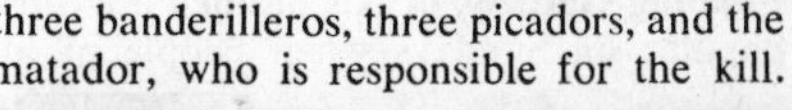

three banderilleros, three picadors, and the matador, who is responsible for the kill.

'on of bullfight is effectively told Hemingway's *Death in the Afternoon*.

The audience at a bullfight is perhaps most interesting part of the spectacle.

os: Richard Joseph

Floating Gardens of Xochimilco are most popular on Sundays when people of all social classes come to ride the flo decked boats, poled by Aztec Indi

Xochimilco punts are called *canoas,* are furnished with chairs and table for food.

Chapultepec Park is one of world's n lovely natural parks, with shaded wa

Photos: Kurt Severin (Black Star); bo left, Pan American World Airways; tom right, Victor de Palma (Black S

stivals, like this Harvest festival at oyoacac, are very colorful, interesting.

Conversation piece: From balcony of your hotel you observe scenes like this.

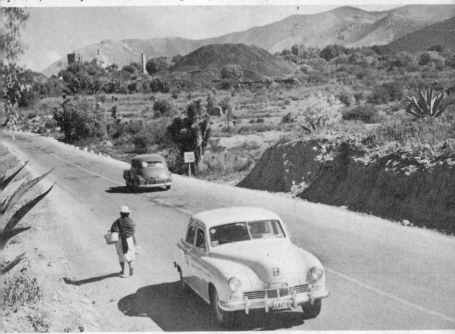

ter-American Highway traffic at Zima-n: This road is great building achievement, sometimes at sea level, sometimes rising to heights more than 8,000 feet.

otos: Samuel E. Lessere; top right, orgia Engelhard (Camera Clix); tom, Herbert Lanks (Black Star)

Massive cathedral in Cuernavaca was begun by Cortez in 1529, is very Spanish in character. Much of the city re atmosphere of days of the conquistad

Tepoztlán, Aztec for *Where there is Copper,* puts on an outstanding festival.

Teloztlán, unspoiled village 12 miles f Cuernavaca, adheres to old ways of

Photos: Georgia Engelhard (C Clix); bottom, Samuel E. L

ommunity laundry is a feature of old cturesque silver-mining town of Taxco.

Perched on side of a mountain, Taxco rivals the hill towns of Italy for beauty.

eavy Traffic" in fascinating Taxco: ere's "a picture around every corner."

Indian market, on Sundays, offers baskets, silver, tinware, many other handicrafts.

os: A. L. Koolish; top right, gia Engelhard (Camera Clix)

Morelia's main square: Towers of great cathedral are more than 200 feet high.

Aqueduct at Morelia was built, 1785–89 to give employment during a famine

Spectacular mountains and lush tropical foliage are reflected in swimming pool near Veracruz, city whose name ste from Cortez landing on Good Frida

Photos: George Pickow (Three Lions); top rig Three Lions; bottom, Victor de Palma (Black St

necameca ("Many Water Holes" in tec) is point of ascent to Popocatepetl and Ixtaccihuatl (in background of photo), the two magnificent volcanoes.

Castillo is huge 100-foot pyramid at aya ruins of Chichén Itzá, near Mérida.

Temple of the Warriors surrounds 4½ acre area that was probably a Mayan market.

hurch of San Francisco at San Miguel Allende is in Spanish colonial style.

Monterrey, 3rd largest city, is 140 mi. from Laredo, on Inter-Am. Highway.

otos: De Cou (Ewing Galloway); center left, L. Koolish; center right, Jim Mitchell (Black ar); bottom left, George Pickow (Three Lions); ttom right, Burton Holmes (Ewing Galloway)

Deep-sea fishing is famous at Acapulco; witness this magnificent sailfish catch.

Favorite "morning" beach is Caleta. In the afternoon, Los Hornos is preferred.

Photos: A. L. Koolish

Mirador Hotel, on Quebrada Cliffs, low) has a magnificent water view.

Daredevil divers leap from 100-foot cliff into waters between Quebrada rocks.

Photo: Above, Eric M. Sanford (Black Star)

Loaves of bread aren't cellophane-wrapped in rural areas, but taste is good!

The festival for blessing the sugar can almost every day sees a fiesta somewher

Mexican musicians start young, and play impromptu concerts anywhere, any time.

This is the sort of café entertainmer you get anywhere in the south of Mexic

Street merchant in Oaxaca offers Aztec patterns in hand-loomed cotton and wool.

Mexicans excel in making costumes out c things at hand; note inverted lampshade

Photos: Samuel E. Lesse

UATEMALA IS LAND F HILLS AND LAKES

If you're seeking a land of great scenic beauty, with jungle highlands, ancient cathedrals, Indian villages, you'll find them all in Guatemala. But you won't get night life or conventional entertainment.

'alvary Church, built 1618, is located t Chichicastenango, the Indian village that is a "must" for Guatemalan visitors. Faithful worshipers come by thousands.

oto: National Tour- Bureau, Guatemala

COFFEE DOMINATES ECONOMIC LIFE OF TINY EL SALVADOR

El Salvador is almost a one-crop nation, coffee—mostly of the "mild" variety—furnishing 80% of all exports. Country has 170 mile coastline on Pacific, but none on Atlantic, is not easily reached. Smallest of the Central American repu lics, El Salvador is the most dens populated, with 144 persons per squa mile. The climate is subtropical, wi moderately heavy rainfall of 68 inch

San Salvador, capital of El Salvador, centers on Parque Barrios, with the National Palace (above) being the m imposing building in city of 160,0

Photo: El Salvador Governm

gucigalpa was founded 1578 as mining tlement, became capital of Honduras in 1880. City centers on Plaza Morazán, site of cathedral and municipal palace.

ONDURAS EXPORTS TS BANANA GOLD

nanas, the golden agricultural crop of onduras, are grown in the north on ıntations once run by big U.S. fruit mpanies, now controlled by local in- ests. It's little-known by tourists.

Inspector looks over bananas. At left, Mayan seat in the park at Tegucigalpa.

Photos: Copyright, Charles Perry Weimer

NICARAGUA OFFERS SECOND CANAL SITE

Lake Nicaragua, Lake Managua and t
Tipitapa River that connects them ha
long been considered for a canal fr
the Atlantic to the Pacific. Nicaragua
largely mountainous, thinly peopl

La Merced church is one of many colonial churches in León, once the capital.

Las Isletas, in Granada, is lovely ar
reached by the Inter-American highw

Managua was made capital of Nicaragua in 1855 to end the rivalry between the cities of León and Granada. This is th
National Palace, facing Parque Centra

Photos: National Tou
ist Board of Nicaragu

que Darío, in Managua, is named for t Rubén Darío. City was almost destroyed by an earthquake in 1931, and the government was moved temporarily.

ıb Managua is one of city's numerous ›ressive buildings. Beauty of the city is enhanced by its location on the southeast shore of 38-mile-long Lake Managua.

ıistry of Public Health, Managua, ls with a population that is principally of mixed Spanish and Indian extraction. The main agricultural crop is coffee.

os: National Tour-
3oard of Nicaragua

PANAMA CANAL IS "A DREA
OF CENTURIES COME TRUE"

An idea that occurred to the earliest Spanish explorers, the Panama Canal took many years to build and surpasses all other man-made waterways both in cost and in difficulty. It is 50.72 m long from channel entrance in the Ca bean to deep water in the Pacific. Beca the canal runs generally southeast fi

Atlantic ports of Colón and Cristobal,
Pacific entrance is paradoxically
miles east of the Atlantic one. Trip
ough the canal takes 7 to 8 hours.

tos: A. L. Koolish

Constant dredging is required to keep channels at proper depth. Landslides have sometimes blocked passage of the Gaillard cut, 8 miles long, 45 feet deep.

Ship's passengers have excellent view of the locks in action. Traffic moves in both directions, since all locks are double. Over 5,000 ships a year use canal.

PANAMA IS A MINIATURE SPAIN

Fiestas, bullfights, colorful costumes a the gay nightlife of Panama City m make you think you're in Spain. By sh Panama is 5 days from New York. air, it's only 4½ hours from Miar

Ruins of Cathedral in old Panama remind you of country's historic past, when it was route by which treasures the Inca empire were carried to Spai

Photo: Copyright, Charles Perry Weir

tel Internacional, Panama City, has to-date facilities, old world charm.

Panama has Cabana Sun Club by l, roof garden, air-conditioned rooms.

Panama City is near Pacific end of canal, is capital of Panama, industrial center.

mous San Blas Indians make their me on the picturesque Mulatas Islands, near Cape San Blas, a point in north Panama which juts out into Caribbean.

tos: Copyright, Charles Perry mer; center left, Kirkeby Hotels

San José, capital of Costa Rica, is a bustling city on main business street.

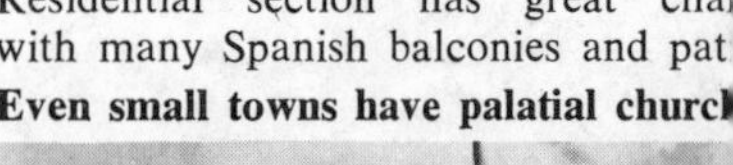

Residential section has great cha with many Spanish balconies and pat

Airport at La Sabana, west of San José.

Even small towns have palatial church

COSTA RICA: HEART OF THE AMERICAS

Located in the geographical center the Americas, Costa Rica is a coun of high culture, education, and politi stability. Coffee is its principal cr Air and steamer services are plentif

Photos: Ewing Galloway; bott left, Ace Williams (Black St

SOUTH AMERICA

.ir travel makes it possible for you) make an extensive trip to South .merica even if you have just two 'eeks for a vacation. For example, anagra's luxurious flight, *El Inter-* *mericano,* leaves Miami every night t eight and reaches Panama at mid-ight. It arrives in Lima, Peru, in me for breakfast, in Santiago, hile, right after lunch. A mere venty-five minutes takes you across ie majestic Andes, then, speeding ver the flat Argentine pampas, the ight touches down at Buenos Aires. ' you prefer to start down the East oast, Pan American will take you n *El Presidente,* a Super-6 Clipper ight, direct to Port of Spain, Trini-ad, then on to Rio de Janeiro, razil, Montevideo, Uruguay, and uenos Aires. Other air lines also rve the continent.

If you have time to travel by ship, iat is the way for a vacation of real laxation. Grace Line's two new iips, *Santa Rosa* and *Santa Paula,* iake 12-day cruises from New York Curaçao, La Guaira (for Caracas), ruba, Kingston, Nassau, and Port verglades (for Miami), continuing New York. Other Grace Line iips go through the Panama Canal id call at all the principal West oast ports down to Chile. On the ast coast, the Moore-McCormack

S.S. SANTA ROSA HAS DECK POOL.

Line, and the Argentine State Line (from New York), and the Delta Line (from New Orleans) take you to Rio, Santos, Montevideo and Buenos Aires. Round trip from New York to Buenos Aires takes about 38 days.

As to climate, South America can offer almost everything. Near the equator, the lowlands and coastal regions have tropical climate, but the high mountain regions are surprisingly cool. Below the equator, countries in the temperate zone have moderate climate with four seasons reversed from those we are used to in North America.

Spanish is the official language of all the South American countries except Brazil, where some 45 million people speak Portuguese. In all the well-traveled centers, however, English is spoken. A short course in Spanish or Portuguese, or at least a phrase book, may add to the comfort and interest of your travels South.

ioto: Grace Line

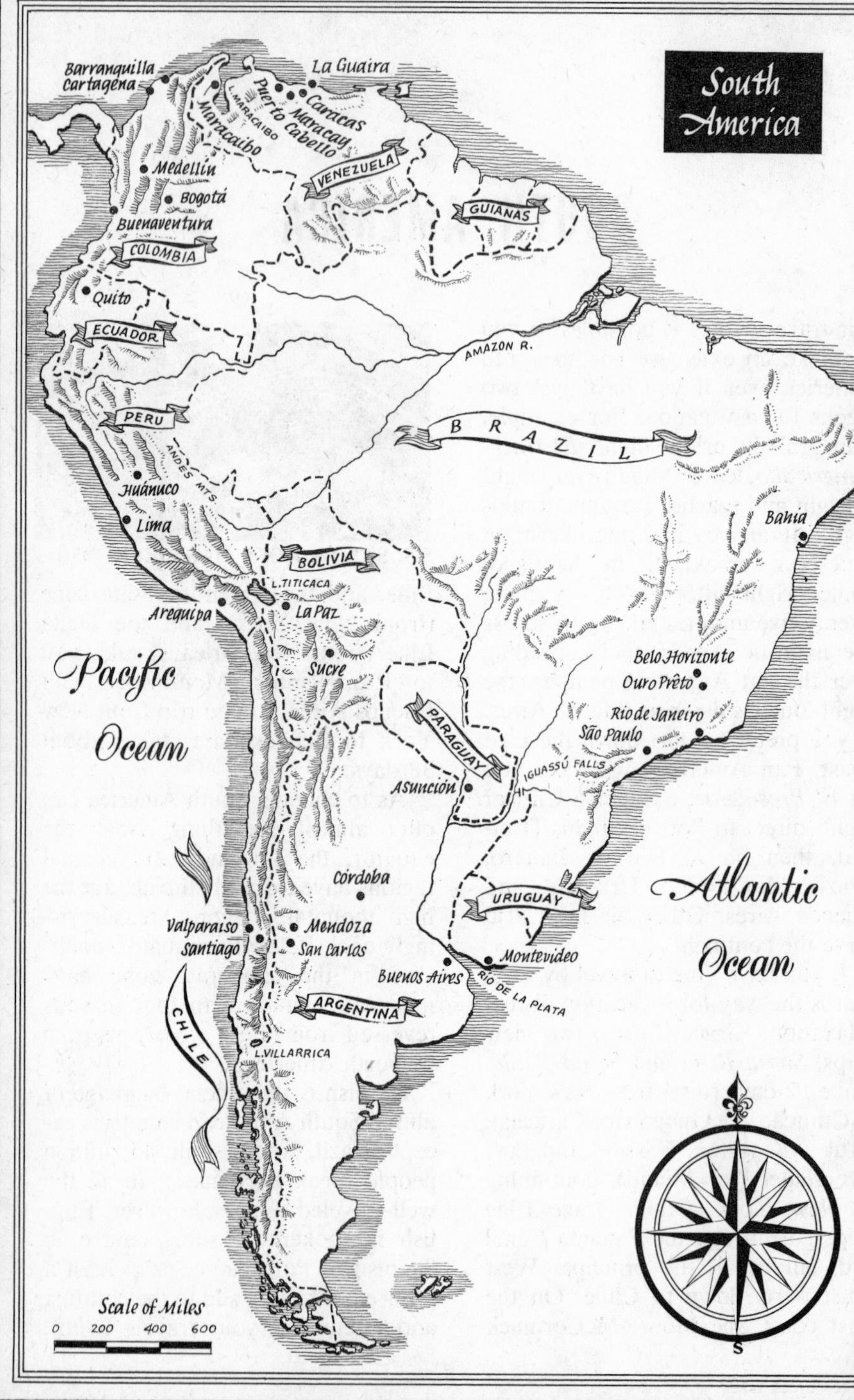
South America
Barranquilla
Cartagena
La Guaira
Puerto Cabello
Caracas
Maracay
L. MARACAIBO
Maracaibo
VENEZUELA
Medellín
Bogotá
Buenaventura
COLOMBIA
GUIANAS
Quito
ECUADOR
AMAZON R.
PERU
B R A Z I L
ANDES MTS.
Huánuco
Lima
Bahia
BOLIVIA
L. TITICACA
La Paz
Arequipa
Sucre
Belo Horizonte
Ouro Prêto
Pacific
Ocean
PARAGUAY
Rio de Janeiro
São Paulo
IGUASSÚ FALLS
Asunción
Córdoba
URUGUAY
Atlantic
Ocean
Valparaiso
Santiago
Mendoza
San Carlos
Montevideo
Buenos Aires
RIO DE LA PLATA
ARGENTINA
CHILE
L. VILLARRICA
Scale of Miles
0 200 400 600
S

BOLIVAR AND THE ANDES DOMINATE VENEZUELA

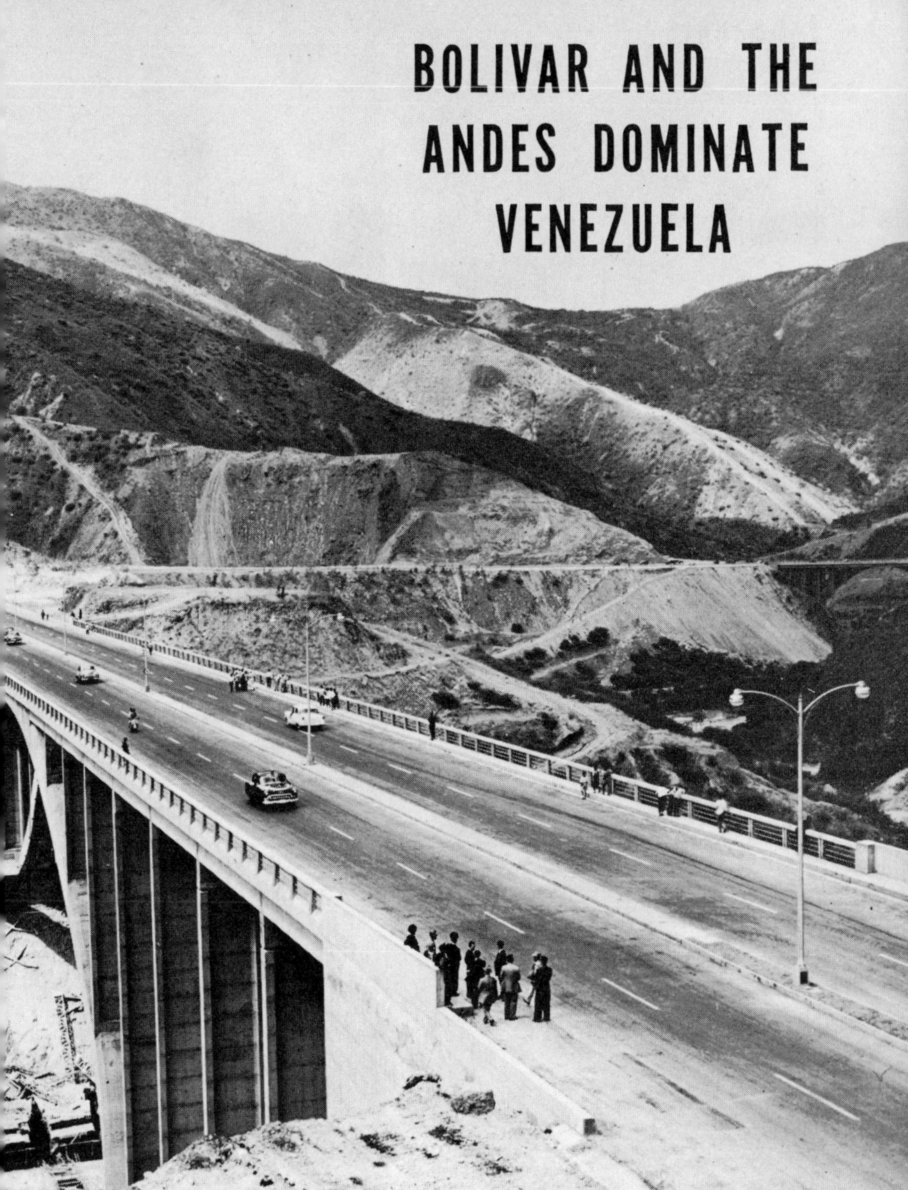

EW AUTOPISTA HIGHWAY, LA GUAIRA TO CARACAS, COST $70,000,000.

non Bolivar was born in Caracas, 1783. w, more than a hundred years after his ath, the people remember with awe and erence "the great Liberator" who freed nezuela and five other countries and ended Spanish power in South America. The fabulous human career of Bolivar is matched by a stupendous natural phenomenon, the great *cordillera* of the Andes flowing from Venezuela 4,600 miles south.

oto: Hamilton Wright

Venezuela

Capitol building's most famous room is the Salon Eliptico, with heroic paintings.

The Pantheon is the "Westminster Abbe of Caracas, with tombs of national hero

Center of Caracas is Plaza Bolivar, with statue of Liberator, important buildings.

"Casa Natal," birthplace of Bolivar, h become a national shrine, with mementc

Cathedral is one of impressive buildings of old Spanish city, with narrow streets.

Country club has swimming pool, go course, view of surrounding mountain

Photos: Grace Line; center left, Richc Joseph; bottom right, Hamilton Wrig

tamira is one of several new residential ctions of Caracas, with broad boulevards. The city is in a hollow, with the mountains towering around it on every side.

-story twin sky-scrapers overlooking ntro Bolivar will house government offices when finished. Beneath the Centro lies a bus station, parking space for autos.

otos: Hamilton Wright

Rio de Janeiro's trade-mark is 1,296-foot Sugar Loaf Mountain, guarding the entrance to Guanabara Bay. The summit reached by aerial railroad, has fine vie

Photo: A. L. Koo

BRAZIL'S CITIES DEFY WILDERNESS

Brazil, covering almost half the land area of South America, is larger than the continental United States and is exceeded in size only by the U.S.S.R., China and Canada. Most of the country is vast, untamed wilderness, but its pioneers have carved out some of the world's most interesting cities, fabulous Rio de Janeiro, modern São Paulo, and the port of Santos.

opacabana Beach is the promenade spot : Rio, like the Champs-Elysées in Paris.

Praça Paris is one of Rio's bayside parks, its formal gardens unsurpassed in world.

losaic sidewalks, palm-lined boulevards ake walking pleasant for Rio's citizens.

Palatial residences like this testify to wealth of fashionable Avenida Beira Mar.

otos: A. L. Koolish; top right and tom left, Charles Perry Weimer

Brazil

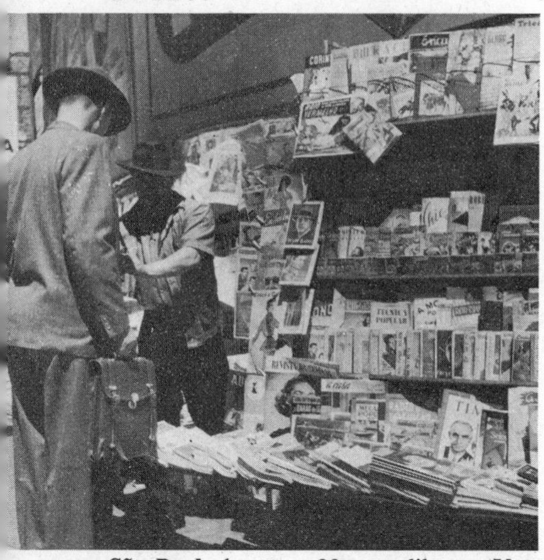

São Paulo boasts a 22-story library. You will find familiar magazines on the stands.

Business buildings in São Paulo, "worl fastest growing city," suggest Hollywoo

São Paulo's great avenues have underpasses and viaducts to speed traffic. The Triangulo at heart of city is much l Chicago's Loop. Population is 2,600,0

Photos: Charles Perry We

RUGUAY, WITH ITS FAMOUS BEACHES,
S PLAYGROUND OF SOUTH AMERICA

allest, but one of most progressive of uth American nations, Uruguay is often npared to Denmark and to Switzerland, d its renowned beach area is known as e Riviera of South America." Uruguay about size of New England. It was imed by both Portuguese and Spanish. ter the wars of independence, it emerged as a buffer state between Brazil and Argentina and was recognized by foreign powers in 1828. Uruguayans make no attempt to match power with their larger neighbors, but concentrate on earning a living—largely from agriculture—and on making their country a well-run republic with a deep belief in democracy.

aza Independencia, on Montevideo's ain artery, features statue of national hero, José Gervasio Artigas. Calle Sarandi leads downtown, Avenida 18 de Julio up.

oto: Copyright, Charles Perry Weimer

Uruguay

Another view of Plaza Independencia shows the modern Victoria Plaza Hotel.

Skyscraper Palacio Salvo contains Hot Palacio Salvo, with 10th fl. dining roon

La Carreta monument in the Parque de los Aliados (Park of the Allies) represents the spirit of undiscourageable pioneerin Done in bronze, it is wonderfully rea

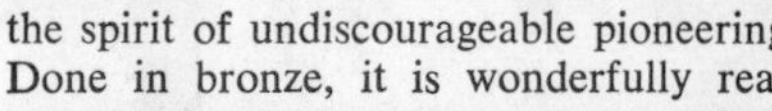

Avenida 18 de Julio takes name from date of Uruguay's proclamation of freedom.

Avenida Agraciada, lined with beautifu buildings, leads to Legislative Palac

Photos: Oficina Nacional de Turismo d Uruguay; top right and center, A. L. Koolis

tinctive modern apartment has ıboyant exterior decoration.

Playa Carrasco is just outside city limits of Montevideo. The beach has an immense casino.

sic, dancing and gaiety feature annual Montevideo carnival.

Playa Pocitos is another in the string of famous beach resorts that surround Montevideo.

ıta del Este is one of the top resorts of all South America.

Legislative Palace, containing 30 kinds of marble, is matched in splendor only by Cuba's *Capitolio.*

ʼos: Oficina Nacional de Turismo del ıuay; center left, bottom left, Copyright, ʼles Perry Weimer; top left, A. L. Koolish

ARGENTINA BOASTS MIGHTY METROPOLIS

Buenos Aires, the "City of Fair Breezes," is as cosmopolitan a city as any in the world. It is largest in South America, with population of nearly three million, and covers 80 square miles. It offers theaters, opera, concerts. There's a modern subway system, hundreds of trams and thousands of busses. Café-sitting has developed almost to the point it has in Paris. In spite of strange new winds, Buenos Aires can be a place to have a lot of fun.

Palermo Park has fine rose gardens, statue of Carlos María de Alvear, hero of revolution.

Luxurious Plaza Hotel faces Plaza San Martín, is well known to North American visitors.

Argentine National Congress bu ing faces Congress Plaza, with mc

Plaza de Mayo is in the heart old Buenos Aires. Directly acı

Photos: Copyright, Charles Perry Wei two in center of spread, Pan

ents and fountains that recall the
and manner of European capitals.

Kavanaugh Building is second tallest in South America. Alvear Palace Hotel is next door.

see the dusty-pink Casa Rosada
k House), residence of President.

Subway stations (entrance above) have artistic tile work depicting scenes in Argentine life.

Teatro Colón, municipal opera house, seats 3500 and is one of best equipped in world.

Mendoza (San Martín monument above) is wine and fruit center, "Garden of Andes."

Córdoba, 400 miles northwest of Buen Aires, is noted for beautiful Cathedra

Gauchos are more colorful than U.S. co boys. Pampas cover 200,000 square mil

Hotel Llao-Llao (pronounced by Argentines Jao-Jao, with the "j" soft as in French) is most famous of the mou tain inns in the Lake District, near Chi

Photo: Copyright, Charles Perry Weim

onte Tronador is an Andean peak of ,200 feet, with number of waterfalls and glaciers. Nearby is Swiss-settled San Carlos de Bariloche, like Alpine village.

ectacular Nahuel Huapí National Park, Argentine Lake district, is one of most scenic regions in all Latin America. It's a thousand miles west of Buenos Aires.

os: Charles Perry Weimer; bot- Copyright, Charles Perry Weimer

PARAGUAY IS OFF BEATEN TRACK

Paraguay and Bolivia are South Amer two wholly inland countries. Paragu Asunción (founded Assumption I 1536) has a strong lure for travelers are fed up with big cities. It is thorou primitive, and thoroughly charm

Asunción may be reached easily by air, or by 4-day voyage by river steamer from Buenos Aires, up Paraná and Parag Lace made at Itaguá village is fam

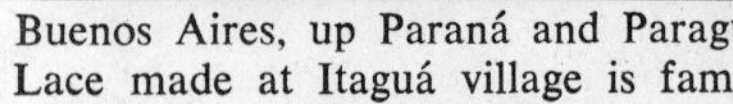

Asunción Palace is newest hotel. Gran Hotel del Paraguay was once residence.

You'll often see countrywomen ridin market, sitting side-saddle on donk

Photos: Ewing Gall

CHILE'S MOUNTAINS STRETCH 2,600 MILES

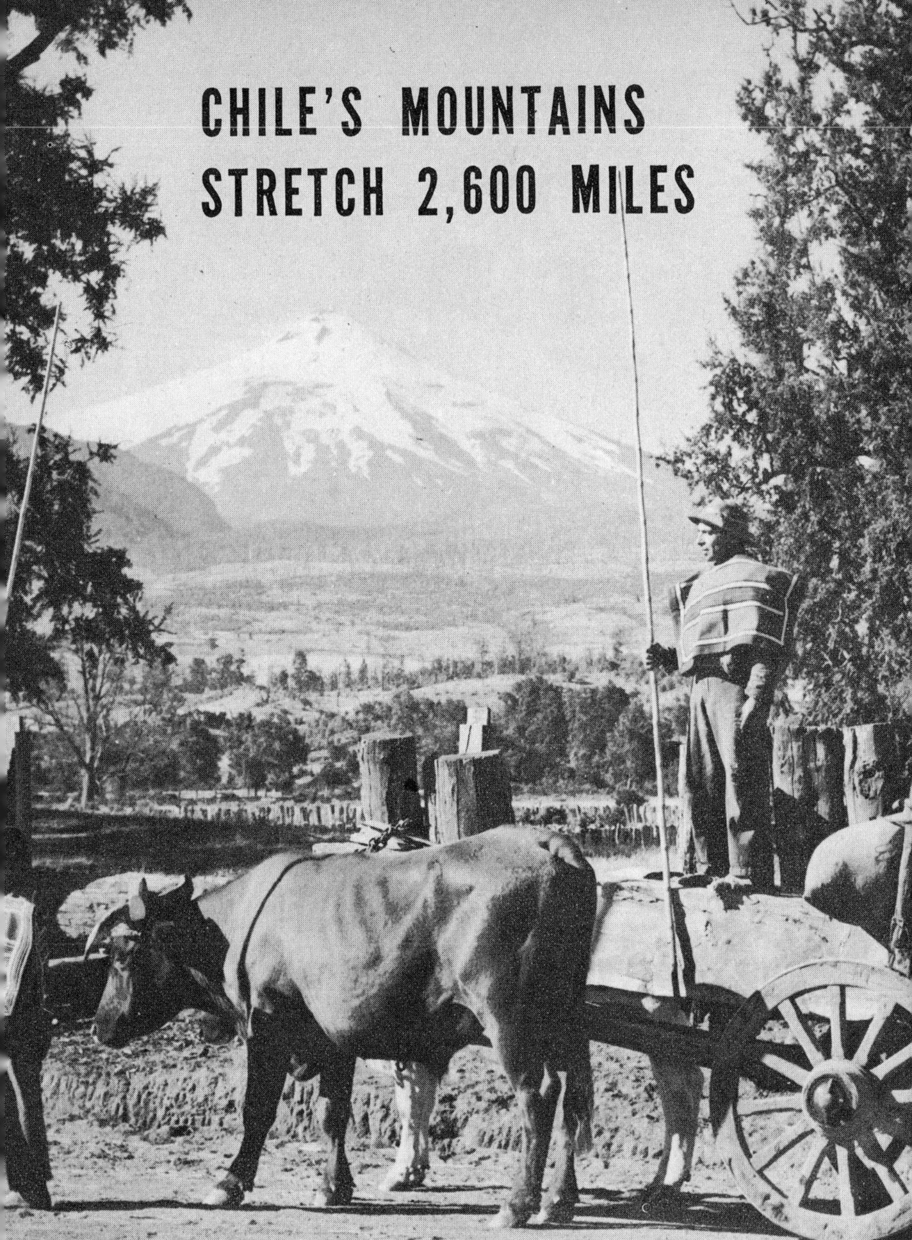

NDIAN PONCHOS SHOW YOU THIS IS NOT SWITZERLAND BUT CHILE.

veraging barely 110 miles in width, Chile a narrow strip extending from Peru own to the tip of South America, a distance greater than that from New York Los Angeles. Within a short distance of the coast the formidable Andes rise to some of the hemisphere's highest peaks. The Chilean lake district, with 12 lakes all differing in the color of their water, offers magnificent scenery, great sport.

noto: Pan American World Airways

The Alameda, in Chile's capital of Santiago, is also known as Avenida Bernardo O'Higgins, named for one of the patriot who led the movement for independence

Hotel Puyehue, famed hot springs resort, is among most sumptuous in South America.

In a Chilean rodeo, *huasos* are judged b speed and accuracy in stopping steer

Golf Club at Los Leones: Sports in Chile take precedence over almost everything.

Club Hípico in Santiago, offering horse racing, is one of show places of continent

Photos: Grace Line; center left, Pan American World Airways; bottom left, Pan American-Grace Airways; bottom right, Panagra

Valparaiso, most important port on west coast of South America, is terminus of the Transandine Railroad to Argentina. City is bounded by hills, reached by funiculars.

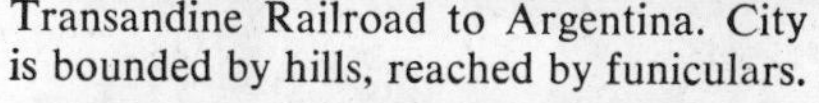

Pucón on Lake Villarrica is outstanding resort, dominated by snowy volcano.

Valparaiso attracts tourists to its nearby beaches, like Playa Torpederas (above).

Photos: A. L. Koolish; bottom left, Grace Line; bottom right, Panagra

One of main streets of La Paz is Avenida 16 de Julio. At left is office of Patino Mines, fabulous enterprise that put B
livia 3rd among world producers of ti

Cathedral at La Paz, on Plaza Murillo, is one of largest churches in South America.

Equestrian statue of General Antoni
José de Sucre is prominently locate

Photos: Panag

BOLIVIA'S LA PAZ IS HIGHEST BIG CITY IN WORLD

At an altitude of 11,909 feet, La Paz is the highest large city in the world, with 320,000 residents living more than two miles above sea level. Some say it's the world's highest capital, but accurate research indicates that Lhasa, Tibet, is slightly higher, although it is a comparatively small place with only 20,000 population. Then too, La Paz is not the legal capital of Bolivia (Sucre is), but La Paz developed more rapidly because of better transportation and has been since 1900 the actual seat of the government. Nearest seaport is Mollendo, in Peru.

Lake Titicaca is largest lake in South America and highest large lake in world.

El Prado is the main boulevard of La Paz. Visitors often find high altitude hard to get used to at first; it is advisable to take cabs for sightseeing rather than walk.

Photos: Grace Line

PERU IS QUEEN OF WEST COAST

Lima, capital of Peru, is one of t world's most fascinating cities. A mi ture of Indian and Spanish tradition, is gay and sophisticated. It's a spectacul country physically: the narrow strip alo the coast, the stupendous Andes, t Amazon lowlands. The road from Lin up the Andes rises 15,948 feet in 85 mile

This mountain valley is near Huánuco, reached by rail, crossing 15,000 ft. passes.

Torre Tagle Palace in Lima is a beautiful survival of seventeenth-century design.

Peruvian folk dancers exhibit their gay costumes. February has 3-day carnival.

Cornerstone of the Cathedral, on Pla de Armas, was laid by Francisco Pizarr

October is month of annual Fair. And Memorial stands before Fair Ground

Photos: A. L. Koolis top left, Panag

n Lima's streets, advertising signs con-
rast with dignified Spanish buildings.

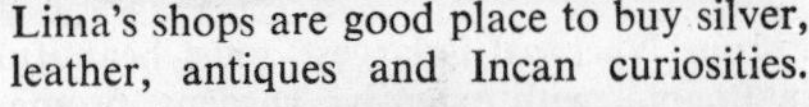

Lima's shops are good place to buy silver, leather, antiques and Incan curiosities.

hurch of San Marcello, an excellent ex-
mple of Spanish style, was built in 1584.

Arequipa, in the south, is a picturesque city. This is the Church of San Augustin.

roya Indians (Peru's population has 3
nillion Indians) sell silver and baskets.

Machu Picchu ruins, amazing Inca city, weren't discovered by white men till 1911.

hotos: A. L. Koolish; center, Pan American
Vorld Airways and Pan American-Grace
irways; bottom left, Copyright, Charles
erry Weimer; bottom right, Grace Line

COLOMBIA HA
COLOR, CULTUR

Parque Nacional is largest, most beautiful park in Bogotá, with extensive gardens, promenades.

Colombia, perhaps the most pur Spanish of all South American tions, is a country of infin variety and color. In Bogotá, isolated mountain capital, th are more bookshops than cafés, a the city is frequently referred as the "Athens of America." theaters are very fine and there an excellent conservatory of mu and a national orchestra. Orchi grow in wild profusion in Colomb and are one of the principal sig in Cali and Medellín. Colombia only South American country whi fronts on both Atlantic and Pacif

Bell Tower of the San Felipe Fortress, Cartagena, gave warning of enemy ships.

Circo de Santamaria, in Bogotá, is c of world's greatest bull-fighting rin

Cartagena is one of oldest cities in the Western Hemisphere, founded 1533. It became "treasure city" of the Spanish Mai where conquistadores kept their spoi

Photos: Grace Lir bottom, Foto Mangi

Swimming pool of the Del Prado Hotel, Barranquilla, is a favorite tourist spot.

Medellín is Colombia's leading industrial city, center of the rich gold-mining area.

A visitor picks orchids growing wild in jungle near Buenaventura, a leading port.

Cali is old colonial city with eight fine parks, churches, magnificent haciendas.

Puente Roman in Cartagena is the bridge which joins the city with island of La Manga, one of main residential sections. Principal beach resort nearby is Marbella.

Photos: Grace Line; top left, Intercontinental Hotels; bottom, Foto Mangini

ECUADOR CLAIMS OLDEST CITY OF THE NEW WORLD

Quito, capital of Ecuador, makes what may prove a valid claim to being oldest city in Western Hemisphere. Once occupied by the Quitu Indians, it was captured in the 15th century by the Incas.

Plaza de Independencia, in Quito, is flanked by Cathedral and Government Palace. Quito, under Spanish till 1822, joined Gran Colombia, then broke away.

Guayaquil is largest city of Ecuador and its principal seaport, about 60 miles from ocean on the Guayas River.

Simple monument marks the Equatorial Line in Ecuador.

Photos: Pan American-Grace Airways; bottom, Grace Line

SOUTH PACIFIC

World War II opened up new interest in the South Pacific for thousands of Americans. You may never have been nearer than reading *Tales of the South Pacific* by James Michener, or seeing the great musical show based on it, but you have an idea of its romance, and the vigor of the great frontier lands, Australia and New Zealand.

Here's a typical flight by Pan American: You leave San Francisco a minute before midnight. At 6:45 in the morning, Honolulu time, you are in the Hawaiian islands for a brief rest. You leave at noon and arrive at Canton Island 7:45 p.m. Between there and Suva in the Fiji Islands, you cross the International Date Line and lose a day! If you've left San Francisco at midnight Sunday, you arrive at Suva's Nandi Airport at 12:01 a.m. Wednesday. For New Zealand, you take off an hour later, at 1:00, and are in Auckland at 8:15 p.m. If you are headed for Australia, you leave Nandi at 1:30 a.m. and arrive at Sydney at 8:00 p.m.

From London, BOAC and Qantas (the Australian Government-owned airline) run flights by way of Cairo, Karachi and Singapore. From Vancouver, you take Canadian Pacific or Qantas Empire Airways. And between Australia,

Qantas Super Constellation belongs to fleet that flies around the world.

New Zealand and Fiji there is service by TEAL'S DC6's.

Good ship service from North America is now provided by the Orient Line. If you have plenty of time, there are freighters that plod their leisurely way across the Pacific, some from New York by way of the Panama Canal. From London, several liners make the trip via the Suez canal in less than a month. Others go around Africa and take thirty to forty-five days, calling en route at Madeira or one of the Canary Islands, Cape Town and Durban.

Within Australia, there's good transportation by railways, air services, and busses. Distances are not as great in New Zealand which is about as big as New York and Illinois combined. Renting a car is good way to see all of its beauties.

Photo: Qantas Empire Airways

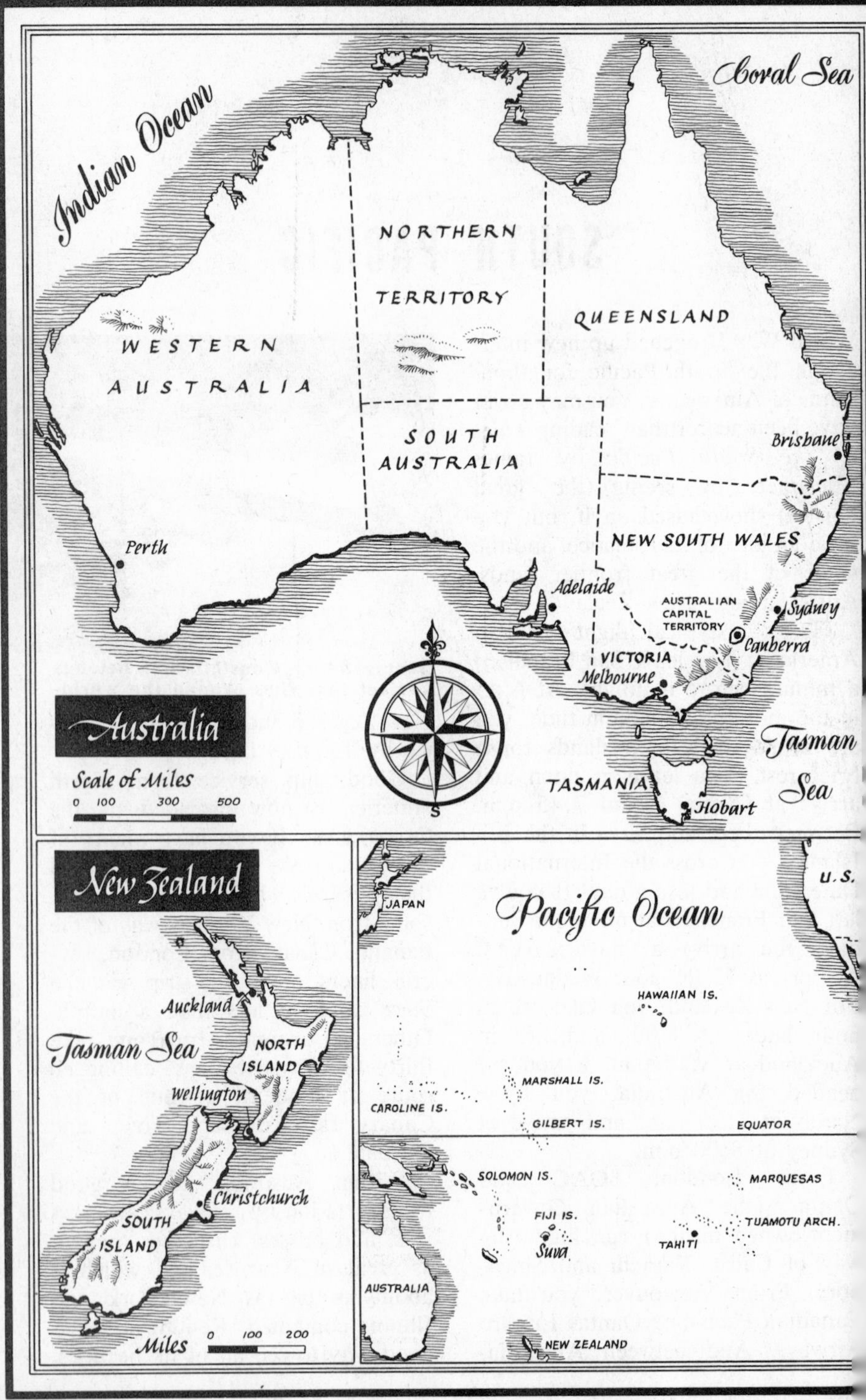

Indian Ocean
Coral Sea
NORTHERN TERRITORY
QUEENSLAND
WESTERN AUSTRALIA
SOUTH AUSTRALIA
Brisbane
NEW SOUTH WALES
Perth
Adelaide
AUSTRALIAN CAPITAL TERRITORY
Sydney
Canberra
VICTORIA
Melbourne
Australia
Scale of Miles
0 100 300 500
Tasman Sea
TASMANIA
Hobart
S
New Zealand
JAPAN
Pacific Ocean
U.S.
HAWAIIAN IS.
Auckland
Tasman Sea
NORTH ISLAND
Wellington
MARSHALL IS.
CAROLINE IS.
GILBERT IS.
EQUATOR
SOLOMON IS.
MARQUESAS
Christchurch
FIJI IS.
Suva
TUAMOTU ARCH.
TAHITI
SOUTH ISLAND
AUSTRALIA
Miles
0 100 200
NEW ZEALAND

JI'S 250 ISLANDS RE TROPIC HEAVEN

Most important British colony in Pacific, the Fiji Islands are 2500 miles southwest of Hawaii. Some say there are 250 isles, others up to 320. 80 are inhabited. The largest is Viti Levu, with capital of Suva.

atives of Suva were once cruel canni-ls; converting them was a religious triumph. Population is now about 40% Fijian, 50% Indian and 10% other races.

rand Pacific Hotel in Suva is one of e best known Pacific hostelries. It entertained during the war hundreds of U.S., British, and other Allied officers.

otos: Ewing Galloway; bot-n, Rob Wright (Black Star)

SYDNEY IS DOMINATED BY GREAT BRIDGE OVER ARM OF THE HARBO

AUSTRALIA IS BIG AS UNITED STATES

The smallest of the continents, Australi is still very nearly as large in area a the United States—but it has only abo nine million inhabitants. Known as "th sunshine continent," it is a land whe you can live outdoors much of th time, with such sports as golf, skiin fishing, bathing on wonderful beache

Photo: Pan Ame
ican World Airwa

Eighteen footers take part in yachting regatta in beautiful harbor of Sydney.

dney is the largest city, with over million and a half population. Other incipal cities are Brisbane, Melbourne, lelaide, Perth, and Hobart on island of smania, lying to the south, 150 miles om Melbourne. Australia, up-and-com- British dominion, has a vitality and optimism that appeal to Americans.

Canberra is federal capital of Australia, with Parliament House, lovely gardens.

otos: Australian National Publicity Associa- n; Australian News and Information Bureau

Melbourne from bank of the Yarra River: Australia's second largest city lies at

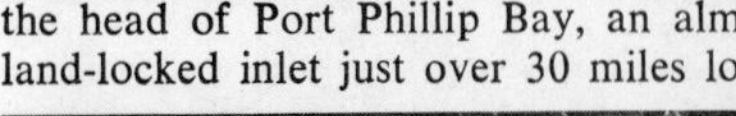

the head of Port Phillip Bay, an alm land-locked inlet just over 30 miles lo

There's good fishing for trout in mountain streams and in spillways of big dams.

Riding is popular in Melbourne, and has the Melbourne Cup race each f

Photos: Australian Nat al Publicity Associa

Melbourne's trim Fitzroy Gardens cottage in which Captain Cook lived.

Skiiers find new chalets at Mt. Hotham (above), Mt. Buffalo, Mt. Kosciusko.

bart, capital of island of Tasmania, at the foot of Mt. Wellington. It has swinging bridge across Derwent River, with a floating portion 3,168 feet long.

tos: Australian Nation-
Publicity Association

The Great Barrier Reef extends over 1,200 miles along the Queensland coast.

Australian bushland is world-famous f its dense growth of trees, ferns, flowe

Cattle crossing at river in Queensland: Dairy cattle are raised in the richer coastal areas, and much beef is raise for local use and for export to Englan

Photos: Australian Natio al Publicity Associati

owering trees of Brisbane frame its ty Hall. Brisbane is capital of the pastoral state of Queensland with its coastal plantations of fruit, sugar cane.

e wattle, with pale-golden blossoms, Australia's national tree and flower.

Koala Bears are easily tamed, perfectly harmless, feed exclusively on eucalyptus.

tos: Australian National Publicity Association; rom right, Pan American World Airways

NEW ZEALAND HAS MATCHLESS BEAUTY

New Zealand is a wonderland of scenery. The Southern Alps have over 200 peaks of 7,500 feet and more, with Mount Cook rising to 12,349. There are lakes and waterfalls, fertile farms and bushland

lington, capital of the Dominion, is on steep hills about a magnificent or, 3 miles wide and 12 long. The are climbed by trams, cable cars iniscent of those in San Francisco.

Rotorua is center of Maori life, with wonderful carvings; also has thermal spa.

Wanganui River runs through primeval forest in beautiful thermal wonderland.

tos: Pan American World Airways; v Zealand Government; Three Lions

New Zealand

Auckland, built on the shores of deeply indented Waitemata harbor, is chief port

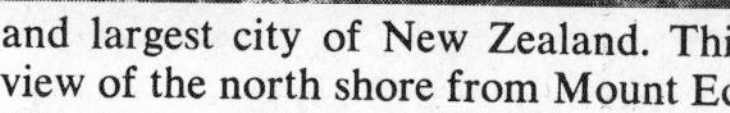

and largest city of New Zealand. Thi
view of the north shore from Mount Ed

Wellington has tunnels that take roads, trolley lines through encircling hills.

University Tower, Auckland: Nation proud of education, social legislatic

Photos: New Zealand Governme
Three Lions; Ewing Gallow

istchurch, the largest city on South
d, is the most typically English 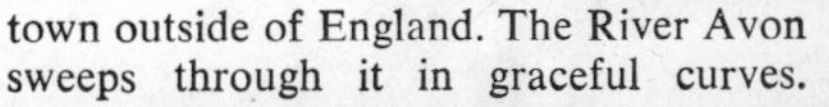 town outside of England. The River Avon sweeps through it in graceful curves.

erland Falls, 1,904 feet high, is of world's tallest, most beautiful.

Pohutu Geyser is one of many in the Hot Springs district health resort, Rotorua.

: Three Lions; bottom left, Ewing Gal-
bottom right, New Zealand Government

GAUGUIN DID MANY PAINTINGS IN SOUTH SEA PARADISE OF TAH

TAHITI IS THE END OF OUR WORLD TOUR

Kon-Tiki brought home to thousand
readers the lure of primitive lif
the South Seas, and especially the
islands of Polynesia. Queen of then
in the dreams of men is Tahiti, sup
symbol of living for the simple jo
living . . . a good place to end our

Photo: French G
ment Tourist

"AROUND THE U.S.A."

"FROM SEA TO SHINING SEA" —THE MOODS OF AMERICA

by Paul J. C. Friedlander

Mr. Friedlander is Travel Editor, The New York Times

r the purposes of the tourist, .merica the Beautiful," as de- ·ibed in the Katharine Lee Bates em and song from which the head- ; of this Foreword is taken, con- ts of thirteen separate regions. .ch is as big as, if not bigger than, ny world powers. Each is an tity in itself. Each has a personal- , and characteristics of geography d agriculture, of people and indus- , of scenery and climate—both ysical and intellectual—that make distinct from all other regions. st as the traveler can tell when he osses from England to Wales or om German Switzerland into Ital- ı Switzerland, so he can tell in this untry without recourse to an atlas ıen he is in New England, the idsouth or the Deep South.

To aid the vacationist about to an a tour of his own country, the mchair traveler anxious to learn ore about his native land, and the turned traveler who wants to kin- e anew the memories of the places has visited, the editors of this ok have selected well over a thousand pictures showing America in its many moods, at work and at play. They have identified each picture with pertinent and often intriguing facts. And they have reprinted with permission character studies of the eleven regions written by correspondents of *The New York Times* who live and work in the various sections they describe.

Because the editors have already covered in their attractive book, *Around the World in 1,000 Pictures,* such outlying sections of the United States as the Virgin Islands and Puerto Rico, this book deals only with the fifty states of our Union and with the District of Columbia. Emphasis is placed on the natural wonders of our country and the places of greatest interest to the pleasure traveler and the vacationist. Yet these alone cannot convey the moods of America. The strength and spirit of our country today are compounded of 160,000,000 people and of their forebears, and of the things they believed in and worked and fought for, the same principles we honor today at our historic shrines.

So among these 1,000 photographs you will find more than the grandeur of nature as it spreads in a 3,000-mile panorama from sea to shining sea. You will see many of the great historic shrines that bring to life those great occasions in New England, Pennsylvania, Virginia and in many other regions when Americans wrote the history of the New World in bold, unfrightened hands. You'll see their descendants at work today—on the farms, in the automobile factories and the industries that make this nation, and the fishermen who still go down to the sea under sail. And, to complete the picture, you'll see Americans at play in their National Parks where the wilderness of this continent is preserved as it was when the first explorers and hunters came through; on the broad sandy beaches that encircle this land like a golden necklace; and at the fabulous man-made resorts like Reno and Palm Springs and Miami Beach, and the biggest tourist attraction of them all—N
York City.

Many of the pictures were ta
by world-famous photographers,
most of them were made by men a
women who live in the various
gions and have had the opportu
to capture on film the places t
love best. The photos have been
lected, not for the qualities t
would win prizes in a competiti
but for their ability to show Am
ica's colorful scenes and people a
events in the same way you mi
like to preserve them in your c
photo album. This is a tremend
undertaking, to picture this great
tion in one volume. To do it as s
cessfully as they have, the edit
had to touch lightly, or not at al
few sections of the country. T
beg, herewith, the indulgence of
loyal partisans thereof.

It is their hope, and I comm
this volume to you in the belief t
they have achieved their goal, t
this book will help Americans to
come more familiar with their c
ball park, our friends abroad to
us in our true lights, and insp
both to travel from sea to shi
sea to see for themselves the g
sights pictured in these pages.

NEW ENGLAND

by JOHN H. FENTON

westward migration across America ned new lands and new vistas for a wing population. Among the pioneers) opened the new country were Yan- s. But sooner or later the Yankees' endants come back to New England, nly for a visit. And along with them e other Americans, for this relic-filled ner of the United States exerts a com- ing influence. So much of it, from the antic's breakers and Old North Church he piny hills and bouldered fields and Yankees themselves, has been change- for 300 years.

'he sounds of New England are many: wind in the sand dunes of Cape Cod, water lapping the sun-bleached fish- wharves of Maine, the rush of a intain-fed stream in New Hampshire the twitter of birds in the Berkshire s of Massachusetts. Voices from the whisper in the Colonial burying inds of Boston, in the House of Seven oles in Salem, beneath the bridge at icord and in the Old Stone Mill at vport.

'he architecture is a conglomerate id of graceful Colonial, sterner Fed- , utilitarian Cape Cod and the best worst of the contemporary. In places Boston, Newburyport and Newport it ossible to turn a corner and go back years.

y and large, the native Yankee has n pictured as a bleak character, with inborn suspicion of all strangers, in- pitable and clannish. Actually, by na- and heritage, he has a respect for vidual opinion. And he is inclined to p the latchstring of his hospitality idrawn on the theory that he himself ld not knock without good reason.

'here are many aspects to this region,

"The Atlantic's breakers . . . changeless."

but a specific tradition marks New England as the national cornerstone. It is found in Boston, in Lexington, in Concord, in Bennington and Newport and Salem. Visitors from all over the world have come to see the shrines and view the relics of the American Revolution that changed the trend of history.

They walk the Boston streets where British muskets rattled in the massacre. They climb the stairs of the Old North Church where the signal lights for Paul Revere were hung. They drive through the Middlesex countryside where the hoofs of Revere's horse echoed in the night. They visit Plymouth and walk where the Pilgrims marched to church. And they wander through a hundred churchyards where fading slate stones tell the story of departed pioneers and patriots.

o: Frank Kelly

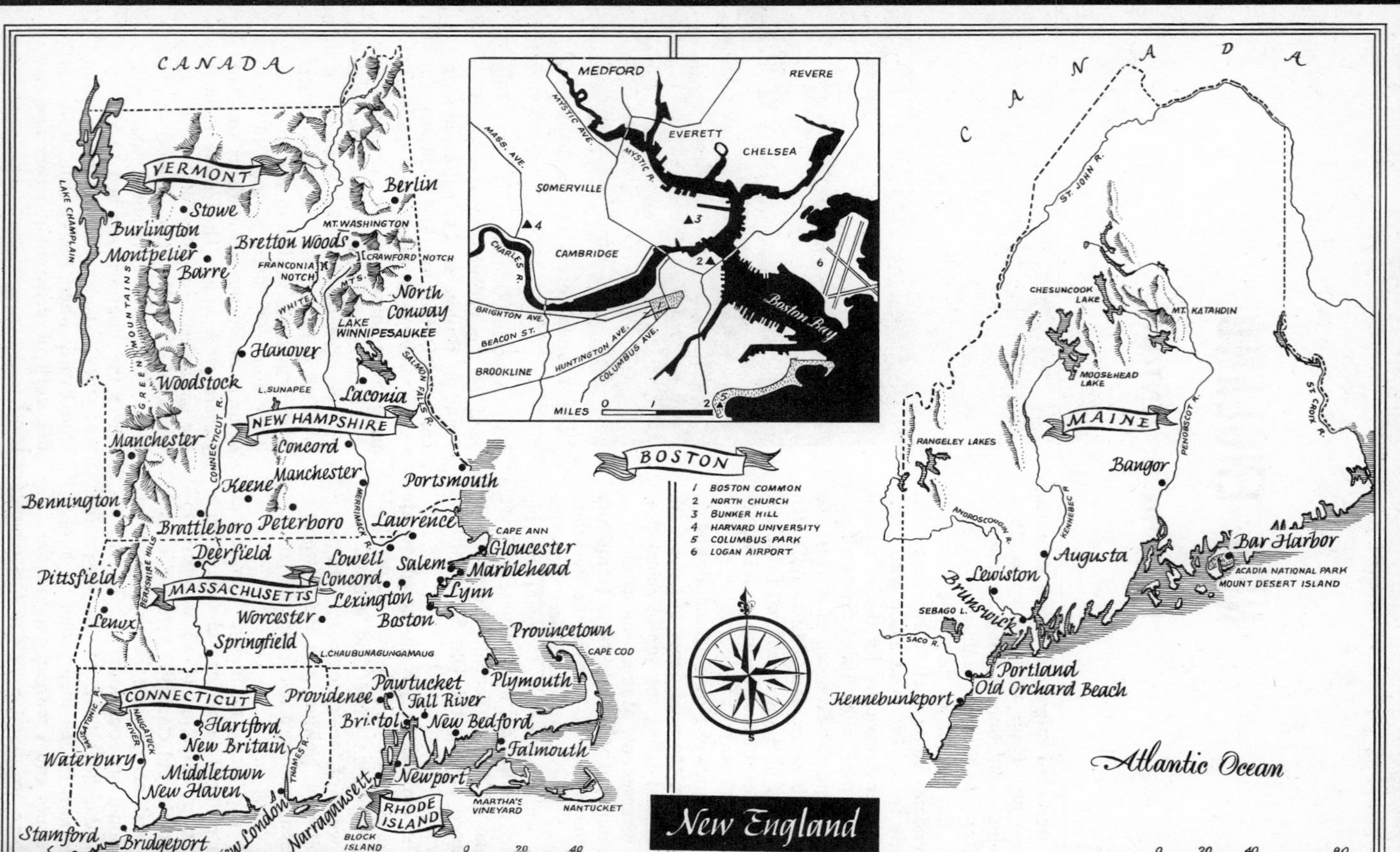
New England
CANADA
VERMONT
NEW HAMPSHIRE
MASSACHUSETTS
CONNECTICUT
RHODE ISLAND
MAINE
LAKE CHAMPLAIN
GREEN MOUNTAINS
Burlington
Stowe
Montpelier
Barre
Woodstock
Manchester
Bennington
Brattleboro
Berlin
MT. WASHINGTON
Bretton Woods
FRANCONIA NOTCH
CRAWFORD NOTCH
WHITE MTS.
North Conway
LAKE WINNIPESAUKEE
Hanover
L. SUNAPEE
Laconia
CONNECTICUT R.
SALMON FALLS R.
MERRIMACK R.
Concord
Manchester
Keene
Peterboro
Portsmouth
Lawrence
CAPE ANN
Gloucester
Deerfield
Lowell
Salem
Marblehead
Pittsfield
BERKSHIRE HILLS
Concord
Lexington
Lynn
Lenox
Worcester
Boston
Springfield
L. CHAUBUNAGUNGAMAUG
Provincetown
CAPE COD
Plymouth
Pawtucket
Providence
Fall River
Bristol
New Bedford
Falmouth
HOUSATONIC R.
NAUGATUCK RIVER
THAMES R.
Hartford
New Britain
Waterbury
Middletown
New Haven
Newport
New London
Narragansett
MARTHA'S VINEYARD
NANTUCKET
BLOCK ISLAND
Stamford
Bridgeport
0
20
40
MEDFORD
REVERE
MYSTIC AVE.
MYSTIC R.
EVERETT
CHELSEA
MASS. AVE.
SOMERVILLE
CAMBRIDGE
CHARLES R.
BRIGHTON AVE.
BEACON ST.
HUNTINGTON AVE.
COLUMBUS AVE.
BROOKLINE
Boston Bay
MILES 0 1 2
BOSTON
1 BOSTON COMMON
2 NORTH CHURCH
3 BUNKER HILL
4 HARVARD UNIVERSITY
5 COLUMBUS PARK
6 LOGAN AIRPORT
ST. JOHN R.
CHESUNCOOK LAKE
MT. KATAHDIN
MOOSEHEAD LAKE
ST. CROIX R.
PENOBSCOT R.
RANGELEY LAKES
Bangor
ANDROSCOGGIN R.
KENNEBEC R.
Augusta
Bar Harbor
ACADIA NATIONAL PARK
MOUNT DESERT ISLAND
Lewiston
Brunswick
SEBAGO L.
SACO R.
Portland
Old Orchard Beach
Kennebunkport
Atlantic Ocean
0
20
40
80

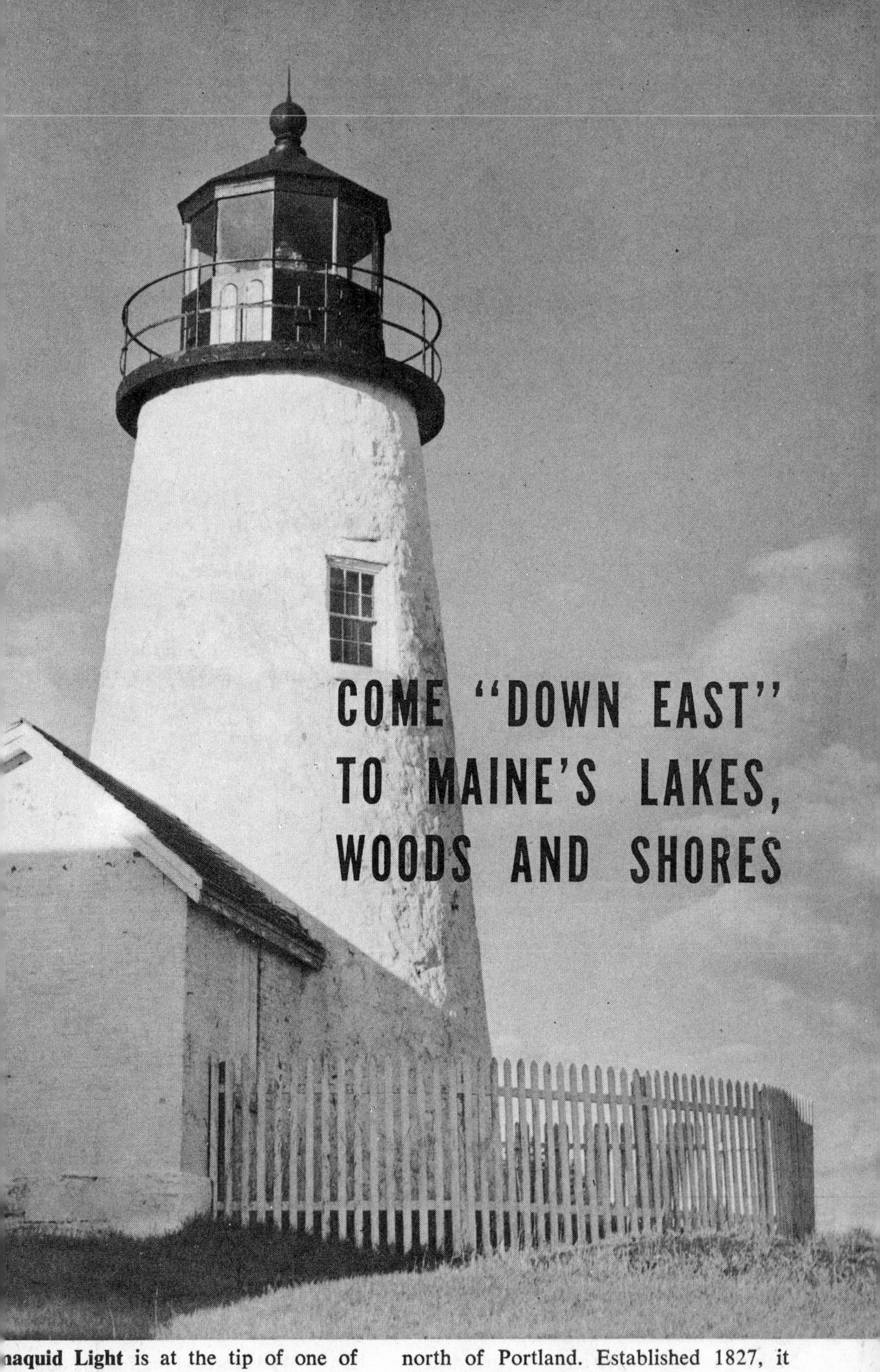
COME "DOWN EAST" TO MAINE'S LAKES, WOODS AND SHORES

naquid Light is at the tip of one of many points that jut into the ocean north of Portland. Established 1827, it warned clipper ships of rocky peninsula.

o: Grant M. Haist

New Harbor is fishing village and resort three miles from Pemaquid Point. It was

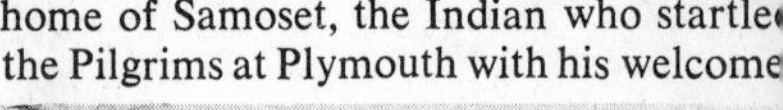

home of Samoset, the Indian who startle[d] the Pilgrims at Plymouth with his welcome

Maine's rolling slopes and the consistency of its snows make for ideal ski country.

Henry Wadsworth Longfellow taught [at] Bowdoin College. This is the Chap[el]

• Photos: Grant M. Haist; Ko[n]stantin Kostich; Stephen Mer[...]

cadia National Park is on Mount Desert land which also includes Bar Harbor.

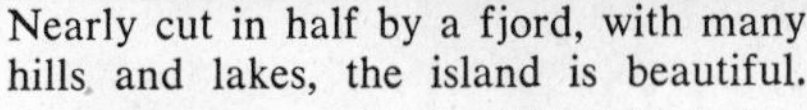

Nearly cut in half by a fjord, with many hills and lakes, the island is beautiful.

ockland and Camden on Penobscot Bay, re home ports for windjammer cruises.

"Alice S. Wentworth" is one of sailing ships offering salt-water vacation trips.

This scene in Camden harbor is typical of many of Maine's bay and river harbors.

Early morning stillness made possible the perfect reflections in this Maine cove.

hotos: National Park Service; Alice . Wentworth Cruises; Maine Devel- opment Commission; Grant M. Haist

Maine

Pleasant Point is up near Passamaquoddy Bay, on the Canadian border. Lobster pots show it's one of the many places whe Maine lobsters are caught for mark

Lakes near Bridgton, 35 miles northwest of Portland, are good for trout and bass.

The Rangeley Lakes have such love names: Mooselookmeguntic, Umbago

Photos: Maine Development Commission; Ko stantin Kostich; Alfred E. Reichenberg

GREAT WHITE HILLS, LOVELY LAKES BECKON TO NEW HAMPSHIRE

The Old Man of the Mountain stands guard at Franconia Notch, scenic defile in the White Mountains. There is an aerial tramway and the famous Flume is nearby.

Photo: White Mountains Region Association

New Hampshire

Concord has been the capital since 1808; imposing State House was built in 1819.

Mt. Washington Cog Railway, completed in 1869, was first of its kind in the world.

Boyhood home of Franklin Pierce, 14th President of U.S., is in Hillsborough.

Skimobile Tramway at Mt. Cranmore, near North Conway, carries passengers

Dartmouth College, founded 1769, is on of country's most distinguished libera

nearly a mile, with vertical lift of 1300 ft. It's used by skiers, summer sight-seers.

arts colleges for men. Dartmouth Winter Carnival is big social event at Hanover.

Berlin's 80-meter ski jump has highest steel ski tower (171½ ft.) in the U.S.

The White Island lighthouse, Isles of Shoals, lies off the coast near Portsmouth.

The Balsams, at Dixville Notch, is Swiss-like hotel on sparkling Lake Gloriette.

Photos: Eric M. Sanford; Cranmore Skimobile, Inc.; Dartmouth College News Service; Berlin Chamber of Commerce; Douglas Armsden; The Balsams

Newmarket is attractive little industrial community on shores of the Lamprey.

Village of Walpole has distinguished Unitarian Church, many lovely old homes.

New Hampshire granite has been used to fashion many U.S. buildings, monuments.

John Goffe's Mill, made famous by recent best seller, attracts many art students

Visitors enter Hall of Ships at Lost River Reservation, near North Woodstock.

Chair lift at Mt. Sunapee State Park offers summer visitors a superb view

Photos: Douglas Armsden; Monadnock Region Association; John Swe Granite Company, Inc.; White Mountains Region Association; Eric M. ford, from New Hampshire State Planning and Development Commi

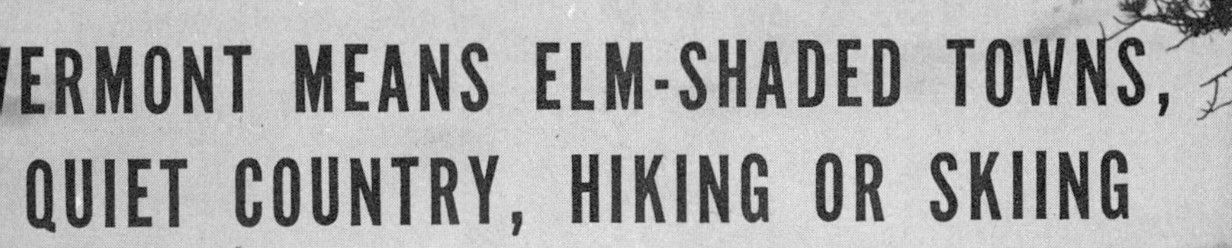

VERMONT MEANS ELM-SHADED TOWNS, QUIET COUNTRY, HIKING OR SKIING

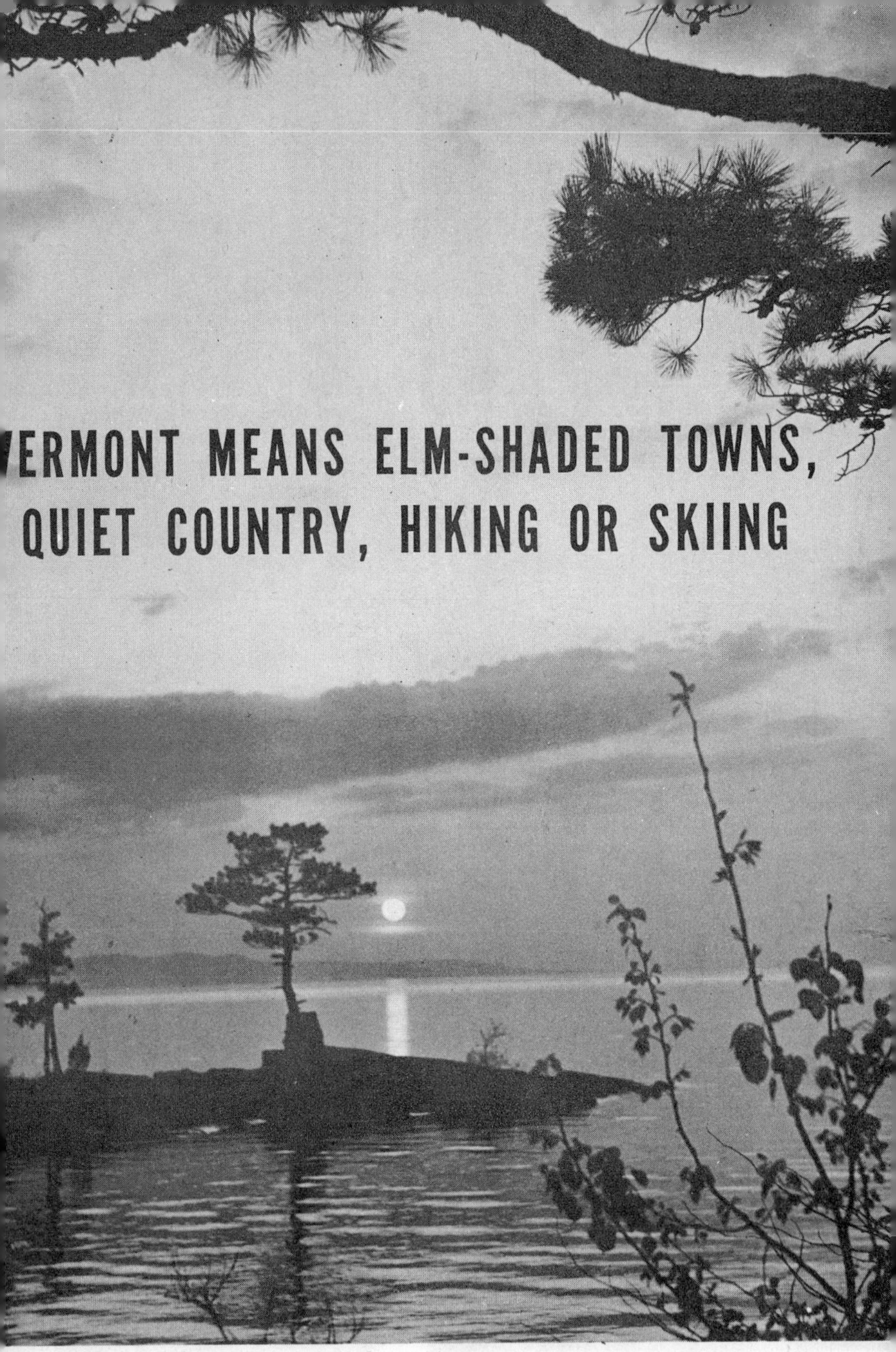

Lake Champlain at sunset is typical of the peaceful scenes to be found in the Green Mountain State. This tremendous lake borders western Vermont for 100 miles.

Photo: Vermont Development Commission

Playhouse at Weston is a fine 100-year-old structure that was formerly a church.

Ethan Allen, colonel of "Green Mounta Boys," stands at State House, Montpeli

Half a hundred centers have been built up to accommodate winter sports fans in

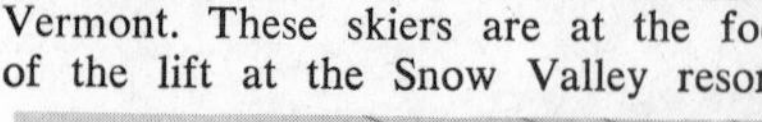

Vermont. These skiers are at the foo of the lift at the Snow Valley resor

Derrick hoists granite block at Rock of Ages quarry, Barre, world's granite center.

Famous "Round Church" at Richmond actually 16-sided. It was built in 181

Photos: Vermont Development Commissi

Basin Harbor Club, Vergennes, is one of delightful resort areas along shore of Lake Champlain. This air view shows the Adirondacks across the lake in New York.

Hikers arrive to spend night at one of bunk houses on the 261-mile Long Trail.

State constitution was adopted here at Old Constitution House, Windsor, in 1777.

Photos: Basin Harbor Club; Vermont Development Commission

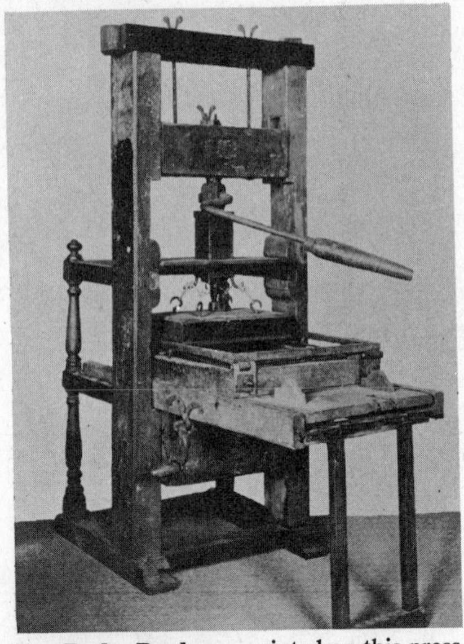

Bay Psalm Book was printed on this press, now at Historical Museum, Montpelier.

Hazen Road Monument at East Hardwick commemorates military road built in 1779.

Historical Museum at Bennington has relics, documents, utensils of early days.

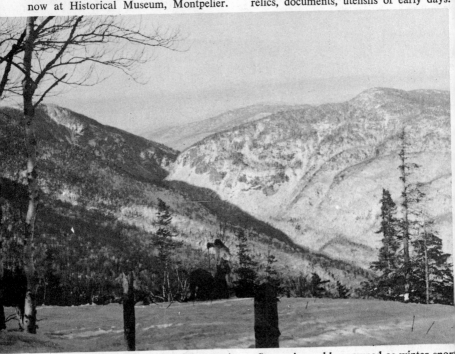

Mt. Mansfield, 4,393 ft. high, is summit of the Green Mountains. This area, near Stowe, is world renowned as winter spor center and also as summer vacationland

Photos: Vermont Development Commissio

IN MASSACHUSETTS
YOU RE-LIVE THE
BIRTH OF AMERICA

unker Hill monument on Breed's Hill, harlestown, commemorates the stand of raw American militia against the cream of British troops, at start of Revolution.

oto: Massachusetts Department of Commerce

Massachusetts BOSTON

Old South Meeting House shares with Faneuil Hall momentous oratory of 1770's.

Blooming magnolias indicate that Spring has come to Commonwealth Avenue.

Iron grillwork distinguishes old houses on Beacon Street, opposite Boston Common.

Faneuil Hall, scene of important protest meetings, is called "Cradle of Liberty."

Paul Revere statue stands near the Old North Church, where the lanterns hung.

Old waterfront, once host to ships from a over world, now has mostly fishing boat

Photos: Massachusetts Department of Cor merce; center right, TWA Trans World Ai lines; bottom right, Konstantin Kosti

rom Memorial Drive in Cambridge, you ok across the Charles River Basin to

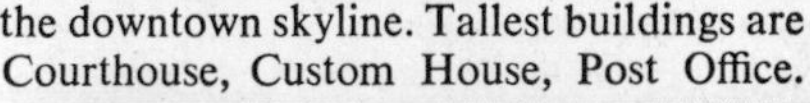

the downtown skyline. Tallest buildings are Courthouse, Custom House, Post Office.

gassiz House is recreation building at adcliffe College for women, Cambridge.

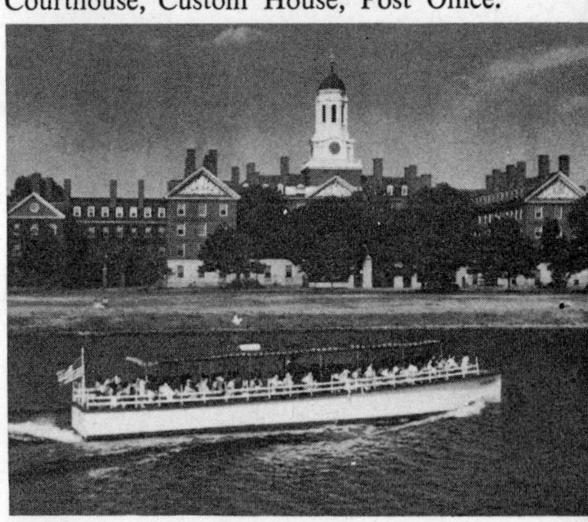

Sightseeing boat on Charles passes one of Harvard's dormitories, Dunster Hall.

ublic Garden, with its celebrated swan oats, has been treasured feature of city for generations, as has also the Common where free speech is honored every day.

otos: Henri Cartier-Bresson (Magnum), bot-m left; TWA Trans World Airlines, bottom ght; Massachusetts Department of Commerce

Old Deerfield is known for its historic houses. This is room of "Indian House."

Nearby Conway has beautifully simple ol house with a "ballroom" on second floo

Berkshire Music Festival is annual series of public concerts at Tanglewood estate in Stockbridge. Famous conductors dra music lovers from all of North Americ

Farm house kitchen at Old Sturbridge village shows early American methods.

House of the Seven Gables, in Salem, said to be setting of Hawthorne's nove

Photos: Alfred E. Reichenberger, center and botto right; A. Milton Runyon, top right; Pioneer Vall Association, top left; Old Sturbridge Villa

Mt. Greylock, some 3,500 feet, is tallest of the Berkshire Hills and highest mountain in the state. In winter dress, or autumn colors, it has majestic beauty.

Williams is known as "the college of gentlemen." This is Chapin Hall auditorium.

"Sweetheart Gate" is revered fixture of Mohawk Trail curio shop, Charlemont.

overed bridges are a New England feare that may disappear before onslaught of wide new roads. This fine example spans the Deerfield River near Charlemont.

otos: Mohawk Trail Association; center t, Massachusetts Department of Comrce; bottom, Pioneer Valley Association

Gloucester fishermen unload cod at this port with 300-year seafaring tradition.

Hadley's First Congregational Church has spire designed by Christopher Wren

This view of Connecticut River valley from Mt. Sugarloaf is typical of lovely farm country around South Deerfield and Sunderland, part of the "Pioneer Valley"

Photos: Konstantin Kostich, left; Pioneer Valley Association

'lymouth Rock, one of America's most :evered shrines, is protected by imposing

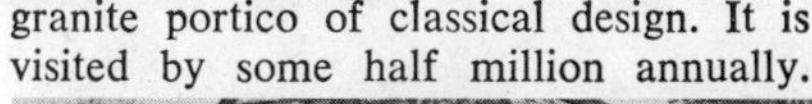

granite portico of classical design. It is visited by some half million annually.

ock itself bears 1620 date as reminder year Pilgrims used this stepping-stone.

Each May traditional corn-planting is re-enacted at the Old Fort-Harlow House.

ree famous statues: "Hail to the Sun-:" greets visitors to Mohawk Trail. Kitson's "Minuteman" stands on green at Lexington, the one by French at Concord.

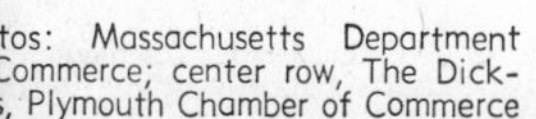

tos: Massachusetts Department Commerce; center row, The Dick-;, Plymouth Chamber of Commerce

Giant blue fin tuna, weighing 300 to 600 pounds. are landed at a Cape Cod harbor.

Cape Cod's 300 miles of coast provi scores of safe bays, inlets for sailir

Provincetown's narrow streets and lanes delight visitors to its famous art colony.

Sandwich Congregational Church: Fam colored Sandwich glass was made in to

Photos: Cape Cod Chamber of Commerce; b tom left, Massachusetts Department of Comm

arvesting cranberries: The September ndscape is brilliant with the crimson bogs and the colorful costumes of the berry pickers, some of Indian descent.

lelody Tent at Hyannis presents operetta, usical comedy in theater-in-round style.

oked rug exhibition shows present-day nples of favorite early American art.

Stoney Brook Mill at Brewster is first water power grist mill in the country.

tos: Cape Cod Chamber of Commerce; bot- right, Massachusetts Department of Commerce

Nantucket Island (25 mi. off Cape Cod) once was the great whaling port of world.

Jethro Coffin house, genuine "salt box" style, is oldest on island, built 1686.

Old Mill on Nantucket has spar so fixed that vanes will turn only for West wind.

Martha's Vineyard is triangular isle of elbow of Cape Cod. This is Edgartown

Gay Head Cliffs on Martha's Vineyard are noted for brilliant colors, especially when reflected by the late afternoon sun. Wampanoag Indians make souvenirs of cla

Photos: Massachusetts D partment of Commer top right by Eric M. Sanf

NEWPORT HEADS STYLISH RESORTS OF RHODE ISLAND, OUR SMALLEST STATE

Newport's famous 3-mile Cliff Walk along the Atlantic Ocean passes many fabulous summer residences built by millionaires. At left is Vanderbilt's "The Breakers."

Photo: Rhode Island Development Council

Rhode Island

Slater Park in Pawtucket has 193 acres of winding drives, flower gardens, a lake, 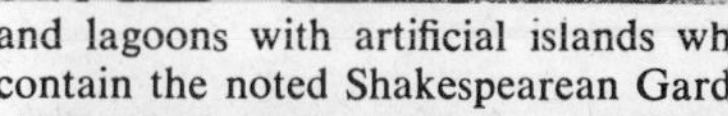and lagoons with artificial islands wh contain the noted Shakespearean Gard

State House overlooks busy Providence. It has world's second largest marble dome.

Craftsman at Gorham Company wo on an exquisite sterling silver tea serv

At Brown's University Hall, French and U.S. troops were housed in Revolution.

Green Hall at University of Rhode Isla houses library and administrative offic

Photos: Rhode Island Development Counc bottom left, Brown University News Bure

n Brown House, built 1786, is now the dquarters of R. I. Historical Society.

Samuel Slater built first textile mill in America on this Pawtucket site in 1790.

aval War College at Newport teaches ficers, logistics to advanced tactics.

Huge yachts line up at Newport for start of race to Bermuda, a sailing classic.

otos: Rhode Island Development Council; top left, ode Island Historical Society; bottom left, U. S. Navy

Rhode Island

All-steel Motor Vessel "Viking" takes to water at Blount Marine Works, Warren.

Block Island, fishing center and
is 12 miles off the Rhode Island

"The Towers" at Narragansett, designed by Stanford White, has been a landmark

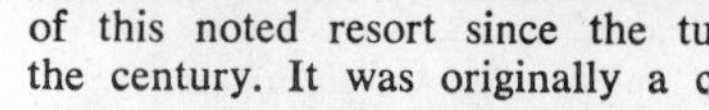

of this noted resort since the tu
the century. It was originally a c

Old Colony House, Newport, is considered one of nation's best Colonial buildings.

Newport's Old Stone Mill was pro
windmill, but legend calls it Norse

Photos: Rhode
Development C

ONNECTICUT IS KNOWN FOR SKILLED RTISANS, EDUCATION, TRIM COUNTRY

d **Lyme,** where "a sea captain once ed in every house," is an elm-shaded village that typifies Connecticut. Present Congregational Church copies 1816 one.

oto: Connecticut Development Commission

The Sterling Memorial Library at Yale: According to tradition, the founders of the college donated books from thei libraries to start the school in

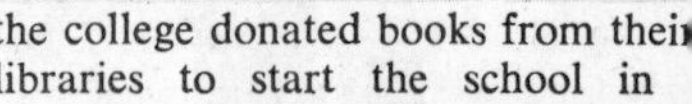

U.S. Naval Submarine Base, New London, operates "submarine escape training tank."

Choate School, exclusive prep schoc boys, has 500-acre campus at Walling

Photos: Connecticut Development Commission; C United States Navy Photograph; The Choate

The Corps of Cadets of the United States Coast Guard Academy, New London, lines up for review on the parade ground. Academy is "Annapolis" of Coast Guard.

Cadet Training Ship "Eagle" is part of floating equipment of $2,500,000 school.

Stanton House in Clinton is one of the many historic early homes in Connecticut.

Home office of the Aetna Life Affiliated Companies in Hartford is the largest colonial-style office building in the world. It's one-eighth of a mile long.

Photos: U. S. Coast Guard Academy; Connecticut Development Commission; Aetna Life Affiliated Companies

Connecticut

Intricate work of skilled craftsmen is shown at U. S. Time plant in Middlebury.

Nathaniel Allis House, at Madison, is kept as in old days. This is the kitchen.

Clock Tower at Waterbury was modeled after the Torre del Mangia, Siena, Italy.

Stonington lighthouse, now a museum stood up under bombardment by British

The Barnum Museum, Bridgeport, ho ors founder of Greatest Show on Eart

Gillette Castle, Hadlyme, is perched cliff like medieval strongholds it copi

Photos: Connecticut Development Commission; Madison Historical ciety; Al Mathewson, Bridgeport Scientific and Historical Soci American-Republican, Inc. and Waterbury Chamber of Comme

ystic **Seaport** is 19th century coastal lage being recreated by the Marine Historical Association. At left is the *Charles W. Morgan,* Yankee whaleship.

att & **Whitney Aircraft** plant at East artford shows state's industrial power. In 1851 the Sharps Company began making the famous Sharps rifles on this site.

otos: Official Mystic Seaport Photo, uis S. Martel; Pratt & Whitney Aircraft

Meriden's Broad Street-Memorial Boulevard parallels the long Green. World War I monument stands in front of churches, both over a hundred years

The War Office at Lebanon was supply headquarters for Revolutionary troops.

Nathan Hale, of "I have but one l fame, taught school here at East Hadd

Photos: Meriden Chamber of Comm
Connecticut Development Commi

MID-ATLANTIC STATES

by PAUL J. C. FRIEDLANDER

The Middle Atlantic States — New York, New Jersey, Pennsylvania and Delaware — constitute a kind of old, established and, therefore, respectable *avant garde* of the United States of America. They set the pace for the rest of the country in finance, communications, industry, science, education, and in the civilizing influences of culture and of fashions.

With their roots deep in the history of pre-Colonial days, these four states need not bluster over their origins, their patriotism or devotion to America's ideals, for they were among the very first to fight for, achieve and practice them since the days when this continent was parceled out in royal grants. They are able to face life more calmly, with the stability of a mature population, than some of their sovereign cousins to the west. Their outlook is of necessity broader, international and global because of their vantage point on the Atlantic seaboard.

The highest compliment a visitor can give a San Franciscan is to tell him that his city has the feel, the pace of an eastern metropolis. A traveler through the United States, and particularly an Easterner come home again, immediately feels this drive, this concentration of purposeful energy that moves people, that gets things done. This is the keen spirit of the "major league" of accomplishment, the sophistication of a cruelly competitive market for talent and ideas.

Here, too, are the universities, the book publishing houses, the newspaper and magazine offices where much of the nation's thinking is shaped. Here are headquarters for the media of communications—radio, television, advertising, entertainment. Here are the highest buildings, the deepest subways, the largest cities and biggest seaside playgrounds, and even deserted, barren areas remote in time and customs, if not miles, from seaboard civilization. Here are the largest banks, the biggest corporations, the richest of the rich, and just down the block in cold-water hovels the poorest of the poor. Here parade the intellectuals and the very smartest smart set and, by extension of this law of superlatives, the dumbest of the dumbbells.

The region owes much of its character to the Appalachian Mountain Range that runs from northeast to southwest, paralleling the Atlantic Coast. They were a barrier against the earliest arrivals, forced the colonizers to build cities and towns on the coastal plain. The few water gaps to the west channeled trade and commerce to and from the great deep-water ports of New York, Newark and Philadelphia, making these big cities grow bigger than ever.

Over 30 million people — one-fifth of the nation's total population—live in these four states, a population cosmopolitan because of the diversity of its origins, yet homogeneous in the sense of being "Easterners." Immigrants and sons of immigrants sit in the legislatures, on the courts and in the governors' mansions, and so do descendants of the men who signed the Declaration of Independence. There are regional and city accents within each state; election campaigns show conflicts between farmers and industrial centers.

Perhaps it is these great diversities in such a great concentration of people in a comparatively small area that gives this region its peculiar character — not as a cross section of America, not the common denominator, but rather a kind of show window of what this country has been, what it is and what it can hope to be.

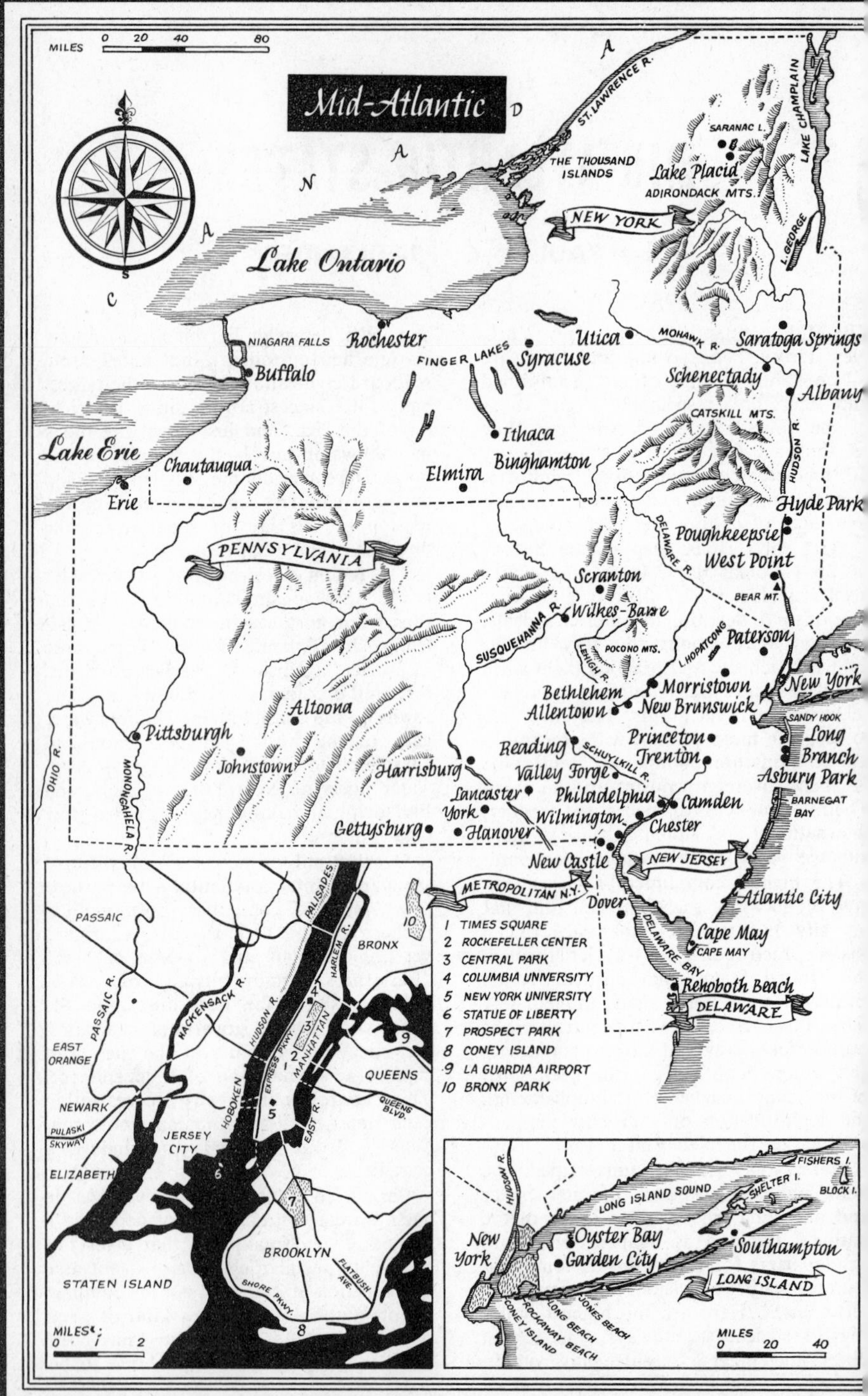

Mid-Atlantic
MILES 0 20 40 80
CANADA
ST. LAWRENCE R.
THE THOUSAND ISLANDS
SARANAC L.
Lake Placid
ADIRONDACK MTS.
LAKE CHAMPLAIN
L. GEORGE
NEW YORK
Lake Ontario
NIAGARA FALLS
Buffalo
Rochester
FINGER LAKES
Syracuse
Utica
MOHAWK R.
Saratoga Springs
Schenectady
Albany
CATSKILL MTS.
HUDSON R.
Lake Erie
Chautauqua
Erie
Ithaca
Elmira
Binghamton
Hyde Park
Poughkeepsie
West Point
BEAR MT.
DELAWARE R.
PENNSYLVANIA
Scranton
Wilkes-Barre
SUSQUEHANNA R.
POCONO MTS.
LEHIGH R.
L. HOPATCONG
Paterson
New York
Bethlehem
Allentown
Morristown
New Brunswick
SANDY HOOK
Long Branch
Asbury Park
Altoona
Pittsburgh
Johnstown
OHIO R.
MONONGAHELA R.
Princeton
Trenton
Reading
SCHUYLKILL R.
Harrisburg
Valley Forge
Lancaster
Philadelphia
Camden
BARNEGAT BAY
York
Wilmington
Chester
Gettysburg
Hanover
New Castle
NEW JERSEY
METROPOLITAN N.Y.
Dover
Atlantic City
Cape May
CAPE MAY
DELAWARE BAY
Rehoboth Beach
DELAWARE
1 TIMES SQUARE
2 ROCKEFELLER CENTER
3 CENTRAL PARK
4 COLUMBIA UNIVERSITY
5 NEW YORK UNIVERSITY
6 STATUE OF LIBERTY
7 PROSPECT PARK
8 CONEY ISLAND
9 LA GUARDIA AIRPORT
10 BRONX PARK
PASSAIC
PASSAIC R.
HACKENSACK R.
HUDSON R.
PALISADES
HARLEM R.
BRONX
EXPRESS PKWY.
MANHATTAN
EAST ORANGE
QUEENS
QUEENS BLVD.
NEWARK
HOBOKEN
EAST R.
PULASKI SKYWAY
JERSEY CITY
ELIZABETH
BROOKLYN
FLATBUSH AVE.
STATEN ISLAND
SHORE PKWY.
MILES 0 1 2
HUDSON R.
FISHERS I.
SHELTER I.
BLOCK I.
LONG ISLAND SOUND
New York
Oyster Bay
Garden City
Southampton
LONG ISLAND
JONES BEACH
LONG BEACH
ROCKAWAY BEACH
CONEY ISLAND
MILES 0 20 40

NEW YORK BOASTS THE WORLD'S LARGEST CITY AND GREATEST HARBOR

ooking south from 70th floor of RCA uilding at dusk, you see lights aglow in Empire State Building (1472 ft. with television tower) and lower Manhattan.

oto: Grant M. Haist

New York NEW YORK CITY

Bartholdi's Statue of Liberty welcomes ships as they arrive in New York harbor.

Ferry "Miss Liberty" carries half million visitors yearly from Battery to Statue.

Sightseeing yachts provide pleasant way of viewing all of Manhattan's skyline.

United Nations Secretariat Building ha two sides entirely of glass, two of marbl

Sub-Treasury Building, Wall and Nass streets, is of Greek Revival architectu

Photos: New York State Department of Comm Trans World Airlines; Circle Line-Statue F Circle Line-Sightseeing Yachts, Inc.; Konstan

New York's City Hall has welcomed visitors from all over world for 150 years.

Ieart of financial district, at lower tip f island, is seen from across river.

The Bowery," famed in song and story, a battered relic of its early days.

The "canyons" of the financial center are pictured at Pine Street and Broadway.

otos: Konstantin Kos-
ch; right, G. A. Reims

New York NEW YORK CITY

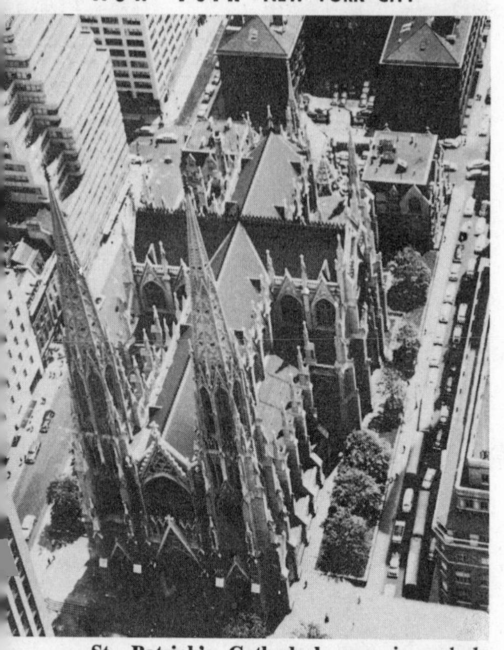

St. Patrick's Cathedral occupies whole block across from Rockefeller Center.

Riverside Church has impressive towe containing carillon of seventy-two bells

Cathedral of St. John the Divine, when completed, will be the largest Gothic cathedral in the world. It has seve chapels clustered around soaring aps

Photos: Konstantin Kosti

-story **RCA Building** dominates 15-unit ckefeller Center, "Radio City."

Looking east from RCA Building you see UN, East River, Grand Central, Chrysler.

oking to south you see of Lower Manhattan.

View to west from observation roof shows the *Queen Mary* in Hudson River, with New Jersey shore beyond.

ı **Lower Plaza** is noted rometheus Fountain.

Northward view pictures Central Park, lined on all sides with impressive apartment buildings, hotels, museums.

hotos: Rockefeller Center, Inc.; top right and lower left, rant M. Haist; center left and lower right, Konstantin Kostich

"Sunday in the Park" is favorite recreation of New Yorkers who boat or skate

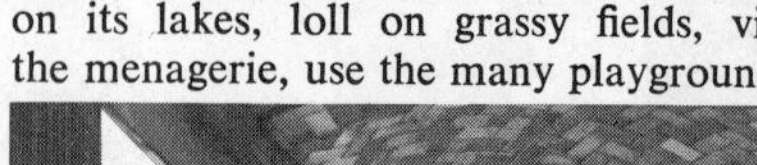

on its lakes, loll on grassy fields, vi the menagerie, use the many playgroun

Columbia University, founded in 1754 as Kings College, has over 22,000 students.

Hall of Fame at New York Universi honors American men and women of no

Photos: G. A. Reims; bo tom left, Konstantin Kosti

.t Times Square, Broadway becomes the Great White Way," aglow with hundreds of spectacular electric signs. Theaters make it the amusement center of nation.

herman Billingsley's Stork Club is one ' most famous night clubs in country.

ack & Charlie's "21" always has autograph hunters waiting for celebrities.

Christmas brings enormous decorated tree to Rockefeller Plaza, songs by Choristers.

Stage shows at Radio City Music Hall are famous for precision *Corps de Ballet*.

'hotos: TWA Trans World Airlines; Stork Club; Edward
Ratcliffe; Jack & Charlie's "21"; Konstantin Kostich

New York NEW YORK CITY

Brooklyn Bridge, built in 1883 by the Roeblings, was first to span East River.

George Washington Bridge, with Linco and Holland tunnels, cross Hudson Rive

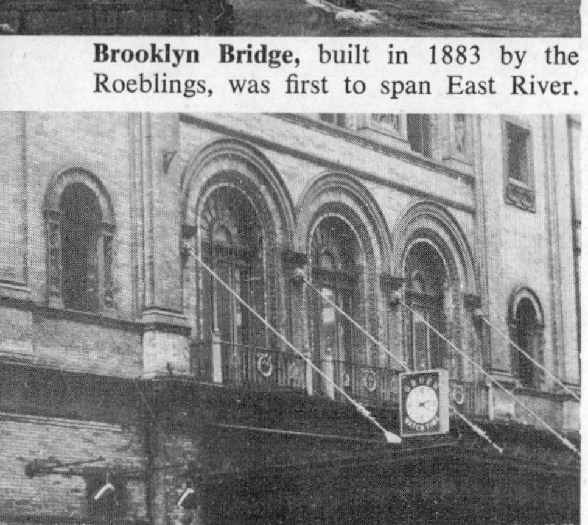

Metropolitan Opera House is premier home of grand opera in the United States.

Washington Arch, at lower end of Fif Avenue, is gateway to Greenwich Villag

Chinatown is center for restaurants and curio shops, about 4,000 Chinese residents.

Grant's Tomb, Riverside Drive landmar honors Civil War general, 18th Preside

Photos: Northwest Orient Airlines: top right, center left, Konstantin Kostic United Air Lines; Grant M. Haist; New York State Department of Commer

oney Island often attracts a million to its
ean beach, boardwalk and amusements.

Rockefeller Plaza outdoor ice skating pond has twenty onlookers to each skater.

lamas from Peru are among the curios
Bronx Zoo, one of world's largest.

Japanese Garden, Rose and Rock Gardens are found in Brooklyn Botanical Garden.

arades up New York's great Fifth Ave-
ue honor holidays, heroes, special events.

Sidewalk art shows encourage looking and buying in bohemian Greenwich Village.

hotos: Konstantin Kostich; top right, Edward Ratcliffe;
nter left, New York State Department of Commerce

Montauk Point is the eastern tip of Long Island. Its lighthouse, with black-and-white-striped tower, was built in 179 Fishing grounds off the point are famou

Ducks on the hoof: Duck farms flourish along the many creeks of the South Shore.

Whalers Church at Sag Harbor lost i spyglass-shaped tower in 1938 hurrican

Shelter Island nestles between the two eastern points of Long Island, Orient Point on the north and Montauk to t south, connected with both by ferrie

Photos: top, Charles L. Sherman; N York State Department of Comme

nce an almost inaccessible sandbar, nes Beach is now state's best play spot.

Watertower, floodlighted at night and visible for 25 miles, dominates Jones Beach.

agamore Hill, recently opened to public, as home of Pres. Theodore Roosevelt.

Souvenirs of Rough Rider days, of big-game hunting, fill Teddy Roosevelt home.

'alt Whitman Birthplace in West Hills: ood Gray Poet was born here in 1819.

Country Life Press, Garden City, is one of world's great book publishing centers.

otos: New York State Department of mmerce; bottom right, A. Milton Runyon

Franklin D. Roosevelt Library, at Hyde Park, houses six million of his papers.

Taylor Hall is at entrance to Vass College for women, at Poughkeeps

At West Point, the buildings of the U. S. Military Academy seem carved out of the hillside rocks. Admitted as cadet graduates are named second lieutenant

Harness racing at Goshen is climaxed by the internationally famous Hambletonian.

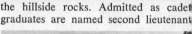

Mid-Hudson Bridge is at Poughkeepsi half way between New York and Albany

Photos: New York State Department of Commerc

ar Mountain Bridge, about 40 miles ·rth of New York, leads to Palisades

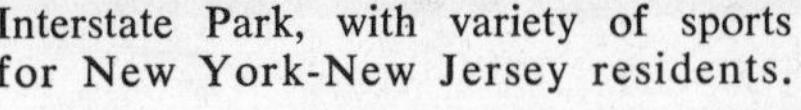

Interstate Park, with variety of sports for New York-New Jersey residents.

atskill Game Farm, in Greene County, :hibits animals from all over the world.

ctors' rehearse for summer theater at 'oodstock, widely known artist colony.

Tower in Catskills gives wide view. This is noted as "Wish You Were Here" land.

ıotos: New York State Department of Com-ɛrce; bottom right, Konstantin Kostich

New York ADIRONDACK REGION

Kayak sailing on Seventh Lake: There are hundreds of lakes in the Adirondacks.

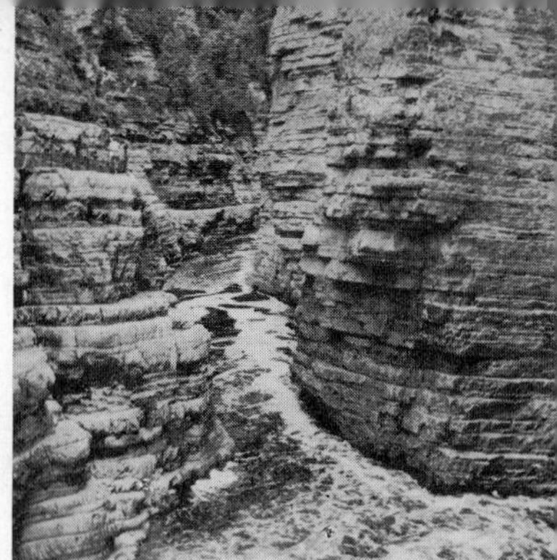

Ausable Chasm is a wonderland of ro forms: Pulpit Rock, Devil's Oven, e

Schroon Lake is lovely 9-mile-long body of water that attracts many vacationists.

Legend says it was named after Madar de Maintenon, widow of Paul Scarro

State operated bathing beach is one of many facilities of 33-mile Lake George.

Whiteface Mountain has elevator to loo out tower that gives a magnificent vie

Photos: New York State Department Commerce; center, Konstantin Kosti

aratoga Race Track, Saratoga Springs, is ;ene of internationally famous horse races during August, including the Travers and the Hopeful, test for two-year-olds.

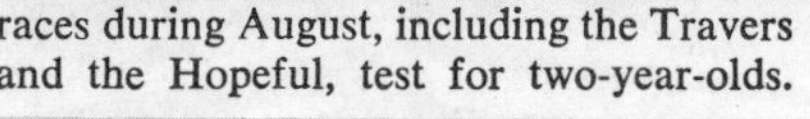

entral Adirondacks offer winter sports :rills for youngsters and for grownups.

10w tractor transports skiers in com- ›rt at the Whiteface Mt. ski development.

Lake Placid ski jump: This village on Mirror Lake is famous as sport center.

ıotos: New York State Department of Com- erce; top, Henri Cartier-Bresson (Magnum)

Y-shaped Keuka Lake is the only one of the Finger Lakes with irregular outline.

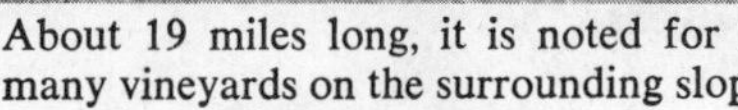

About 19 miles long, it is noted for t many vineyards on the surrounding slop

The Krebs, Skaneateles, is one of most famous eating houses in upstate area.

Baseball Museum at Cooperstown reve Abner Doubleday's invention of the spo

McKinley Circle, Buffalo: This is the second largest city (580,000) in state.

Elmira was summer home of Mark Tw for many years. This is writer's stud

Photos: New York State Departmen Commerce; center left, A. G. Tc

boats are towed to anchorage after a e on Cayuga Lake, largest of the six Finger Lakes. Chief city on the lake is Ithaca, the home of Cornell University.

tkins Glen: The Gorge Trail is 2 miles g, has some 700 steps, many bridges.

Taughannock Falls, 50 feet higher than Niagara, is highest east of the Rockies.

tos: Bill Ficklin; Alfred E. Reichenberger; York State Department of Commerce

The "Thousand Islands" actually number about 1700. About 20 of them are visible in this picture of the American cha of the St. Lawrence near Alexandria I

Boldt Castle was built on Heart Island by George C. Boldt, who rose from dishwasher to presidency of the company owned New York's Waldorf-Astoria h

Photos: Alexandria Bay Chamber of Comm
New York State Department of Comm

;hthouse on Cape Vincent:** Many French tled here at time of Napoleon's exile.

Water tours visit the six state parks and view Thousand Island luxury estates.

ternational highway, with several idges, crosses the St. Lawrence via Wells and Hill islands. It was opened in 1938. From mainland to mainland, it's 6 miles.

otos: New York State Department of Commerce

Niagara Falls is the largest cataract in North America with total width of 4,750 feet. This is American Falls which tered shape with recent erosion of r

Photo: Grant M.

FIFTY MILLION A YEAR ENJOY NEW JERSEY'S FAMOUS BEACHES

ntic City's fabulous boardwalk, im-
se hotels, Municipal Auditorium, Steel Pier all combine to make it one of world's most patronized year-round resorts.

o: New Jersey Department of Con-
ation and Economic Development.

Skyline of Trenton, New Jersey's capital, is dominated by dome of Statehouse.

This tall electric beacon marks Thor A. Edison's workshop at Menlo Pa

Princeton University Chapel ranks with Chicago and Cambridge as world's largest.

This is Voorhees Chapel of N. J. Colle for Women, a part of Rutgers Universi

Photos: New Jersey Department of Co servation and Economic Developme

ıry Park is best-known of the resorts ; the northern part of New Jersey's

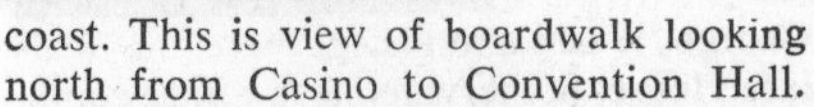

coast. This is view of boardwalk looking north from Casino to Convention Hall.

lfonte-Haddon Hall is meeting-place ıany of Atlantic City's conventions.

Cape May is at southernmost point of the state, between Delaware Bay and Atlantic.

ıegat Lighthouse was re-ed by lightship off-shore.

Manasquan and Brielle, on the Manasquan River where it flows into the Atlantic, are fishing headquarters.

ɔs: Asbury Park Municipal Publicity Dept.; fonte-Haddon Hall; New Jersey Department Conservation and Economic Development.

George Washington slept here, at Wallace House, Somerville, near winter camp.

Walt Whitman lived in this modest C den residence from 1884 until his d

Alexander Hamilton monument, in a small park on the brink of the Palisades at

Weehawken, marks spot of Burr-Hami duel. Across Hudson is New York skyl

Basking Ridge oak, in Somerset County, has amazing branch spread of 140 feet.

Paulins Kill is one of many lakes a streams that provide good sport-fishi

Photos: center, G. A. Reims; New Jersey Dep ment of Conservation and Economic Developn

ENNSYLVANIA HAS HISTORIC SHRINES ROM EARLY DAYS OF INDEPENDENCE

ladelphia's Independence Hall, which ses Liberty Bell, witnessed the signing of the Declaration of Independence in 1776. Constitution was framed here, too.

o: TWA Trans World Airlines

Franklin Institute has many exhibits, including Benjamin Franklin Printing Shop.

University of Pennsylvania was first in the country officially designated as such.

Old Original Bookbinder's is a favorite restaurant, filled with mementoes of past.

Liberty Bell developed crack in 1835 whe tolling death of Chief Justice Marshall

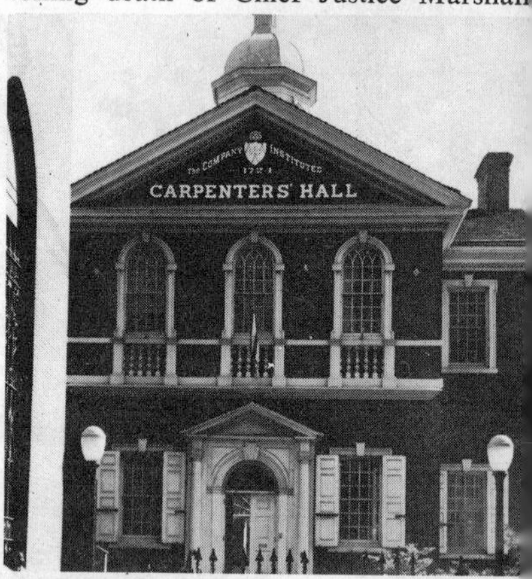

First Continental Congress assembled her in Carpenters' Hall on September 5, 177

Old Swedes Church, built in 1700, is t oldest church building in Philadelphi

Photos: Pennsylvania State Department of Cor merce; bottom left, Old Original Bookbinde

sy Ross House is reputed place where t American Flag was designed, sewn.

Wissahickon Valley, Walnut Lane Bridge show a pastoral section of Philadelphia.

Custom House was originally home he second Bank of the United States.

In front stands a statue of Robert Morris, a chief financier of American Revolution.

ɔs: Pennsylvania State rtment of Commerce

These soldiers' huts at Valley Forge are similar to those used by Washington's 11,000 ragged Continentals who camp here during crucial winter of 1777–17

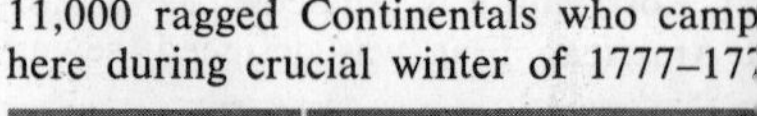

Washington's Headquarters was scene of conferences with Lafayette, Knox, others.

Washington Memorial Carillon has bells, one for each state, one for Un

Photos: Pennsylvania
Department of Comm

ysburg was scene of three-day battle marked turning point of Civil War.

Monument honors General Meade who led Union forces against General Lee's.

iers' National Cemetery has graves ,604 soldiers who died in battle between forces numbering 70,000 to 80,000 on each side. Cemetery covers 17 acres.

sylvania Memorial honors 34,530 of state who took part in the battle.

National Monument is near spot where Abraham Lincoln gave Gettysburg speech.

s: Pennsylvania State
tment of Commerce

Pennsylvania

Bucknell University, Lewisburg, is one of state's leading educational centers.

University of Pittsburgh's 42-story scraper is called "Cathedral of Lear

Pittsburgh's "Golden Triangle" is area between Allegheny and Monongahela rivers.

One of the great steel centers of is Pittsburgh's gigantic "Steel Va

Quaint buggies, homespun garb typify the Amish, one of state's many religious sects.

Hopewell Village, near Reading, has re-created as it was in Revolutionary

Photos: Pennsylvania State Department of Commerc left, A. Milton Runyon; center left, Robert V. Pi

elaware Water Gap Bridge spans river tween New Jersey and Pennsylvania.

Capitol at Harrisburg was dedicated by President Theodore Roosevelt in 1906.

bria Inclined Plane connects Johns- n with Westmont, 504 feet higher.

Shaft commemorates Washington's cross- ing of Delaware in attack on Trenton.

s: top left, Copyright Aero Service Corpora- courtesy Delaware River Joint Toll Bridge Com- n; Pennsylvania State Department of Commerce

Pennsylvania

U. S. Brig "Niagara" took decisive part in Battle of Lake Erie, during War of 1812.

Buck Hill Falls is hidden in deep gor Photo shows the Upper and Middle Fa

The Inn at Buck Hill Falls in the Pocono Mountains was established in 1901 by a group of Philadelphia Quakers. It is of America's prominent resort hot

Horseshoe Curve of the Pennsylvania Railroad, constructed in 1852, is an outstanding engineering feat. The curve, 220-degree central angle, is 2,375 ft. lo

Photos: Pennsylvania State Department of C merce; top right and center, Buck Hill Falls

DELAWARE IS PROUD OF ITS HISTORIC LANDMARKS

he County Court House at New Castle ?as served Delaware's government since the days of William Penn, making it oldest U. S. Court House in continuous use.

hoto: Delaware State
evelopment Department

First powder mill of E. I. duPont de Nemours used power of Brandywine Creek.

University of Delaware pioneered i
Foreign Study, with exchange students

Christ Church, Dover, possesses a Bible presented in 1767 by Benjamin Wynkoop.

Old State House, built in 1787, stands on the Green in Delaware's capital, Dover

Photos: Delaware State Development Department

Rehoboth Beach, largest summer resort in Delaware, occupies one of the few spots along the South Atlantic coast where the mainland extends right to surf's edge.

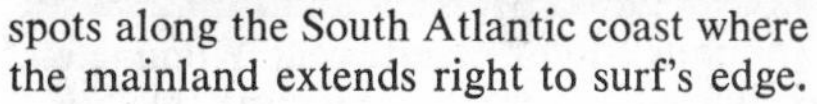

Wilmington is Delaware's one big city, of 110,000 people. This is old City Hall.

Zwaanendael Museum, Lewes, commemorates settlement by the Dutch in 1631.

Photos: Delaware State Development Department

Tourinns Motor Court, near Wilmington, is typical of modern highway facilities.

Old Swedes Church, built at Wilmington in 1698, has mementoes of many pioneers.

Old Drawyers Presbyterian Church dates from 1773. It is located near Appoquinimink Creek, in Odessa. Many founders of the state are interred in its cemetery.

Photos: Delaware State Development Department; top left, Tourinns, Inc.

THE MIDSOUTH

by STACY V. JONES

͡The Midsouth is New England with the corners rounded. It is more Colonial than Confederate, and this in spite of the fact that roadside markers recall Manassas and Appomattox. Perhaps it would be fairer to call New England a rough-edged Midsouth, for the adventurous businessmen of Jamestown did beat the Puritans to the New World by a few years. At any rate, there are similarities between the two regions: oldness and reverence for age; a pervading sense of duty and the fitness of things; close identification with the finding and founding of America and with the Revolutionary War.

The tourist is likely to see more boxwood than battlefields, for much of the area's history is preserved in the old homes and gardens of the men who made it. Energetic clubwomen have restored numerous eighteenth-century mansions; they collect visitors' half-dollars and see that everything indoors is dusted and everything outdoors is green. Stratford Hall, on Virginia's northern neck, was the birthplace of Robert E. Lee, and also of two earlier Lees, who signed the Declaration of Independence. There is George Washington's birthplace on what was once Pope's Creek and his later home at Mount Vernon on the Potomac; George Mason's Gunston Hall just below the latter, and Jefferson's Monticello at Charlottesville. A whole Colonial capital has been restored at Williamsburg. And Colonial plantation houses dot Maryland's Eastern Shore and the banks of the James in Virginia.

Mount Vernon was George Washington's later home and place of burial. It is on Potomac, 14 miles south of Washington.

The Midsouth has great topographic variety, which makes it congenial country for casual touring. In orderly progression tidewater plains cut by widening estuaries give way to rising piedmont farmland, which in turn is broken by the wooded Appalachians—a handsome but tamed range in these parts, well suited to vacationing. And of course there is Washington, a national capital but definitely a Southern city.

Photo: Grant M. Haist

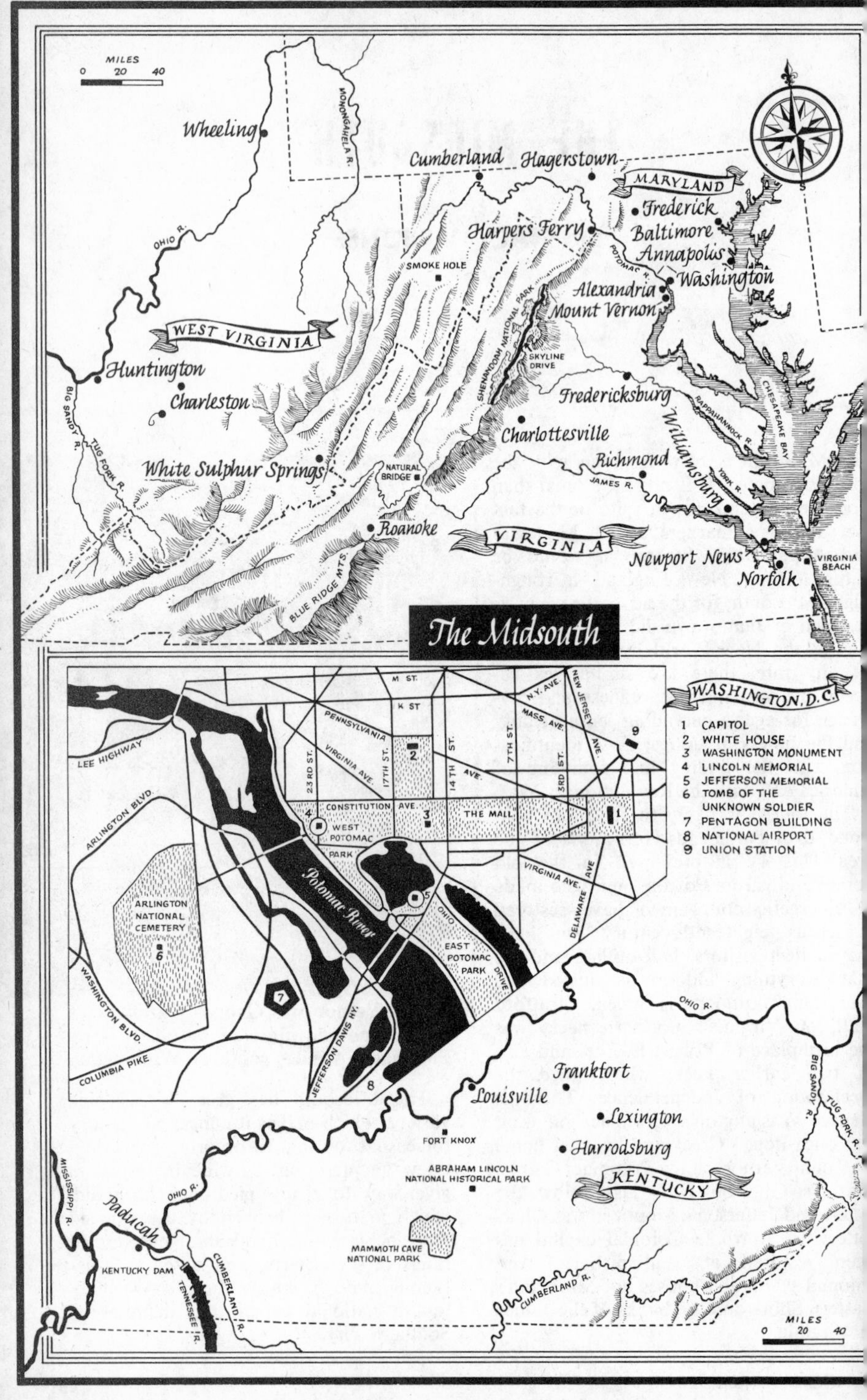

The Midsouth
MILES
0 20 40
Wheeling
MONONGAHELA R.
OHIO R.
Cumberland
Hagerstown
MARYLAND
Frederick
Baltimore
Annapolis
Harpers Ferry
POTOMAC R.
Washington
Alexandria
Mount Vernon
SMOKE HOLE
SHENANDOAH NATIONAL PARK
SKYLINE DRIVE
WEST VIRGINIA
Huntington
Charleston
BIG SANDY R.
TUG FORK R.
Fredericksburg
RAPPAHANNOCK R.
CHESAPEAKE BAY
Charlottesville
Williamsburg
Richmond
JAMES R.
YORK R.
White Sulphur Springs
NATURAL BRIDGE
Roanoke
VIRGINIA
BLUE RIDGE MTS.
Newport News
Norfolk
VIRGINIA BEACH
WASHINGTON, D.C.
1 CAPITOL
2 WHITE HOUSE
3 WASHINGTON MONUMENT
4 LINCOLN MEMORIAL
5 JEFFERSON MEMORIAL
6 TOMB OF THE UNKNOWN SOLDIER
7 PENTAGON BUILDING
8 NATIONAL AIRPORT
9 UNION STATION
M ST.
K ST
PENNSYLVANIA
N.Y. AVE.
NEW JERSEY AVE.
MASS. AVE.
VIRGINIA AVE.
23RD ST.
17TH ST.
14TH ST.
7TH ST.
3RD ST.
AVE.
LEE HIGHWAY
ARLINGTON BLVD.
CONSTITUTION AVE.
THE MALL
WEST POTOMAC PARK
Potomac River
VIRGINIA AVE.
DELAWARE AVE
OHIO DRIVE
EAST POTOMAC PARK
ARLINGTON NATIONAL CEMETERY
WASHINGTON BLVD.
JEFFERSON DAVIS HY.
COLUMBIA PIKE
OHIO R.
BIG SANDY R.
TUG FORK R.
Frankfort
Louisville
Lexington
FORT KNOX
Harrodsburg
ABRAHAM LINCOLN NATIONAL HISTORICAL PARK
KENTUCKY
MISSISSIPPI R.
OHIO R.
Paducah
MAMMOTH CAVE NATIONAL PARK
KENTUCKY DAM
CUMBERLAND R.
TENNESSEE R.
CUMBERLAND R.
MILES
0 20 40

WASHINGTON IS WORLD CITADEL OF FREEDOM

J. S. Capitol dominates Washington from ummit of Capitol Hill. George Washington laid the cornerstone in 1793; statue of Freedom was placed atop dome in 1863.

hoto: Grant M. Haist

Washington Monument, opened in 1888, is the world's tallest structure of masonry.

Air view of the Capitol shows its 12 acres of grounds. In the north wing,

ʟe left, is the Senate, and in the south ʼing, the House of Representatives meets. The building is 751 feet long, 350 wide, and its dome rises to height of 285 feet.

ʰotos: Greater National Capital ɔmmittee; American Airlines

Visitors to the top of 555-ft. Washington Monument have a spectacular view of the city, and especially of the White Hou and its 18 acres of grounds. Every U

esident has lived here since President hn Adams moved to the unfinished building in 1800. It was completely rebuilt, within the original walls, in 1950–1952.

oto: Grant M. Haist

Arlington Memorial Bridge, built at cost of $10 million crosses Potomac from the Lincoln Memorial to Arlington Nationa Cemetery. Photo shows end-of-day traffic

Lincoln Memorial, built in general form of a Greek temple, is one of the world's most impressive memorials. 36 colum represent states at time of Presiden

Photos: Grant M. Haist; Grec
National Capital Commit

terior of Lincoln Memorial contains gantic 19-ft. seated figure of Lincoln by Daniel Chester French, in which the artist has captured his brooding sadness.

oto: Grant M. Haist

Washington, D.C.

Jefferson Memorial, completed in 1943, was dedicated on the 200th anniversary of the birth of Thomas Jefferson. Pantheon design was one he often us

Photo: Konstantin Kos

owering statue of Jefferson, the great atesman who wrote the Declaration of Independence, is principal feature of the Memorial. Quotations are carved on walls.

oto: Grant M. Haist

National Gallery of Art is one of most famous in world. It was gift of Andrew W. Mellon. This view shows Constitution Avenue entrance and the 7th Street side.

Rotunda in National Gallery has fountain surmounted by Giovanni Bologna's bronze Mercury. In famed collection are painting by Stuart, Renoir, Vermeer, Home

Photos: National Gallery of A

ntagon Building is across Potomac in irginia, but so much a part of life in Washington that we include it here. It's the largest office building in the world.

ithsonian Institution houses amazing entific exhibits, most popular being *The Spirit of St. Louis,* the plane in which Lindbergh made solo flight to Paris.

tos: Ewing Galloway;
rary of Congress

The Supreme Court, completed in 1935, is one of newest and most beautiful of the major buildings in Washington. Decision by Court reflect history of the nation

Abraham Lincoln was fatally shot, here at Ford's Theater, by John Wilkes Booth.

Old Peterson House, where Lincoln die in April 1865, is across from theate

Occidental Restaurant is noted eating place next door to famous Willard Hotel.

Photographs of military men and oth celebrities line walls of the Occident

Photos: Library of Congre
bottom, Occidental Restaur

UST BELOW THE MASON-DIXON LINE, ARYLAND BLENDS NORTH AND SOUTH

he Third State House to be built on ıe same site in Annapolis, this one ates back to 1772. It is the oldest state capitol in America still in daily use, and the only one in which the Congress of the United States has convened.

ıoto: Maryland Department of Information

"Tecumseh" is revered by midshipmen at United States Naval Academy, Annapolis.

Academy Chapel has crypt containin tomb of daring hero, John Paul Jones

St. John's College, Annapolis, was the first free school in original 13 colonies.

Annapolitans model fashions of ancesto at historic Hammond-Harwood hous

Photos: Maryland Department of Informat

cean City is Maryland's only resort by e sea. Located on sandy strip between

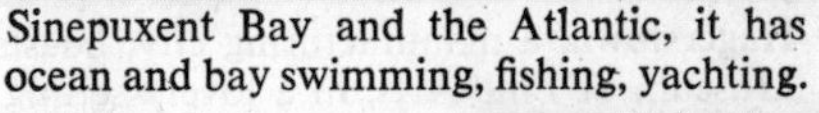

Sinepuxent Bay and the Atlantic, it has ocean and bay swimming, fishing, yachting.

ort McHenry repulsed British in 1814; vas birthplace of "Star Spangled Banner."

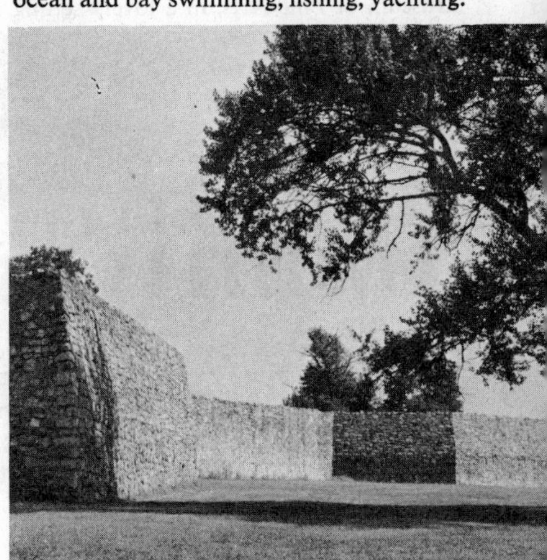

And battle-scarred Fort Frederick dates back to 1756, in days of the Indian wars.

ntietam Battlefield, near Hagerstown, vas scene of one of the hardest-fought Civil War battles, on September 17, 1862. Markers show ebb and flow of fierce battle.

hotos: M. E. Warren, Mary-
and Department of Information

Maryland

Hagerstown, a manufacturing city, boasts Museum of Fine Arts, in a lovely setting.

The "Narrows," near Cumberland, was famous gateway to the west 200 years ago.

Fairchild Aircraft plant, near Hagerstown, is responsible for the city's nickname, "The Home of the Flying Boxcars." Other plants make furniture, pipe organs, shoes.

Wye Oak is the state tree. Maryland has twelve extensive park and forest areas.

Princess Anne, one of the earliest settlements, has old homes like Teackle House

Photos: top left, Raup, Maryland Department of Information; top right, Cumberland Chamber of Commerce center, Maryland Department of Information; bottom M. E. Warren, Maryland Department of Information

IRGINIA, "MOTHER OF PRESIDENTS," HAS WEALTH OF SCENERY, HISTORY

oto: Court House, Charlottesville,
Henri Cartier-Bresson (Magnum)

Williamsburg is delightful replica of our Colonial past. Magazine was built 1715.

In this 18th century Capitol, Patric Henry made speech against the Stamp Ac

Bruton Parish Church has been restored to its appearance when built in 1710–15.

Raleigh Tavern has been refurnished a cording to inventories of early keepe

Public Gaol: Minor offenders were pu ished in the stocks and pillory in fro

Photos: Colonial Williamsb top right, Konstantin Kos

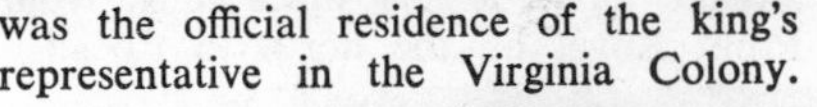

overnor's Palace, considered one of the ndsomest estates in colonial America, was the official residence of the king's representative in the Virginia Colony.

lliamsburg Inn, just outside restored ea, has fine facilities for visitors.

Early costumes recreate lavishness of colonial life under the British crown.

tos: Colonial Williamsburg; bottom right, Vir- a Department of Conservation and Development

Skyline Drive is 107 miles long, from Front Royal on the north to Rockfish Gap near Waynesboro on the south. The it links up with the Blue Ridge Parkwa

Shenandoah National Park is 300-square-mile tract of mountains and ridges that extends on either side of the Sky Drive. It has 200 miles of hiking tr

Photos: Virginia Department of Conservation and Develop

e **Homestead,** at Hot Springs, is one the world's famous hotels. First inn

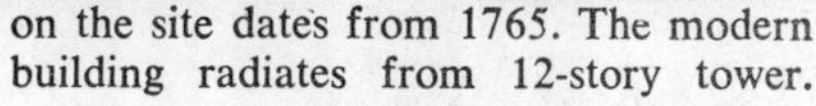

on the site dates from 1765. The modern building radiates from 12-story tower.

ıes **Monroe,** as a young attorney, used modest Law Office, Fredericksburg.

University of Virginia was founded 1819 by Thomas Jefferson. This is the Rotunda.

ıes **Monroe built Oak Hill,** near Aldie, ing his first term as President. He spent much time here, making journeys to and from the Capital on horseback.

tos: James Monroe Memorial Foundation; top, The Homestead

Monticello, the home of Thomas Jefferson, was designed and built by the statesman himself. He died here on July 4, 18 fiftieth anniversary of Independence D

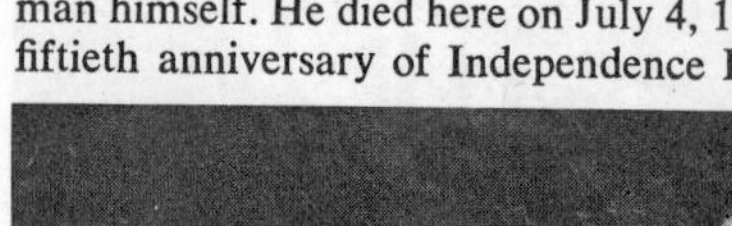

Luray Caverns, beneath western slopes of Blue Ridge, have great underground halls.

Shenandoah is another of Virginia's n caverns. This is the Grotto of the Go

Photos: Virginia Department of Conservation and Developn

re at Mount Vernon, plantation home erlooking the Potomac River, George

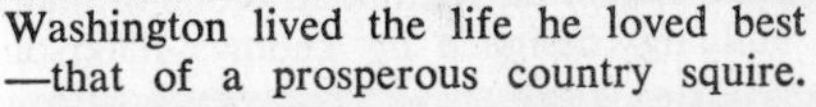

Washington lived the life he loved best —that of a prosperous country squire.

onewall Jackson taught at "V.M.I."— rginia Military Institute, Lexington.

Natural Bridge, 215 feet high, is one of the seven natural wonders of the world.

otos: Virginia Department of nservation and Development

Virginia

State Capitol at Richmond is one of many buildings designed by Thomas Jefferson.

It contains Houdon statue of Washing only one of the President made from

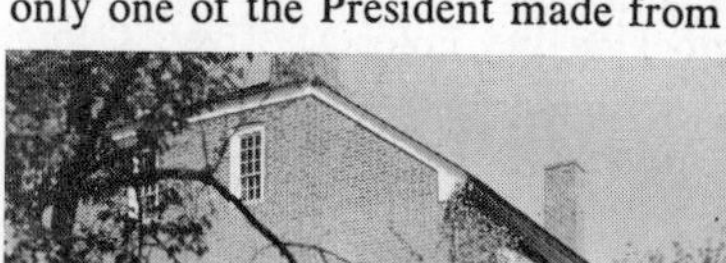

Kenmore was home of Washington's sis Betty, and her husband, Colonel Lev

Westover, home of the famous Byrd family of Virginia, is along the James River.

Girls from Mary Washington College se tea in the stately dining room at Kenm

Photos: Virginia Departmen Conservation and Developm

Valentine Museum, Richmond, houses work of sculptor Edward V. Valentine.

White House of Confederacy, at Richmond, was the home of Jefferson Davis.

Stratford was birthplace of the Lees of Virginia, including the famous Robert E.

"Mother's Room" at Stratford: The great plantation, now restored, borders Potomac.

This is gracious dining room of house in which George Washington was born, 1732.

Exterior of Birthplace: Rebuilt like the original, it is now a National Monument.

Photos: Virginia Department of Conservation and Development; bottom right, U. S. Department of the Interior

Arlington House, in Arlington National Cemetery, was built by step-grandson of

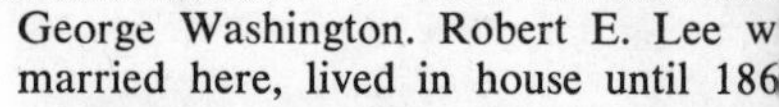

George Washington. Robert E. Lee w married here, lived in house until 186

Woodrow Wilson was born in this square house at Staunton, on December 28, 1856.

Presbyterian Meeting House, Alexandr Unknown Soldier of Revolution lies he

Gunston Hall was home of George Mason, outstanding author of the Bill of Rights.

St. Luke's Church, near Smithfield, one of nation's oldest, built in 16

Photos: Virginia Departmen
Conservation and Developm

hirley, one of the largest of Tidewater 'irginia mansions, was built between 1720 and 1740 by Thomas West and his three brothers. Lawn slopes to James River.

ames Monroe built Ash Lawn near Mon-cello, so he could be near his friend and mentor, Thomas Jefferson. Estate is, known for its beautiful boxwood hedges.

hotos: Virginia Department of
onservation and Development

Old church tower, Jamestown: This was site of first permanent English settlement.

St. John's Church, Richmond, echoed to Patrick Henry's cry for "liberty or death."

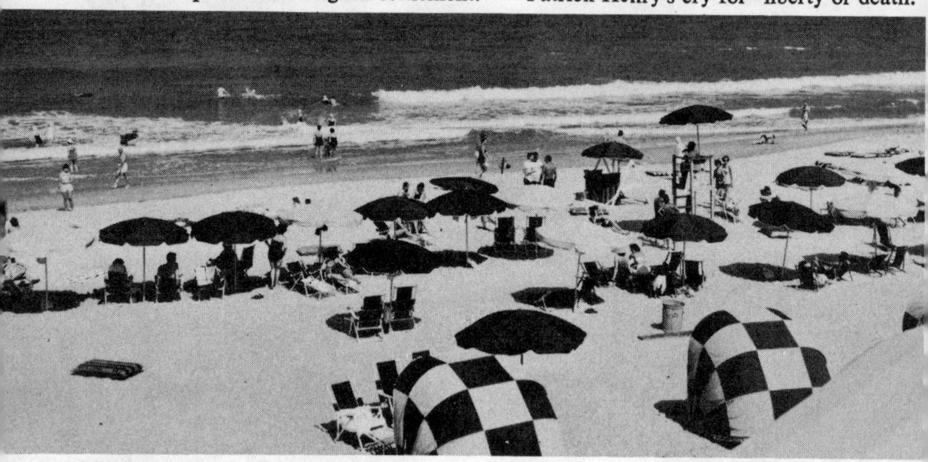

Virginia Beach, on the Atlantic near Norfolk, is an outstanding shore resort.

Virginia's best-known Chesapeake Bay resorts are Ocean View, Buckroe Beach.

George Washington Masonic National Memorial Temple towers over Alexandria.

Boyhood home of Patrick Henry, this old house became Michie Tavern in 1746

Photos: Virginia Department of Conservation and Development; bottom right, Michie Tavern

WHITE SULPHUR IS NOTED RESORT OF "MOUNTAIN STATE," WEST VIRGINIA

he original White Sulphur Springs Hotel as renowned for more than half a century as the Old White. Belle, in front of Greenbrier, re-creates ante-bellum days.

ıoto. Greenbrier News Bureau

Woodburn Hall is symbol of West Virginia University, situated at Morgantown.

West Virginia's State Capitol is located at Charleston, in Appalachian foothills.

Greenbrier College for Women, originally Lewisburg Seminary, was founded in 1812.

Harewood, in Eastern Panhandle, was built by Washington for his brother, Samuel.

"Old Stone Face" gazes across creek a Beckwith Cut-Off, near Chimney Corner

Photos: West Virginia Indus trial and Publicity Commissio

awks Nest State Park provides breath-king view of the New River Gorge, east of Charleston. The towering rock is named for the fish hawks that once nested there.

t **Blackwater Falls,** the dark hued river ops over broken ledge to huge boulders.

Smoke Hole Cavern was used by Indians and early white settlers to cure meats.

onument above and "John Brown's Fort" right commemorate the stand which the famed abolitionist made against force of marines prior to start of the Civil War.

otos: West Virginia Indus-
al and Publicity Commission

West Virginia

Indian Burial Mound, in Staunton Park at South Charleston, is 175 feet around at base and 30 feet high. Many Indian o nаments, stone weapons have been foun

The Castle, Berkeley Springs, was built by Judge Soult as a "castle in the air."

Carbide and Carbon Chemicals Corpora tion is one of state's many industrial plant

Photos: West Virginia Indu trial and Publicity Commissi

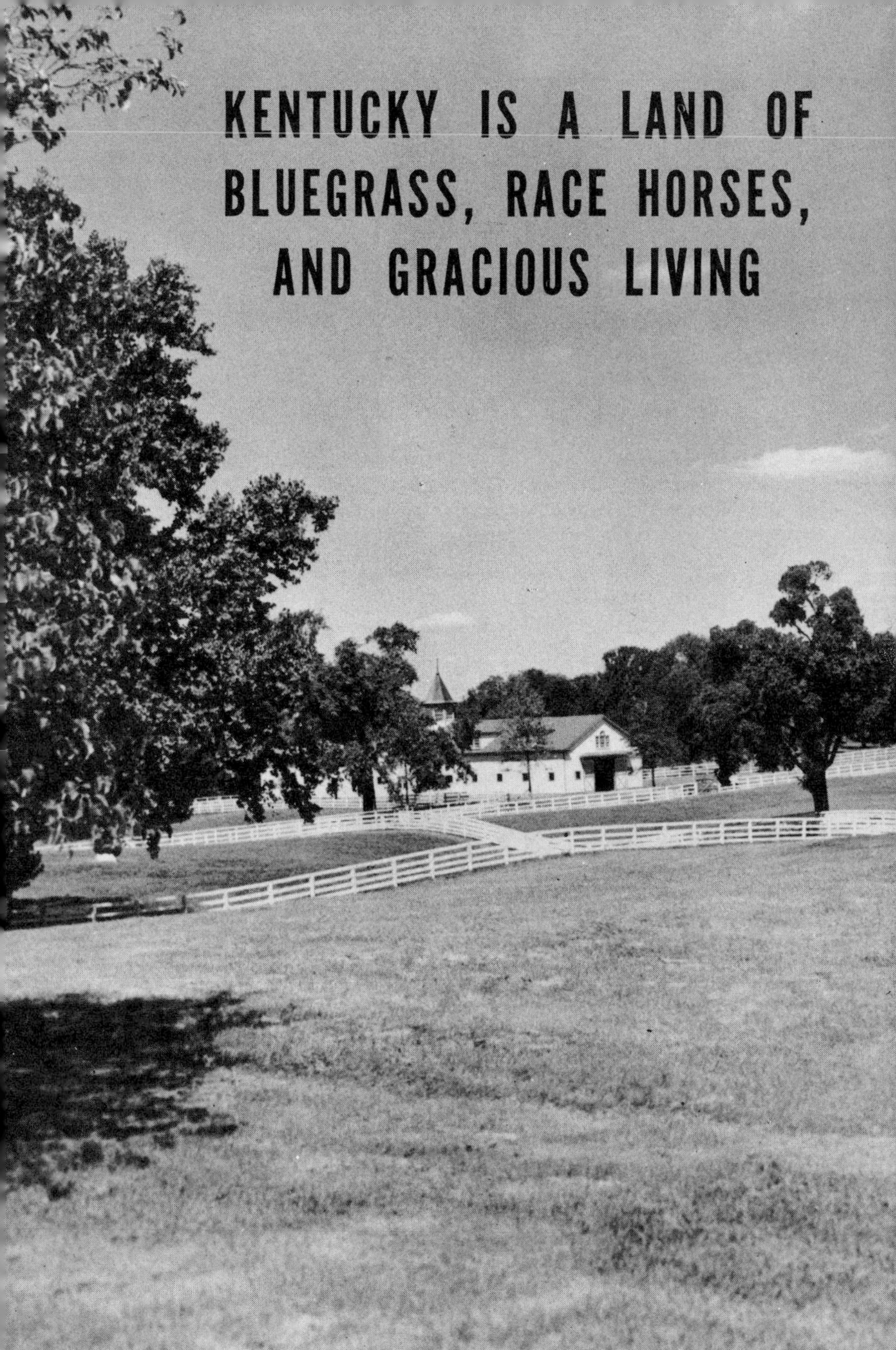

KENTUCKY IS A LAND OF BLUEGRASS, RACE HORSES, AND GRACIOUS LIVING

orse farm region of Kentucky centers ound Lexington. Visitors may see the thoroughbreds that have made history and watch gambols of promising young colts.

oto: Kentucky Division of Publicity

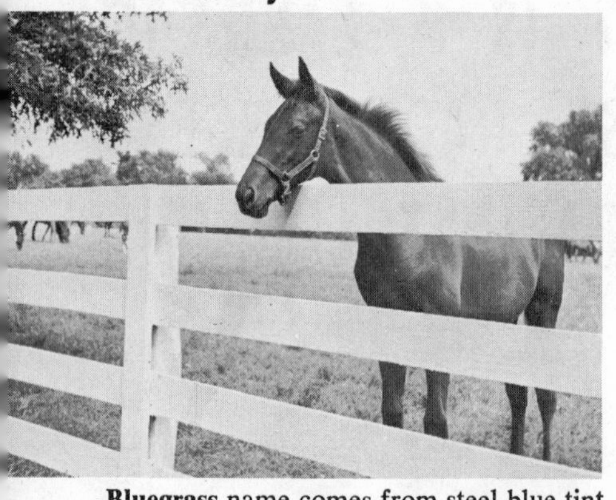

Bluegrass name comes from steel-blue tint of May blossoms. It's ideal for grazing.

Capitol, built in 1909, is at Frankfo in center of state, along Kentucky Rive

Mammoth Cave covers an area ten miles in circumference and has 325 explored passageways which extend 150 miles. Th is Crystal Lake, an outstanding featur

Photos: Kentucky Division of Publicity; botto W. Ray Scott, National Park Concessions, Ir

urchill Downs in Louisville is scene of nerica's most celebrated horse race, the Kentucky Derby. More than 100,000 fans gather here first Saturday in May.

ir view of Calumet Farm shows beautiful rns, outdoor track, miles of rolling blue-grass where many thoroughbred winners have been raised. It covers 1,000 acres.

otos: Kentucky Division of Publicity

Kentucky Dam is major TVA dam, finished 1944, 206 ft. high, 8,422 ft. long.

Kentucky Lake, formed by dam, is sp center with three state parks on shor

Laurel Cove, Pine Mountain State Park, is scene of the annual Mountain Laurel Festival. High point of 3-day event crowning of the queen by the Govern

Liberty Hall, in Frankfort, was home of John Brown, state's first U.S. Senator.

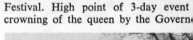

Diamond Point is one of Harrodsbur old homes in southern plantation st

Photos: top left, Robert H. Fo
Kentucky Division of Publi

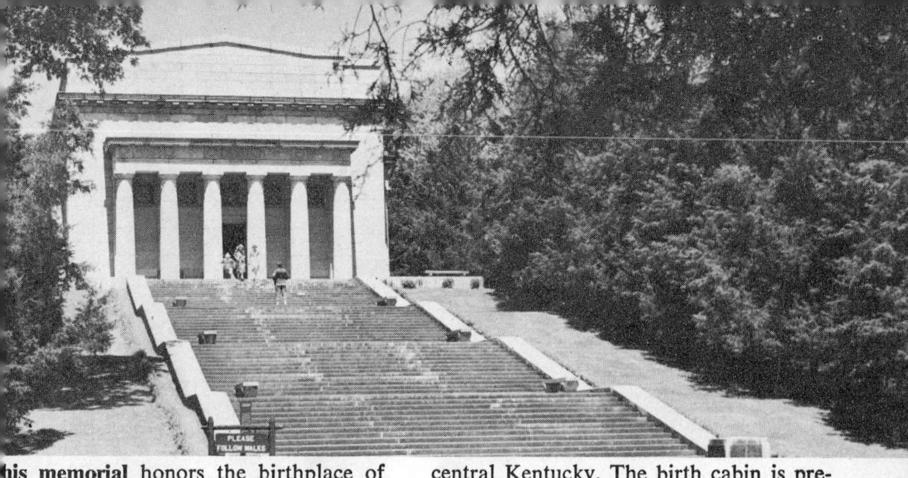

his memorial honors the birthplace of braham Lincoln, near Hodgenville, in

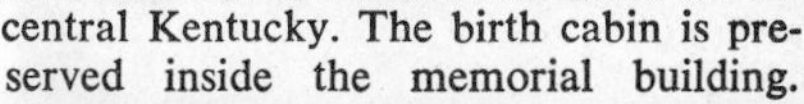

central Kentucky. The birth cabin is preserved inside the memorial building.

g house where Lincoln's parents were ırried stands at Pioneer Memorial Park.

Split-rail fence appropriately marks boundaries at Lincoln Memorial Park.

arriage Temple shelters cabin where ıomas Lincoln married Nancy Hanks.

At Federal Hill, near Bardstown, Stephen Foster wrote "My Old Kentucky Home."

ıtos: Kentucky Division of Public- center right, Robert H. Faith

Restored buildings at old Fort Harrod are furnished in manner of pioneer days.

Monument to Jefferson Davis, Presider of the Confederacy, stands at Fairviev

Fine burley tobacco is grown in bluegrass section and taken to market at Lexington.

Boone Tavern at Berea is operated by Berea College as a student industry.

Graves of Daniel and Rebecca Boone ai on a high bluff in Frankfort cemetery

Photos: Kentucky Division of Publici

THE SOUTH

by JOHN POPHAM

ıe South is a kaleidoscopic parade of .tural scenery and human attitudes, both them etched sharply. The land and the ople are undergoing great economic and cial changes. The past and the present t lances in a setting as colorful as any ıgeantry in history.

The South is a land rich with historical ntinuity, a land of long days, bright in e sun and slow to cool in the evening adows. On a summer's day the heat ınces visibly along macadamized high-ays and dusty country roads. The ubiq-tous screen doors shut with loud re-ort on hollow stillness. Soft Southern ices add to the muted effect.

Everywhere there is a sense of some-ing old and stable. Go west in North arolina through the Great Smokies to herokee at twilight and watch Cherokee ıdians from the near-by reservation act ıt the tragic story of their ancestors' trek ross the "trail of tears" in the days of ndrew Jackson.

Then go down into the valley where ıe Tennessee River forms the famous loccasin Bend at Chattanooga and visit ıe great dams of the Tennessee Valley uthority, where turbines and generators our out the electrical power that has elped remake the face of this section.

At Memphis one reaches the banks f the Mississippi River and for miles round the country is flat, the soil black ith Old Man River's largesse. This ustling city is a modern commercial ub for much of Tennessee, Mississippi ıd Arkansas but over its business sec-on there yet remains the aura of planta-on society. Along the river front cotton is yet the economic king. The shouts of river roustabouts have long since drifted downwind, side-wheelers no longer churn muddy waters and W. C. Handy's jazz is held in escrow on LP records. But trucks loaded with Negro hand-laborers still roll out of the city for chopping and weeding in the cotton fields. Men with necks burned red from the sun, wearing broad-brimmed hats and white shirts with open collars, shop in the stores and talk incessantly of cotton prices and Government parity programs.

Southward from Memphis the hand of history remains heavy, but it is the clash of old and new architecture that catches the eye. There are the great pil-lared mansions in Vicksburg and Natchez, vast stretches of delta cotton land, dot-ted with sharecroppers' cabins.

New Orleans is a special South within the South. The gems of architecture of the French quarter are perhaps un-matched in this country. Eighty miles upriver is Baton Rouge, where Huey Long built a skyscraper capitol.

The Gulf Coast makes a wide arc from Biloxi to the southern tip of Florida's west coast, a coastal vacation land run-ning down to the citrus groves and cattle farms and thriving tourist towns of Florida.

For all the changes, when the mid-day sun has softened, when afternoon shadows dapple tree-shaded streets, when children return to play after their naps, there is always a Savannah or Charleston with red-brick sidewalks and colonial architecture and patio gardens to take the visitor back into the past of the South.

The South
MILES
0
50
100
MAMMOTH SPRING
REELFOOT LAKE
ARKANSAS
Fort Smith
ARKANSAS R.
Little Rock
HOT SPRINGS NATIONAL PARK
MISSISSIPPI R.
Memphis
CUMBERLAND R.
Nashville
TENNESSEE
Chattanooga
TENNESSEE R.
Oak Ridge
Knoxville
GREAT SMOKY MTS. NATIONAL PARK
NANTAHALA NAT. FOREST
MT. MITCHELL
Asheville
Tryon
Greenville
Spartanburg
Gastonia
Charlotte
Greensboro
Winston-Salem
Durham
Raleigh
NORTH CAROLINA
Pinehurst
Southern Pines
Wilmington
ROANOKE R.
Kitty Hawk
ROANOKE IS.
CAPE HATTERAS
PEE DEE R.
Myrtle Beach
Georgetown
SANTEE R.
Charleston
Columbia
SOUTH CAROLINA
Augusta
Aiken
EDISTO R.
SAVANNAH R.
Beaufort
Savannah
Atlantic Ocean
MISSISSIPPI
YAZOO R.
Vicksburg
Jackson
Natchez
PEARL R.
PASCAGOULA R.
Meridian
TOMBIGBEE R.
Mobile
MOBILE R.
Biloxi
Gulfport
ALABAMA
Birmingham
Tuscaloosa
Montgomery
KENNESAW MT.
Atlanta
Warm Springs
Macon
Columbus
GEORGIA
OKEFENOKEE SWAMP
Jacksonville
Tallahassee
Pensacola
SUWANNEE R.
LOUISIANA
Shreveport
RED R.
SABINE R.
Lake Charles
Baton Rouge
New Orleans
Gulf of Mexico
St. Augustine
ST. JOHNS R.
FLORIDA
Daytona Beach
Orlando
Tampa
Lakeland
Clearwater
St. Petersburg
Winter Haven
Lake Wales
Sarasota
LAKE OKEECHOBEE
West Palm Beach
Punta Gorda
Fort Myers
Fort Lauderdale
Hollywood
Miami
EVERGLADES NAT. PARK
Miami Beach
Key West

FROM HATTERAS TO GREAT SMOKIES, NORTH CAROLINA OFFERS INFINITE VARIETY

reat Smoky Mountains National Park shared by North Carolina, Tennessee. The "Great Smokies" take their name from bluish perpetual haze found here.

oto: National Park Service

North Carolina

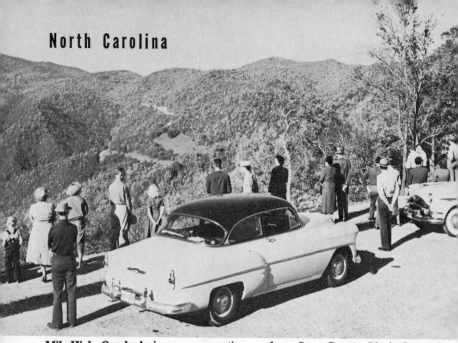

Mile-High Overlook is on new section of the Blue Ridge Parkway, extending

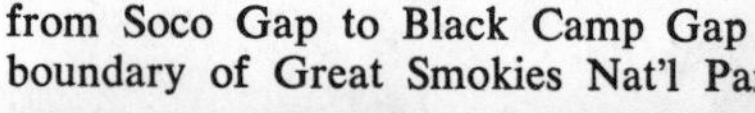

from Soco Gap to Black Camp Gap boundary of Great Smokies Nat'l Pa

Chimney Rock, Eastern America's greatest monolith, rises 315 feet from its base.

Old Market House, built 1838, stan "where all roads meet" in Fayettevill

Photos: North Carolina News Bureau, top Gus Martin; bottom left, Delta-C&S Air Lir

Vear Asheville, the mountain-top Craggy Gardens may be seen from Blue Ridge

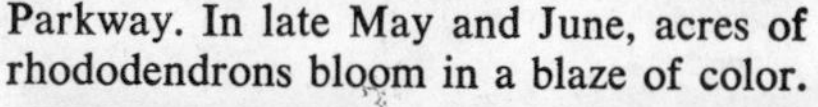

Parkway. In late May and June, acres of rhododendrons bloom in a blaze of color.

ld Well, in classic little temple, is land-ark of University of North Carolina.

Floodlighted, North Carolina's Capitol stands out from surrounding oak grove.

rth Carolina State Fair Arena, five es west of Raleigh, is one of the most remarkable buildings ever constructed. It has seating capacity of more than 9,000.

os: North Carolina News au, bottom by Gus Martin

North Carolina

Mount Mitchell, in western part of state, is 6,684 feet—the highest in Eastern America. State park on the summit ma be reached by five-mile paved highwa

Home Moravian Church is one of historic buildings in industrial Winston-Salem.

A million azaleas greet early spring Wilmington at many garden plantatio

Photos: North Carolina News Bureau, top and l by Gus Martin, bottom right by Hugh Mor

ight Brothers National Memorial, near ty Hawk, marks birth of powered flight.

Chapel at Duke University, Durham, is beautiful example of Gothic architecture.

gah National Forest is million-acre ct in western part of state, parts of which may be reached by motor roads. This is trail beside river at North Mills.

tos: North Carolina News Bu-
; bottom, U. S. Forest Service

Nantahala National Forest is another million-acre tract, known as "Land of the Noonday Sun," in southwestern p of state. This is the Nantahala go.

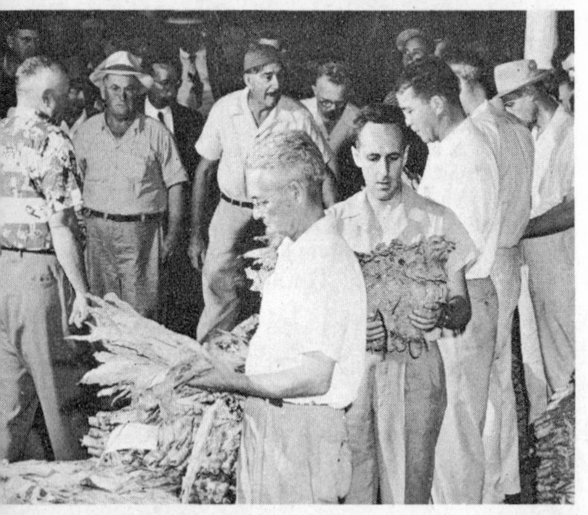

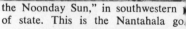

Tobacco production in state is valued at over $460 million. This is auction room.

Principal cigarette factories are locatec Durham, Reidsville and Winston-Sal

Biltmore House, near Asheville, was George Vanderbilt estate, built in 1890.

Governor's Mansion, Raleigh, is Qu Anne style. Furnishings are magnific

Photos: U. S. Forest Service; North C lina News Bureau, center left by Sebas Sommer, bottom right by Gus Mc

VELY OLD GARDENS ARE MEMORABLE FEATURE OF SOUTH CAROLINA

great gardens of South Carolina lure usands of visitors each spring. Among the principal ones are Magnolia, , Cypress, Middleton (above), and Brookgreen.

to: Konstantin Kostich

Fort Sumter, in Charleston Harbor, was scene of first shot fired in Civil War.

Charleston's Dock Street Theater was formerly the famous Old Planters Hotel.

Stuart House, with arched entrance and fluted columns, is beautiful old home.

Lofty octagonal steeple of St. Phil Episcopal Church is Charleston landma

Miles Brewton House is most elegant ample of Charleston Georgian resider

Photos: Charleston Chamber of Comme top left by Ronald A. Reilly, others by A Crenshaw; top right, Delta-C&S Air L

ſany great estates like Bonny Hall were ıilt on rice plantations. The tidewater cultivation of rice, with elaborate dikes and canals, once produced half U.S. crop.

ıky waters of Cypress Gardens reflect ıe great trees and brilliant azaleas. Visitors may view the gardens, open from Thanksgiving to May 1, from little boats.

ıtos: A. Milton Runyon; South Carolina ıte Development Board, Columbia

South Carolina

Aiken, in the west central sandhills, is known as the "Polo Capital" of the South.

State House at Columbia was bombed General Sherman while it was being bu

Library at University of South Carolina was first separate library by U.S. college.

Marine base at Parris Island, Beauf has trained thousands of U. S. Mari

Crofut House is one of many old homes that give Beaufort an Old World charm.

Four former rice plantations were joi to form 4,000-acre Brookgreen Garde

Photos: South Carolina S Development Board, Colur

GRACIOUS GEORGIA HAS VARIED TOPOGRAPHY, VARIED INTERESTS

annah River, 314 miles long, forms the ındary between Georgia, South Carolina. Nicknamed "Cracker State," Georgia is the largest state east of the Mississippi.

to: Southern Photo Service, Inc.,
rgia Department of Commerce

Atlanta, state capital and largest city, is called the "Gateway to the South." Capitol is at right, city hall left, Peachtree Street shopping center at

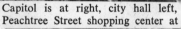

Cyclorama depicts Battle of Atlanta, at start of Sherman's "March to the Sea."

Municipal Auditorium in Hurt Park lanta has many colleges and univers

Photos: Delta-C&S Air
Georgia Department of Comr
lower left by Carolyn

Cloister is famous resort on Sea nd, one of the "Golden Isles" off Georgia's coast, with Atlantic on one side, Intracoastal Waterway on the other.

efenokee Swamp covers 700 square es, is nation's most famous, primitive.

National cemetery at Marietta is burial place of 3,000 soldiers of Confederacy.

tos: Gil Tharp, Sea Island; Flanders lio-Georgia Department of Commerce; ɔ County Chamber of Commerce, Marietta

Savannah, Georgia's oldest city, is port of entry, industrial and shipping center.

Independent Presbyterian Church is or proud buildings in tree-shaded Savan

Old stone wall leading to water: Savannah was once busiest port in the whole South.

Monterey Square is one of more thar parks that dapple the city with gr

Photos: Carolyn Carter, Southern Photo Ser Ralph Jones—Georgia Department of Comm bottom right, Chamber of Commerce of Sava

view of Savannah, looking east, with annah River at the left: City is 17 miles from river's mouth on the Atlantic. Mild climate attracts many winter visitors.

Old Pink House dates from 1771, back in Savannah's days of crinolines.

b House, built as tool shed in 1734, considered oldest building in state.

Cotton merchants once made big fortunes in these historic houses on Bay Street.

os: Chamber of Commerce of Savannah; center Southern Photo Service, Inc., bottom right, iel Benzur—Georgia Department of Commerce

Georgia

Fort Pulaski, on Cockspur Island, is named for hero of the Revolutionary War.

Warm Springs Foundation, for polio aid, was established by Franklin D. Roosevelt.

Henry W. Grady, journalist and orator, lived in this stately mansion at Athens.

Iron lacework decorates porch of Juli Low house, one of ante-bellum hor

Ocmulgee National Monument, near con, has museum run by Park Serv

Grove Point is one of great plantati reminiscent of Gone with the Wind's T

Photos: Southern Photo Service, Hubert Dunlap, Harden, Edgar Georgia Department of Comm

'LORIDA ENJOYS 1,200-MILE COAST, YEAR-ROUND MILD CLIMATE

, **sand, surf and wind-swept** palms e attracted millions of visitors to Florida's coasts, both Atlantic and Gulf. This is Delray Beach, near Lake Worth.

o: Charles L. Sherman

Miami's Crandon Park beach boasts miles of wide, white ocean sand. The "Gold Coast," from Miami north to Hobe Sou is nearest thing to an America Rivi

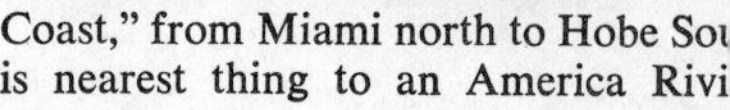

Dade County Courthouse, downtown Miami, is tallest building south of Baltimore.

Horses round the first turn at Gulfstre one of three tracks in Greater Miami a

Miami International Airport is tra center for West Indies, South Amer

Photos: City of Miami News Bur bottom right, Delta-C&S Air L

Miami Beach's fabled mile of gigantic hotels: Each has its own swimming pool

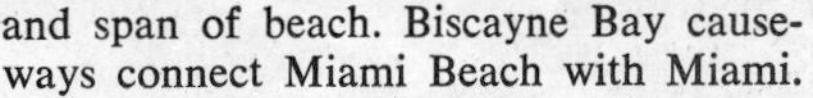

and span of beach. Biscayne Bay causeways connect Miami Beach with Miami.

Orange Bowl has 65,000 capacity-crowd for annual New Year's Day football game.

Flagler Street and Biscayne Boulevard are at heart of Miami business section.

Miami skyline from across Biscayne Bay: The city's growth has been little short of miraculous. Little more than a village 50 years ago, population is now 250,000.

hotos: City of Miami News Bureau; top, Delta-C&S Air Lines

Jacksonville has 4 bridges over St. Johns River. Newest is Gilmore Street Bridge, foreground, opened to traffic in 1954. The city was named for Andrew Jackson.

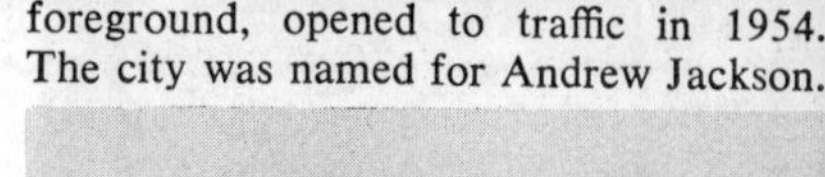

Hemming Park is tropic oasis in midst of bustling Jacksonville business district.

Jacksonville's huge Union Terminal is junction point for East Coast, West Coast.

Photos: Charles Smith Studio; Marsh-Kornegay, Inc.; City of Jacksonville

Castillo de San Marcos, also called Fort Marion, is oldest fort standing in the U.S. Begun in 1672, but not finished until 1756, it is now National Monument.

This well is said to be Fountain of Youth that Ponce de Leon drank from in 1513.

St. Augustine's "Oldest House," now a museum, was reputedly built in 1500's.

Ponte Vedra Club is delightful resort five miles south of Jacksonville Beach.

Photos: Florida State News Bureau; Ponte Vedra Club

Daytona Beach is famed for hard-packed sand on which automobiles can be driven. The 25-mile strip, 500 feet in width, h often been used for auto speed tria

Coral Sands cottages, at Ormond Beach, are typical of modern resort facilities.

Motorcycle races, too, have been he on the hard white sand of Daytona Beac

Marineland, just south of St. Augustine, is the world's largest oceanarium, with leaping porpoises and other denizens c sea in tremendous 700,000 gallon tan

Photos: Florida State News Burea
center left, A. Milton Runy

alm Beach is exclusive resort, on tip f 18-mile island between Lake Worth and the Atlantic. It ranks with Newport as vacation center for the socially elite.

IcKee Jungle Gardens, just south of Vero each, have 80 acres of luxuriant tropical plants, with thousands of orchids and other exotic flowers, trees, shrubs.

hotos: Florida
tate News Bureau

Boca Raton Hotel and Club, once private club for millionaires, is now luxurious

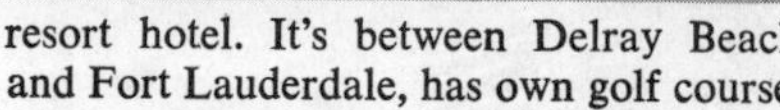

resort hotel. It's between Delray Beac and Fort Lauderdale, has own golf cours

Hollywood Beach Trailer Park: Florida offers world's best facilities for trailers.

Hollywood is winter home of Riverside Academy, a preparatory military school

Palm-lined boardwalk at Hollywood Beach: This resort, south of Fort Lauderdale, was founded by a Californian, bu bears no resemblance to movie capital

Photos: Richard B. Hoit; Florida State News Bureau; Walter Gray, Hollywood By-the-Sea

Mid-winter finds Fort Lauderdale Beach lined with hundreds of gay beach cabanas.

City has many natural waterways, 90 miles of canals, Port Everglades harbor.

Crowd lines Intracoastal Waterway for Fort Lauderdale water-skiing, boat races.

Sightseeing tours by boat leave for New River, Pan-American Park, Everglades.

Pleasure boat traffic on New River: Fort Lauderdale is called "Venice of America."

Fabulous Bahai-Mar yacht basin offers berths for 400 yachts and power cruisers.

Photos: Fort Lauderdale City Publicity Department

University of Florida, at Gainesville, has upwards of 10,000 students enrolled.

Rollins College, Winter Park, has 60 acre campus on shore of Lake Virgini

Singing Tower, near Lake Wales, memorial to Edward Bok, has 71-bell carillon.

More than a hundred ferns and relate tropical plants are found in the stat

Air plants, small spiny growths, deriv their sustenance entirely from the ai

Photos: Florida State News Burea
U. of F. Division of Public Relatio

rlando, from across Lake Eola: Recent apid growth has made it largest inland city in the state. Often called the "City Beautiful," it is year 'round playground.

rlando's Lake Ivanhoe is large enough or sailboat racing. Orlando Yacht Club is on Lake Conway at Pine Castle. There are 44 lakes within Orlando city limits.

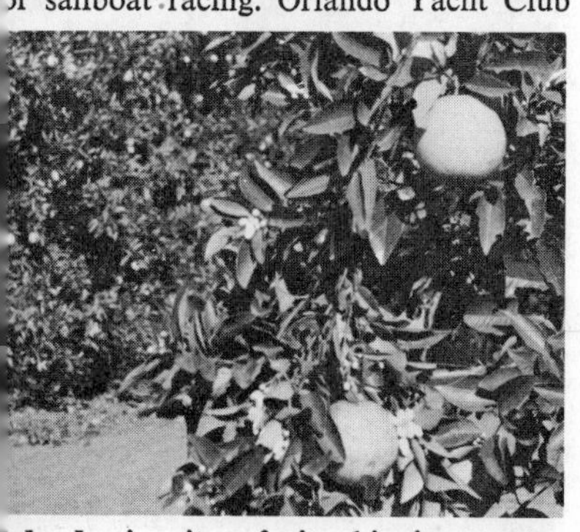

rlando is citrus-fruit shipping center, ith nurseries, packing houses, canneries.

Kissimmee, known locally as Cow Town, is one of the state's chief cattle areas.

hotos: Greater Orlando Chamber of Comerce; bottom, Florida State News Bureau

Tarpon Springs is one of largest sponge markets in world, with fleet of 70 or more boats. Fishing with Greek deep-sea dive begun 1905, is now major industr

Tallahassee, with its State Capitol, is attractively set among hills and lakes.

Silver-scaled tarpon make tremendo leaps as they battle fisherman in Gu

Photos: Florida State News Bure bottom left, Wm. Laven

Clearwater Beach is on island in Gulf, connected by Memorial Causeway with the

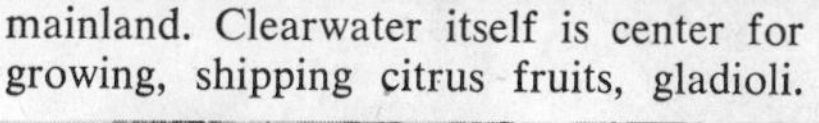

mainland. Clearwater itself is center for growing, shipping citrus fruits, gladioli.

eSoto Oak, one of state's biggest, is at trance to University of Tampa campus.

Latin-American Fiesta is annual event at Tampa, biggest port and industrial city.

otos: Clearwater Chamber of Commerce; Florida te News Bureau; Florida Junior Chamber of Commerce

2,400-ft. Municipal Pier is trademark of the "Sunshine City," St. Petersburg.

Sailboats pass Vinoy Park hotel on way to a day of sport in sheltered Tampa Bay.

New $22 million Sunshine Skyway extends 15 miles, St. Petersburg to Palmetto.

Many of St. Petersburg's 3,800 sidewalk benches are placed along Central Avenue

Al Lang Field: Two major league team Cards and Yankees, train at St. Pe

Spring Fiesta at St. Petersburg is 3-d frolic, with parades and Coronation B

Photos: St. Petersburg News Ser

ıngle Gardens, just north of Sarasota, has ıousands of native and imported trees, plants and shrubs in junglelike setting. It's outstanding tropical botanical garden.

Flamingoes, other rare birds, wade in the beautiful dark waters of Jungle Gardens.

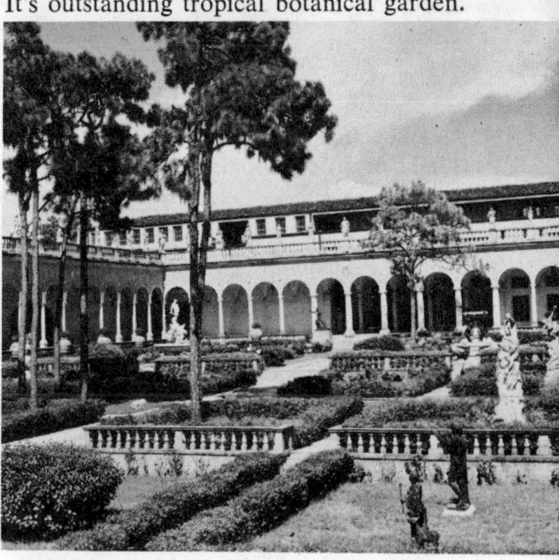

Ringling Museum of Art at Sarasota has 700 old masters collected by showman.

Photos: Atlantic Coast Line Railroad; bottom right, Florida State News Bureau

Thomas A. Edison home at Fort Myers: The inventor came here 1886 for experiments with his incandescent lamp. Ea February, Pageant of Light honors hi

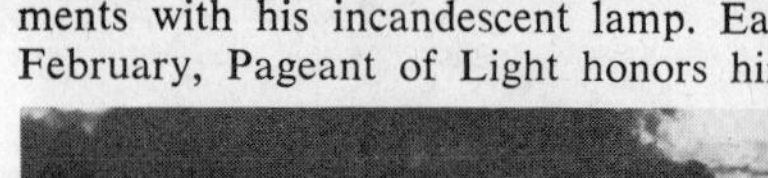

"Money tree" in Edison garden: Over 60 kinds of tropical palms are found here.

Yacht basin: Fort Myers is situated on the mile-wide Caloosahatchee River.

Sanibel Island, in Gulf off Fort Myers, noted for number, variety of sea she

Photos: Florida State News Bureau; b tom left, Atlantic Coast Line Railr

verglades National Park is our newest, edicated in June, 1947. It is 1¼ million acres of tropical scene, a wilderness of strange, exotic plant, bird, animal life.

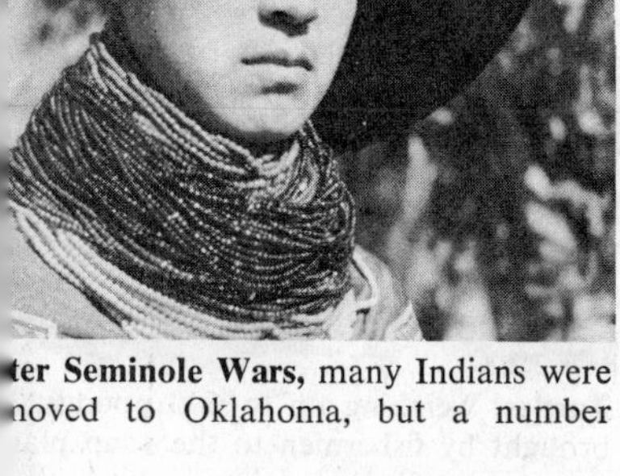

ter Seminole Wars, many Indians were noved to Oklahoma, but a number stayed in Everglades and Big Cypress. Above is Musa Isle Village, in Miami.

tos: Florida State News Bureau; Kon-
tin Kostich; City of Miami News Bureau

Key West is southernmost city in U.S. Fishing boats go after shrimp, turtles.

Lighthouse is known as only one in the country within corporate limits of a city.

Fort Jefferson, now a National Monument, is on Garden Key of the Dry Tortugas, 60 miles from Key West. It was from here that the *Maine* sailed for Havana

Florida National Bank building shows the "different" appearance of Key West.

This home, with its Captain's Walk, i typical of the Bahamas-style residences

Turtles, weighing up to 600 pounds, a brought by fishermen to the soup pla

Photos: top left, Dr. Jacob Klein; Florida State News Bur

ALABAMA MEANS AZALEAS, COTTON, CATTLE, LUMBER

ellingrath Gardens has fabulous collec-
on of rare azaleas and camellias. It is a must on the itinerary of winter and spring visitors to Mobile's Azalea Trail.

oto: Wm. Lavendar

Statue of Vulcan, made for St. Louis Exposition, dominates hill near Birmingham.

Mardi Gras Carnival at Mobile, institut in 1704, rivals the one at New Orlean

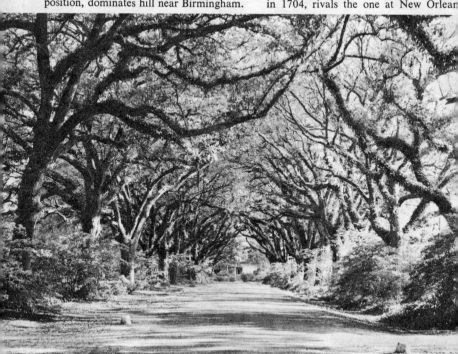

Famous oak drive at Spring Hill College on the Mobile Azalea Trail: The annual flower festival is held in February or ear March when azaleas are in full bloor

Photos: Birmingham Chamber of Commerc
Official State of Alabama; Wm. Lavend

Birmingham, largest city in Alabama, is a leading iron and steel center and is often called "Pittsburgh of the South." Downtown is laid out in planned squares.

First White House of the Confederacy was Montgomery home of Jefferson Davis.

Timepiece above entrance to Capitol was the town clock of Montgomery until 1852.

Members of Azalea Trail "court" are shown during a visit to the Bellingrath Gardens. The trail begins in Mobile's Bienville Square, is well marked by signs.

Photos: Birmingham Chamber of Commerce; Official State of Alabama; Montgomery Chamber of Commerce; Mobile Azalea Trail

Alabama State Coliseum, Montgomery, is outstanding in its modern architecture.

Tuskeegee Monument honors the great Negro educator, Booker T. Washington.

Helen Keller, who won out over deafness, blindness, was born here in Tuscumbia.

Rosemount is 20-room plantation mansio near Eutaw which took five years to build

Gorgas House, with typical portico, is at University of Alabama, Tuscaloosa.

Cotton raising is still a major occup tion, but hand-picking is on way o

Photos: Official State of Alaba

DEEP-SOUTH TRADITION IS STRONG
N MAGNOLIA STATE OF MISSISSIPPI

loucester, open to visitors during the atchez Pilgrimage, is oldest mansion in the district. It was home of Winthrop Sargent, the first Territorial governor.

oto: Mississippi Agricul-
al & Industrial Board

Mississippi River at Vicksburg: A major river port, Vicksburg overlooks junction of Yazoo Canal and the Mississippi. was known as "Gibraltar of Confederacy

Dunleith is stately mansion, with tall Doric columns, on outskirts of Natchez.

This cypress swamp is on Natchez Trac new Parkway following historic old roa

Iuka Mineral Springs were discovered by Indians, later became noted health resort.

MacArthur Hotel, Biloxi: This was fi French settlement in Mississippi Valle

Photos: Mississippi Agric tural & Industrial Bo

elrose is especially popular with visi-
rs during the Pilgrimage because it

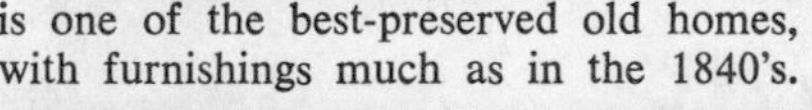

is one of the best-preserved old homes, with furnishings much as in the 1840's.

fferson Military Academy, Washington, as scene of Aaron Burr trial for treason.

Lyceum Building, erected 1848, is center of University of Mississippi at Oxford.

otos: Mississippi Agricul-
ral & Industrial Board

Biloxi Lighthouse dominates new 28-mile sand beach along Mississippi Sound, near the Gulf of Mexico. The city is not as packing center for oysters and shrim

Swimming pool is one of Biloxi's many attractions for entertainment of tourists.

Percy Quinn State Park, at McComb, one of eight state parks in Mississip

The Walter Place, Holly Springs, is fine example of a luxurious home of the 1850's.

Old Capitol Building, Jackson: He Clay, Jefferson Davis spoke from balco

Photos: Mississippi Agri tural & Industrial B

LOUISIANA MEANS PLANTATIONS, BAYOUS, AND FABULOUS NEW ORLEANS

om balcony of Pontalba Apartments, itors to New Orleans' historic *Vieux Carré* see famous St. Louis Cathedral, on Chartres Street and Jackson Square.

to: Louisiana Department Commerce and Industry

"Dinner at Antoine's" added fame to an already internationally known restaurant.

Above is exterior, and at left the fro
desk of Antoine Alciatore's restauran

Pirates Alley runs between St. Louis Cathedral and Cabildo, where Spanish ruled.

French Market coffee stand is place f
coffee and doughnuts in the wee hou

Old Absinthe House has secret room wh
Jackson met Laffite to plan city's defe

Photos: Antoine's Restaurant; Louisiana Department
Commerce and Industry; bottom right, Delta-C&S Air L

rowsing in the numerous antique shops
favorite occupation in the old French

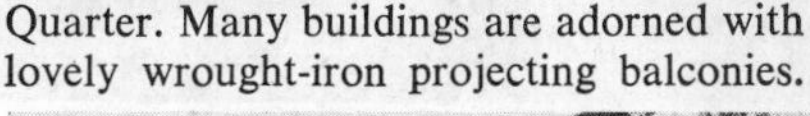
Quarter. Many buildings are adorned with lovely wrought-iron projecting balconies.

here are many shops, too, featuring the outh-watering Creole pecan pralines.

Seen through intriguing doorways are magnificent patios, verdant courtyards.

otos: Henri Cartier-Bresson agnum); Delta-C&S Air Lines

Louisiana MODERN NEW ORLEANS

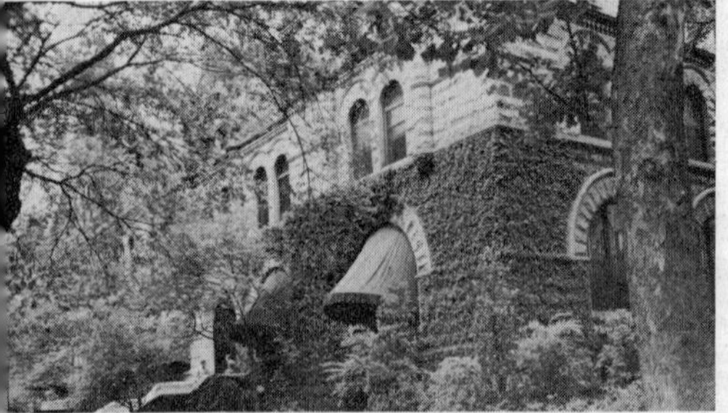

Tulane University's 93-acre campus is scene of the Sugar Bowl football game.

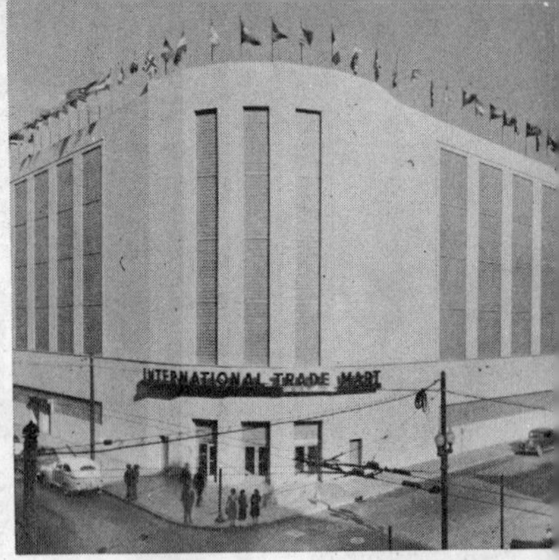

The International Trade Mart exhibits products from South America, Europe

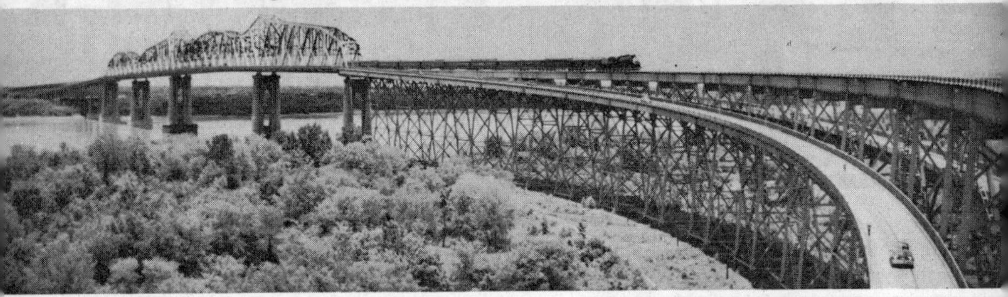

Huey P. Long Bridge is $13 million span carrying automobiles and trains across the Mississippi, which is 2,200 fee wide here, and as much as 180 feet deep

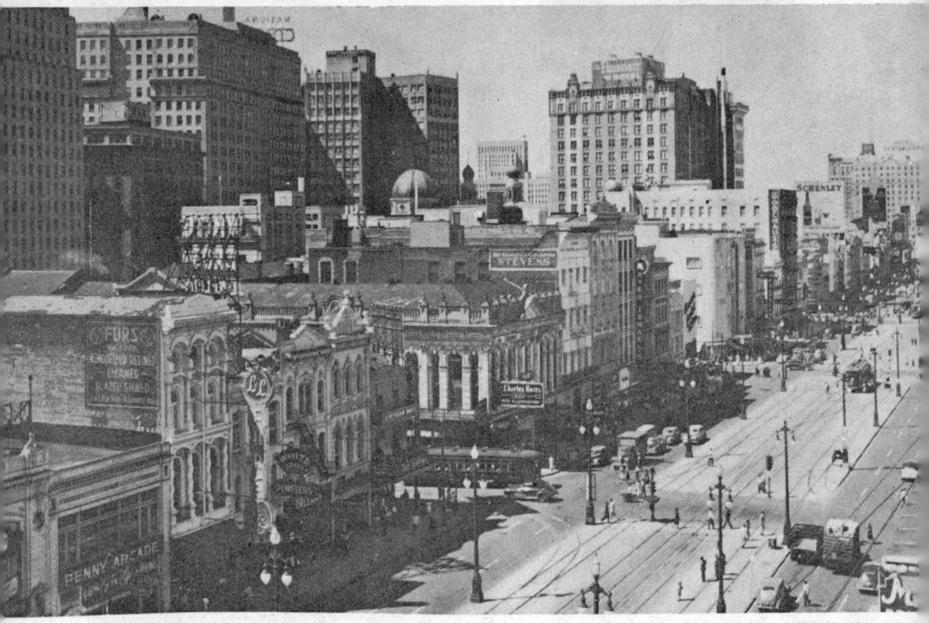

Canal Street extends 3½ miles, from the Mississippi to Metairie. It is one of the widest thoroughfares in the wor 171 feet, and one of most brilliantly

Photos: Louisiana Department of Commerce Industry; center, Bureau of New Orleans N

t Mardi Gras time, and on New Year's ve, Canal Street is real maelstrom. Mardi Gras, the festival that ushers in Lent, brings 100,000 visitors to the city.

e Mississippi winds around New Orleans a great crescent, lined with docks for ships that have come down the river and ships that have come through the Gulf.

otos: Louisville & Nashville
ilroad; Shell Oil Company

Memorial Tower clock and chimes keep time for students at Louisiana State.

Louisiana's towering Capitol at Bat Rouge soars 33 stories, cost $5 millio

Statue of Evangeline is in St. Martinville, the heart of the Acadian country.

Snowy egrets sun themselves in fa Bird City sanctuary at Avery Isla

Photos: Louisiana Depart of Commerce and Ind

ǀ waters of **Bayou Teche** are guarded cypress trees overhung with Spanish moss. Bridge in background crosses over into Longfellow-Evangeline State Park.

Oakley, John James Audubon did much ɜarch for his great *Birds of America.*

San Francisco is "Steamboat Gothic" home, Garyville, built before Civil War.

ɛ **of loveliest** of plantation homes is ɛenwood, 1830–35, St. Francisville.

The Shadows, at New Iberia, stands in lush gardens bordering Bayou Teche.

ːos: Louisiana Department
Commerce and Industry

But for the automboile on deck, this photo of the Mississippi at Baton Rouge might have been taken in Mark Twain's tir Ferries cross from Port Allen to c

Pirogue races are held at Barataria Bay each year. Smugglers and pirates once made this their headquarters. It is r the heart of Louisiana's shrimp coun

Photos: Henri Cartier-Bresson (Magnum); L isiana Department of Commerce and Indu

ARKANSAS IS HOME OF HOT SPRINGS, WORLD FAMOUS SPA

Along the lower reaches of the White River before it joins the Mississippi: Commercial fishing on Arkansas rivers brings an income of $1½ million annually.

Photo: Arkansas Publicity and Parks Commission

Giant bluffs dwarf fishermen on a float trip down the White River. The Arkansas

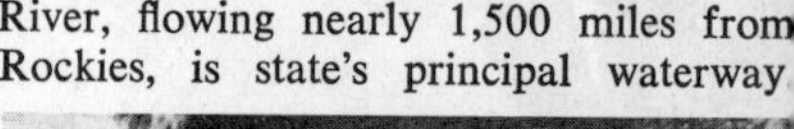

River, flowing nearly 1,500 miles from Rockies, is state's principal waterway.

Mystic Cave, above, Wonderland Cavern, Diamond Cave are underground marvels.

Eden Falls, Lost Valley: In mountai country, streams are clear, swift, col

Photos: Arkansas Publicity and Park Commission, top by Harold Phelp

ot Springs National Park, America's dest, was dedicated in 1832. It covers 1,000 acres in Ouachita Mountains. View shows Army and Navy General Hospital.

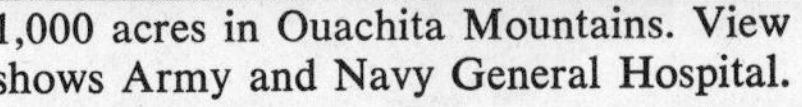

rkansas' old State House, in Little ock, is now official history museum.

Beautiful new State Capitol, designed by Cass Gilbert, was finished in 1916.

Daklawn Jockey Club, Hot Springs, has lass-enclosed, steam-heated grandstand. The climax of each meet is the Arkansas Derby, famous event for three-year-olds.

hotos: Arkansas Publicity and Parks Commis- on, top and center left by John Blundell; enter right, Little Rock Chamber of Commerce

Little Rock Country Club is high above Arkansas River, once busy steamboat route. North Little Rock, on the other sid of the river, is reached by five bridges

Railway ferry "Pelican" carries freight cars across the Mississippi at Helena.

Outboard motor racing is popular at Lak Hamilton, Hot Springs, and at Batesville

Arkansas Post State Park adjoins town which was first capital of the Territory.

Artistry or "land of cross-bow" is show at Blanchard Springs, Mountain View

Photos: Arkansas Publicity and Parks Commission, bottom right by Harold Phelps; top, Little Rock Chamber of Commerce

TENNESSEE IS KNOWN FOR SMOKIES, T.V.A., ANDREW JACKSON, ATOM BOMB

atlinburg is on the edge of Great Smoky ountains National Park, which covers 643 square miles in Tennessee and North Carolina. Photo shows the smoky mist.

oto: Paul A. Moore, nn. Conservation Dept.

"Gordon C. Greene" on the Tennessee River near Chattanooga: After the Civil

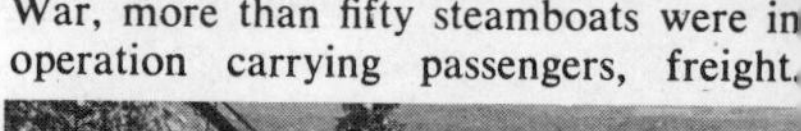
War, more than fifty steamboats were in operation carrying passengers, freight.

Hiking party tackles Mt. LeConte, 6,595-foot peak in the Great Smoky Mountains.

Lookout Mountain Incline Railway goe from Chattanooga to summit of mountain

Photos: Paul A. Moore, Tenn. Conservation Dept.

Memphis, largest city in Tennessee, is a metropolis for that state and for the nearby states of Mississippi, Arkansas. It is named after ancient city on Nile.

Marble quarrying ranks with textiles and furniture as top Knoxville industries.

Spinning, hand-weaving, coverlet-making are prized arts of Tennessee mountain folk.

From top of Lookout Mountain, Chattanooga, you can see more than 100 miles on clear days. This vantage point is near upper end of Incline Railway (photo left).

Photos: Paul A. Moore, Tenn. Conservation Department; top, Delta-C&S Air Lines

Oak Ridge is site of laboratory at which uranium for the world's first two atom bombs was separated. Community housin; 30,000 was built here almost "overnight.

Fort Negley, built 1862, overlooks Nashville from the summit of St. Cloud Hill.

Tennessee State Capitol stands on Ceda Knob, highest point in city of Nashville

Reelfoot Lake, formed by earthquake in 1811, is noted for its huge cypress trees and abundant plant life. 18 miles long 2½ miles wide, it's only 2 to 9 feet deep

Photos: Paul A. Moore, Tenn. Conservatio Dept.; center left, W. Lincoln Highto

THE MIDWEST

by RICHARD J. H. JOHNSTON

Twin Zephyr" with vista-domes rolls along scenic route beside Mississippi River.

ontrary to popular misconception, the lidwest, from the lakes of Minnesota and Visconsin and the Great Lakes down rough Illinois and Indiana and Ohio, is ot barren flat land, always more of the ame. There is, perhaps, more homogeney in the people who live in these states an in their landscapes, though the conasts between the big cities and the rural eas is as sharp as that between one seon of this country and another.

For variety, there are in Indiana and lichigan those strange natural wonders, e sand dunes along the eastern shore of ake Michigan.

One would normally expect the tang of lt air and the roar of ocean surf beyond e dunes, but instead the lake lies quietly midsummer, shimmering in the sun. ike an isolated world by itself stands e dune country; similarly the Midwest ands almost as distinctly a sheltered orld of its own within the United States.

The approach from the East leads rough industrial Ohio, then rural Indiia, and then the traveler plunges into e seemingly endless expanse of smoking ills that border Lake Michigan near the linois line. Here the great works of the ountry's major steel companies belch ot and flames, fouling the air and the pproach that catapults the motorist suddenly from a maze of factories onto Chicago's South Lake Shore Drive.

In Wisconsin, northern Michigan and Minnesota, the country turns woodsy and green, sprinkled with lakes and fishing streams and with wilderness as unspoiled as it was when the French missionaries and explorers and fur traders first opened up this territory. South in Illinois, across the prairie, one reaches the Abraham Lincoln country and the shrines at Springfield.

The Mississippi by now has run its majestic course down through the bluffs and is flowing smoothly across the flat country beyond which the prairie runs off through Iowa into the neighboring Plains States. The nation's railroads and airlines spoke out from the Midwest, her products and her cities feed the nation's industry and commerce.

This is a cross-section of latter-day America. Once the wild Northwest Territory, it has long been tamed. It lacks the majesty of some other regions; it is America at home and at work. After all, the internal combustion engine and the automobile, the truck and powered farm implements and the mail order house—developments that made possible the present state of America at home and abroad—came out of the Midwest.

oto: Burlington Route

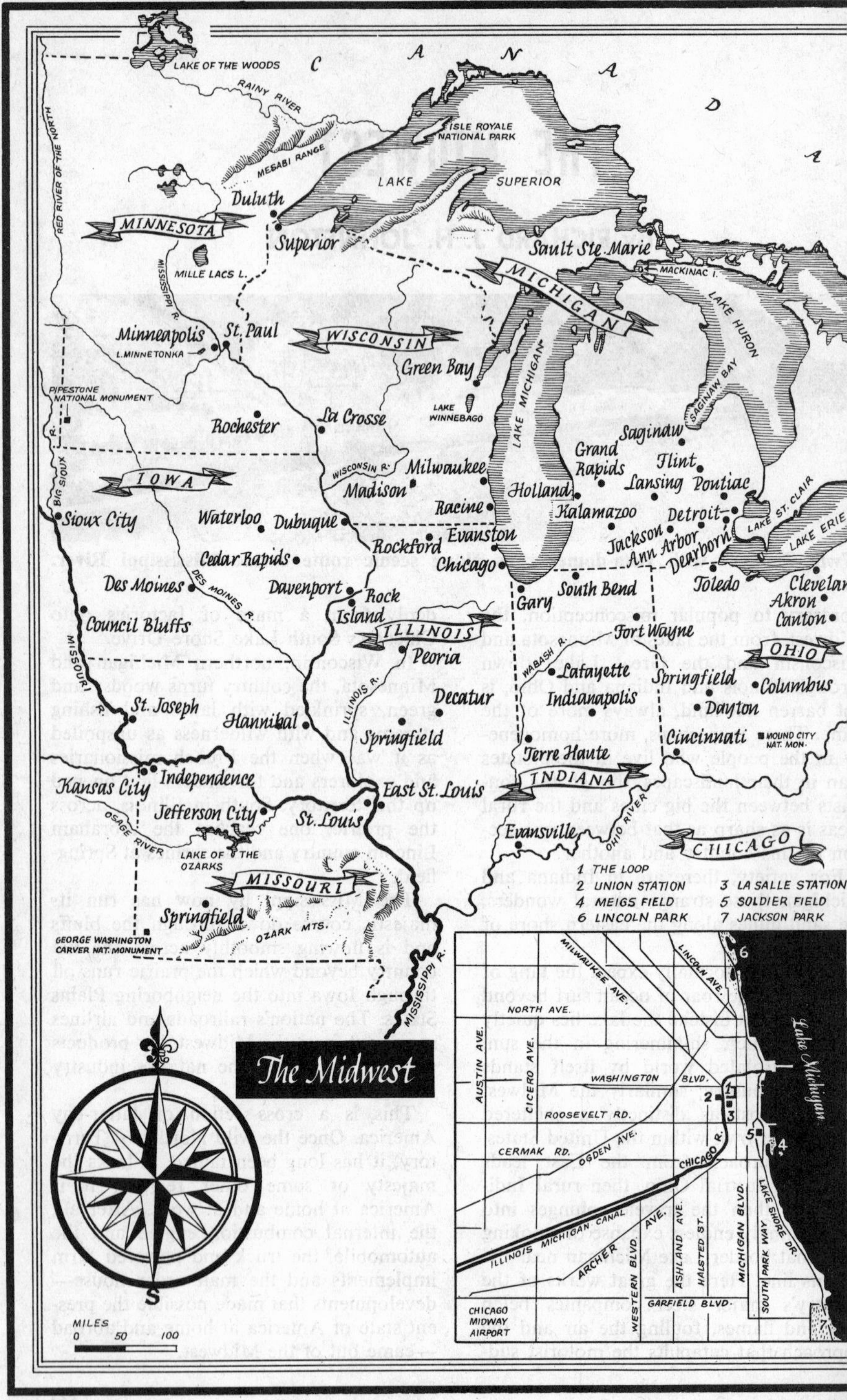

C A N A D A
LAKE OF THE WOODS
RAINY RIVER
RED RIVER OF THE NORTH
ISLE ROYALE NATIONAL PARK
MESABI RANGE
LAKE SUPERIOR
Duluth
MINNESOTA
Superior
Sault Ste. Marie
MACKINAC I.
MICHIGAN
LAKE HURON
MILLE LACS L.
MISSISSIPPI R.
St. Paul
Minneapolis
L. MINNETONKA
WISCONSIN
Green Bay
SAGINAW BAY
PIPESTONE NATIONAL MONUMENT
LAKE WINNEBAGO
LAKE MICHIGAN
Rochester
La Crosse
Saginaw
Grand Rapids
Flint
BIG SIOUX R.
WISCONSIN R.
Milwaukee
Lansing
Pontiac
IOWA
Madison
Holland
Racine
Kalamazoo
Detroit
LAKE ST. CLAIR
Sioux City
Waterloo
Dubuque
Evanston
Jackson
Ann Arbor
Dearborn
LAKE ERIE
Rockford
Cedar Rapids
Chicago
DES MOINES R.
Des Moines
Davenport
Rock Island
Gary
South Bend
Toledo
Clevelan
Akron
Canton
Council Bluffs
ILLINOIS
Fort Wayne
OHIO
MISSOURI R.
Peoria
WABASH R.
Lafayette
Springfield
Columbus
ILLINOIS R.
Decatur
Indianapolis
Dayton
St. Joseph
Hannibal
Springfield
Cincinnati
MOUND CITY NAT. MON.
Independence
Terre Haute
Kansas City
INDIANA
East St. Louis
OSAGE RIVER
Jefferson City
St. Louis
Evansville
OHIO RIVER
CHICAGO
LAKE OF THE OZARKS
1 THE LOOP
3 LA SALLE STATION
2 UNION STATION
4 MEIGS FIELD
5 SOLDIER FIELD
6 LINCOLN PARK
7 JACKSON PARK
MISSOURI
Springfield
OZARK MTS.
GEORGE WASHINGTON CARVER NAT. MONUMENT
MISSISSIPPI R.
MILWAUKEE AVE.
LINCOLN AVE.
NORTH AVE.
AUSTIN AVE.
CICERO AVE.
Lake Michigan
WASHINGTON BLVD.
ROOSEVELT RD.
OGDEN AVE.
CERMAK RD.
CHICAGO R.
ILLINOIS MICHIGAN CANAL
WESTERN BLVD.
ARCHER AVE.
ASHLAND AVE.
HALSTED ST.
MICHIGAN BLVD.
SOUTH PARK WAY
LAKE SHORE DR.
GARFIELD BLVD.
CHICAGO MIDWAY AIRPORT
The Midwest
S
MILES
0 50 100

A 31-MILLION ACRE FARMLAND, ILLINOIS ALSO HAS GREAT MIDWEST METROPOLIS

hicago, with more than 3½ million pop-ation, is the youngest of the world's great cities. Its nickname is the "Windy City." This is North Michigan Avenue.

oto: G. A. Reims

Grant Park's 303 acres provide the mile-long Loop with an open view of the lake. This is Buckingham Fountain, with the new Prudential skyscraper at the right.

Wrigley Building is across Michigan Avenue from Tribune Tower, Sheraton Hotel.

Randolph Street is fun center of Loop at night, with theaters and night clubs

Flaming sword service is a distinctive feature of Pump Room, Ambassador East

Photos: Kaufmann & Fabry Company; bottom left, Delta C&S Air Lines; bottom right, Shiro, Hotels Ambassado

ak Street Beach, most widely used public athing spot, fills a corner on North Lake Shore Drive. Pedestrian tunnel connects it with Michigan Avenue and Drake Hotel.

hicago's Union Stockyards are world's iggest; recently celebrated arrival of one-billionth animal. Nearby Amphitheater had the 1952 presidential conventions.

Ierchandise Mart is second in floor area nly to Pentagon Building, Washington.

Chicago Art Institute has 6,000 students, world-famous paintings and many exhibits.

otos: Chicago Park District; center and lower left, aufmann & Fabry Company; Braniff International Airways

Northwestern University has Chicago campus, above, for professional schools and divisions of night study. Main school at Evanston, on shore of Lake Michiga

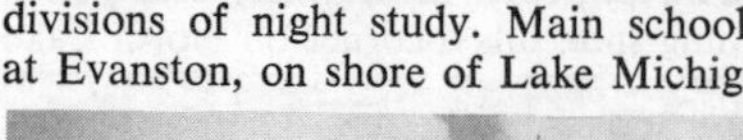

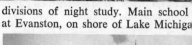

Rockefeller Memorial Chapel is one of stately University of Chicago buildings.

Chicago's great fire of 1871 spared th historic water tower, now much revere

Photos: Northwestern University; Wayne Mill University of Chicago; Kaufmann & Fabry Compa

odgers-Hammerstein Night brought big owd to the Band Shell in Grant Park.

Nationally known guest conductors and soloists are featured at free concerts.

rfield Park Conservatory has 5,000 cies of flowers, valued at $1½ million.

Air view shows North Lake Shore Drive sweeping southward from Lincoln Park.

tos: Chicago
k District

Lincoln Tomb, in Oak Ridge Cemetery, Springfield, was financed by citizens all over the nation. 117-ft. monument ha four bronze groups and statue of Lincol

Lincoln Log Cabin State Park has cabin lived in by Lincoln's father, stepmother.

This is Lincoln-Berry store, now in N Salem State Park, northwest of Springfie

Photos: Illinois Divis of Department Rep

ave-in-Rock, now State Park, was once e lair of Ohio River pirates, outlaws.

Time rolls back millions of years for those who explore canyons of Giant City Park.

yche Stadium, Northwestern University, Evanston, can accommodate 54,000 at football games. McGaw Hall, background, is used for indoor meets, convocations.

otos: Illinois Division of Department eports; bottom, Northwestern University

Since 1850, Illinois has been a top-rank agricultural state, and today its 195,000 farms are valued at $5 billion. 43 field crops are grown, with corn the largest.

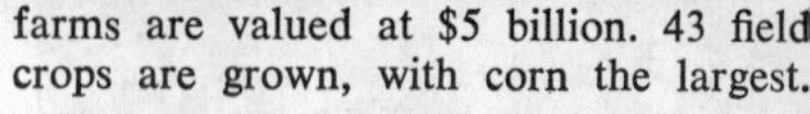

General U. S. Grant received this Galena home as gift on his return from Civil War.

This house in Springfield is the only home that Abraham Lincoln ever owned.

"Wedding of the Wine and Cheese" is a feature of the annual grape festival at Nauvoo, historic old Mormon city buil by the Mormon prophet, Joseph Smith

Photos: Illinois Division of Departmer Reports; bottom, Illinois Division of Park

NDIANA, THE HOOSIER STATE, ADDS BUSTLING INDUSTRY TO RURAL CHARM

cred Heart Church and Administration ıilding with Golden Dome are features of Notre Dame University at South Bend, home of Rockne's "Four Horsemen."

ɔto: University of Notre Dame

Executive Building houses administrative offices of Purdue University, noted for engineering courses. Behind it is Hall o Music Auditorium, seating 6,200 people

Student Building is outstanding landmark of Indiana University, at Bloomington.

The French Lick Springs Hotel has be known since 1840 as a luxurious reso

Photos: David M. Runyon; Indiana U versity; French Lick Springs Ho

ianapolis Motor Speedway, built 1909, ite of the annual 500-mile automobile speed classic. Some 150,000 attend the race, held each year on Memorial Day.

otting races are feature of Indiana ate Fair, held each September at the Indianapolis Fairgrounds. It's been an annual feature for over a hundred years.

otos: Indianapolis Chamber of Commerce; Indi- Department of Commerce and Public Relations

Soldiers' and Sailors' Monument marks heart of Indianapolis, state's chief city.

At far end of impressive World Wa Memorial Plaza is the Central Libr

Indiana State House is located on 9-acre square in downtown Indianapolis. Erected in 1878–88, of Indiana limestone, it Neo-Roman design. Basement is Museu

Photos: Indianap Chamber of Comm

Lincoln Memorial, Lincoln State Park: it was in this neighborhood that Lincoln's family settled in 1816, when he was 7, and Indiana had just been made a state.

From all over world, Christmas parcels come to be mailed from Santa Claus, Ind.

Oldest covered bridge in state, once at Raccoon, now spans Clinton Falls creek.

City park in New Harmony has "golden rain trees" brought from China by Wm. Maclure. These small round-topped trees produce large yellow flowers in June.

Photos: Indiana Department of Commerce and Public Relations

Indiana

Indiana Dunes State Park covers 3½ sq. miles on southern tip of Lake Michigan.

Lanier mansion, at Madison, was though "last word" when built, 100 years ago

Wyandotte Cave is one of largest in th country, with its 23 miles of passage

Brown County State Park and adjoining Game Preserve constitute largest publicly owned land in Indiana. Ten miles of fi roads show off this lovely hill countr

Photos: Indiana Department Commerce and Public Relatic

OHIO FARMS AND INDUSTRIES ARE SERVED BY LAKE ERIE, OHIO RIVER

leveland, Ohio's largest city, is big nter for steel mills and refineries.

Ohio farm and range lands cover 22 million acres, with corn the major field crop.

otos: Ohio Development
d Publicity Commission

Cleveland from Lake Erie: At left is the Municipal Stadium. The city's landmark, tower of Union Terminal, dominates background. City population is 914,8

Ohio's Capitol, at Columbus, is one of purest examples of Greek Doric in U.S.

Toledo is 3rd largest railroad center nation, with new Central Union Termi

Zanesville is divided into three parts by the Licking and Muskingum rivers. It is noted as site of only "Y" Bri in country, spanning both of the rive

Photos: Ohio Developm and Publicity Commiss

kron is known as rubber capital of the orld. B. F. Goodrich Rubber Company, above, produces automobile tires and over 30,000 kinds of other rubber articles.

kron is the chief supplier of tires to arby automobile-making city of Detroit.

Molten steel is "teemed" into molds at Republic Steel's plant at Cleveland.

tos: Ohio Development
Publicity Commission

New group of "fledglings" is graduated from Ohio University, oldest college in what was formerly Northwest Territor Ohio now has 52 colleges and universitie

Memorial at Ft. Recovery marks site of General Wayne's defeat of Indians, 1794.

Air view of Ohio State University, C lumbus, shows 400-acre campus, stadiu

Photos: Ohio Developn and Publicity Commis

Memorial at Hamilton reproduces stockade used in campaigns against the Indians.

Wright Brothers Monument, Dayton, honors inventors of first successful plane.

Allen Memorial Art Building at Oberlin was modeled after Brunelleschi's Hospital of the Innocents. It houses the finest college art museum in the United States.

Campus Martius Museum, at Marietta, has wonderful collection of pioneer relics, including restoration of Rufus Putnam house, built by one of the first settlers.

Photos: Ohio Development and Publicity Commission, bottom left by S. Durward Hoag; center, Arthur E. Princehorn

Ohio

Ohio Caverns, West Liberty, are noted for coloring and diversity of formations.

Old Man's Cave, at Logan, is overhangin ledge that once formed home for hermi

Constructed of stone and yellow clay by prehistoric Indians, the Great Serpent Mount extends for 1,330 feet. It is t most remarkable effigy mound in the U.

Photos: Ohio Developm and Publicity Commiss

MICHIGAN IS WORLD'S AUTO CENTER AND VACATIONLAND OF GREAT LAKES

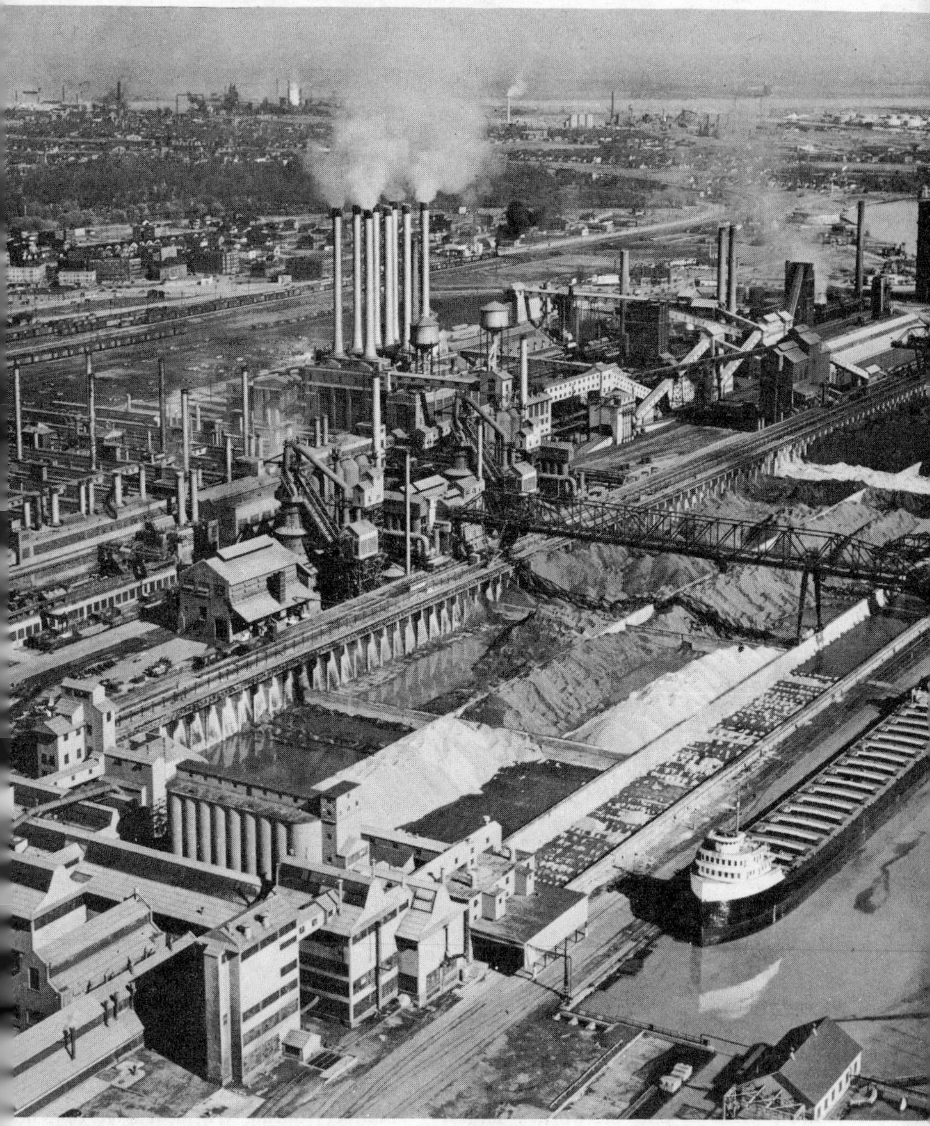

ver Rouge Plant of the Ford Motor mpany, near Dearborn, is one of largest mass-production automobile factories in world. Henry Ford was born at Dearborn.

to: News Department, d Motor Company

Michigan

Detroit, nation's fifth city, is noted as automobile-manufacturing center, with plants of General Motors, Chrysler, and others. It fronts on the Detroit River

A new Chevrolet, just completed, gets polish before assembly line inspection.

New Chryslers near the finish of the intricate step-by-step assembly process

Willow Run is one of world's largest manufacturing plants, built to produce bombers during World War II, and now used by General Motors for transmission

Photos: Michigan Tourist Council; General Motors Corporation; Chrysler Corporation

sle Royale National Park, rock fortress
ı Lake Superior, is a real wilderness.

Lansing's skyline is dominated by the State Capitol and 25-story Olds Tower.

Greenfield Village, at Dearborn, was
stablished by Henry Ford in 1933 to

re-create a colonial village. At left is Martha-Mary Chapel, above, old mill.

General Store at Greenfield Village
s complete with Cigar Store Indian.

Village also has river boat, and complete reproduction of Edison's first laboratory.

Photos: National Park Service; Michigan Tourist Council; center right and bottom, Dr. Jacob E. Klein

The "Soo" Locks at Sault Ste. Marie enable the lake boats to travel along the canal between Lake Huron and La Superior, avoiding St. Mary's rapi

Carriages line main street of auto-less resort on historic Mackinac Island.

Porch of Mackinac's luxurious Gra Hotel is said to be world's longe

Straits of Mackinac cut Michigan in two, between the Upper Peninsula and the Lower Peninsula. Ferries take aut and their passengers across this barrie

Photos: Michigan Tourist Coun

University of Michigan is at Ann Arbor, on Huron River. This is Law Quadrangle.

Tahquamenon Falls: This river plays prominent part in Longfellow's Hiawatha.

On opening day of Tulip Festival in city of Holland, citizens don their Dutch costumes and literally scrub the streets. Merchants scrub sidewalks by their stores.

Port Huron, on St. Clair River, connects with Canada by an international bridge.

Lake o' the Clouds is high in the Upper Peninsula's remote Porcupine Mountains.

Photos: Michigan Tourist Council; center, Holland Chamber of Commerce

Michigan

Ishpeming is the ski center of Northern Michigan, with one of state's first clubs.

State has 18 million acres of farm a range land, varied field and truck cro

Interlochen is scene of summer music camps for high school boys and girls.

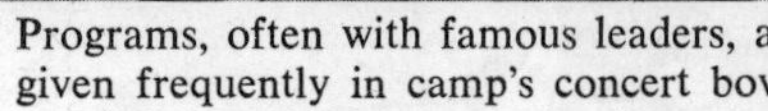

Programs, often with famous leaders, a given frequently in camp's concert bo

Pictured Rocks, multicolored cliffs on Lake Superior shore, extend 27 miles.

Memorial on Au Sable River perpetua spirit of Michigan's pioneer lumberm

Photos: top right, Grant M. Hc others, Michigan Tourist Cou

LAKES, WATERFALLS, GREEN WOODS BLESS WISCONSIN'S VACATIONLAND

Visconsin has some 8,500 lakes, 10,000 niles of trout streams, and 500 miles of shoreline on Lakes Superior, Michigan. This is High Lake, near Michigan border.

hoto: Wisconsin Con-
ervation Department

From dome of State Capitol, Madison, you can see five lakes. Three girdle city, Lakes Mendota, Monona and Wingr Lakes Kegonsa and Waubesa are nearb

Near Wisconsin Dells, seven miles of sandstone rocks have been etched by river.

Wisconsin River is one of many stream in Badger State for canoeing, fishin

First Capitol Building, at Old Belmon was used by the legislature in 183

Photos: Wisconsin Co servation Departme

At Pattison State Park, the Black River plunges 165 feet over Big Manitou Falls.

U. S. Forest Products Laboratory, Madison, conducts research on the use of wood.

A summertime class at the University of Wisconsin meets below Carillon Tower.

St. Croix River cuts through castellated bluffs in Interstate Park, recreation area that is shared between Wisconsin and Minnesota. Park covers 730 acres.

Photos: Wisconsin Conservation Department; top right, University of Wisconsin News Service

Devils Lake is hemmed in by horseshoe of cliffs, some 500 feet high. Formed

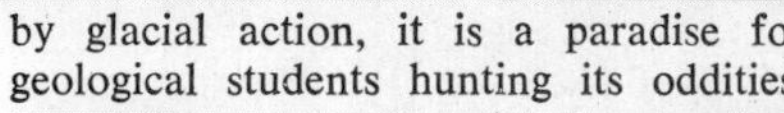

by glacial action, it is a paradise fo geological students hunting its oddities

Tank Cottage, at Green Bay, is the oldest house standing in Wisconsin, built 1776.

Villa Louis was built at Prairie du Chie by the fur-trader, Hercules L. Dousmar

Potawatomi State Park, on the peninsula between Green Bay and Lake Michigan, is one of Wisconsin's 21 state park Many trails wind through Norway pine

Photos: Wisconsin Co servation Departme

'HE "SHOW ME!" STATE OF MISSOURI IS CENTER OF TRANSPORTATION AND COMMERCE

lissouri River joins the Mississippi ıst above St. Louis. Including its 500-mile frontage on the Mississippi, state has over 1,000 miles of navigable water.

ıoto: Massie—Missouri Resources Div.

Union Station with downtown Kansas City skyline: On route of the Santa Fe and Oregon trails, Kansas City is today a important railroad and airline center

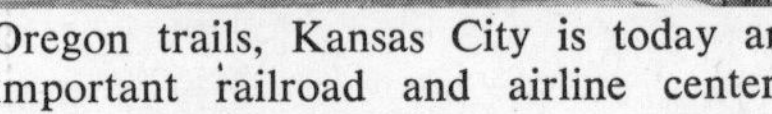

Kansas City's Eleventh Street area has the major stores, theaters and hotels.

Liberty Memorial is 217-foot shaft, in honor of those serving in World War I

Swope Park, with 1,346 acres of hills ravines is the 3rd largest U.S. city park

Photos: bottom left, G. A. Reims
Massie—Missouri Resources Div

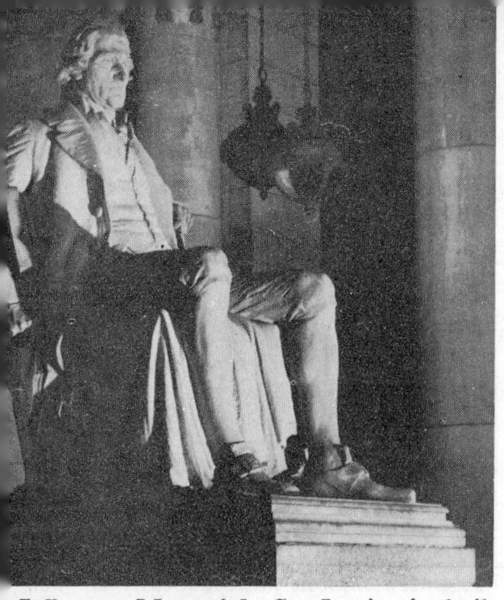

Jefferson Memorial, St. Louis, is built on site of Louisiana Purchase Exposition.

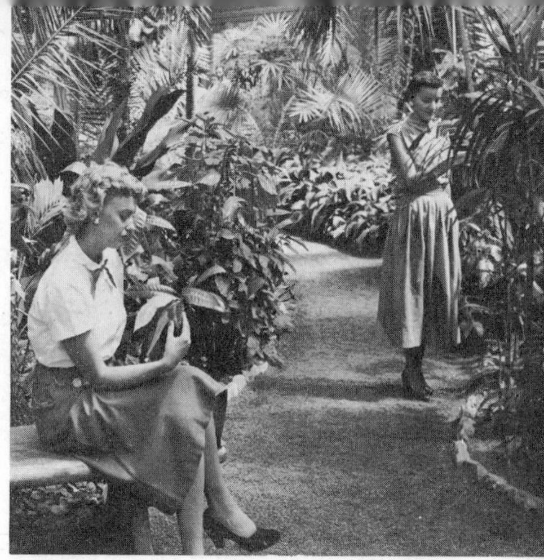

Shaw's Garden, modeled after London's Kew Gardens, has 12,000 plant species.

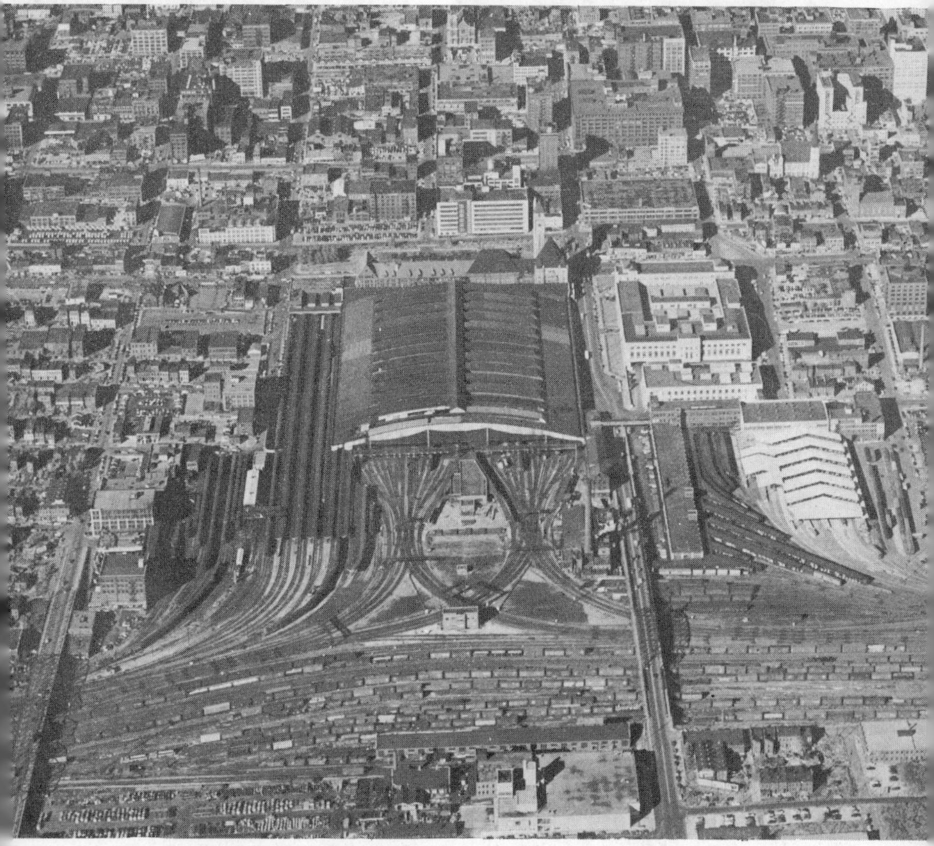

St. Louis, state's largest city, is 2nd only to Chicago in importance as railway center. Union Station, with train sheds and power house, covers more than 20 acres.

Photos: Massie—Missouri Resources Div.

Thomas Hart Benton's lively murals are in house lounge of Capitol, Jefferson City.

Missouri's capital, known locally as "Jeff City" is named after Thomas Jefferson.

Home of Ex-President Truman is in town of Independence, in western Missouri.

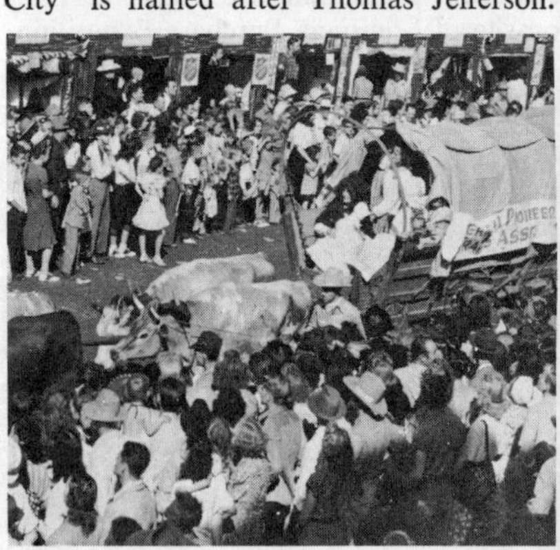

Santa-Cali-Gon Parade, at Independence, commemorates days of wagon caravans.

Champion mules: Missouri mules have long been known for quality, mulishness!

Henry County is noted for its dairy and poultry farms, for these Roberts' horses.

Photos: Massie—Missouri Resources Div.

IOWA, SYMBOL OF CORN BELT IS RICHEST FARM STATE

Old Capitol Building, Iowa City, now administrative center of State University of Iowa, was State Capitol from 1846 to 1857, when Des Moines became capital.

Photo: State University of Iowa

Old water mill, Panora: Town's name is contraction of "panorama," the story being that pioneers, viewing site from a hill, exclaimed, "What a beautiful panorama!"

Davenport stretches along Mississippi River for five miles, where it widens to form Lake Davenport. Rock Island and Moline, Illinois, are across river.

Photo: Iowa Development Commission

State Capitol looks down on Des Moines from an eminence east of the Des Moines River. Design of the gilded dome recalls that of the Hotel des Invalides in Paris.

About 30% of Iowa's land is in pasture, with the eastern and western sections leading in meat production, the north-western part being chief dairying region.

Photos: Iowa Development Commission

Iowa

Iowa is symbol of the Corn Belt, with 95% of the land in farms. The state leads the nation in corn and oats, in hogs poultry and eggs, and in fattening cattle

Cutler Bridge, Madison County: Most of the state is a gently rolling plain, with many winding rivers. Hilly northeaster region is called "Little Switzerland.

Photos: Iowa Development Commis-sion, top left by James A. Ker

10,000 LAKES, BEAUTIFUL FORESTS LURE VISITORS TO MINNESOTA

plit Rock Lighthouse, on sheer cliff high bove Lake Superior, warns of dangerous reefs. Light and siren are important because metal in rocks throws compasses off.

oto: W. A. Fisher, courtesy Lake perior North Shore Association

At Silver Creek Cliff, the highway from Duluth to Canada follows the scenic north shore of Lake Superior. Nearby is lak made famous in *Hiawatha,* Gitche Gumee

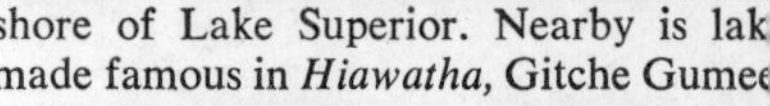

Winter waves of Lake Superior pile up windrows of ice, 20 feet high, miles long.

John Jacob Astor trading post was cente of fur trading more than 100 years ago

Mighty Mississippi, "Father of Waters, has its source here, in Itasca State Park

Ice-bound Iron Ore Carriers: Frequently ships trying to open the season early find further headway impossible. The they must wait for a shift in the win

Photos: Barney Thomas; top, W. A. Fisher; lowe center right, Minnesota Division of Publici

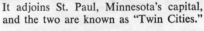

Iinneapolis is state's largest city, the anking and wholesale center of the area. It adjoins St. Paul, Minnesota's capital, and the two are known as "Twin Cities."

'ur trappers use skis to run their lines n the wilderness of Northern Minnesota.

Palisade Head is 80-acre headland of volcanic rock jutting from Lake Superior.

hotos: Northwest Orient Airlines; arney Thomas; W. A. Fisher

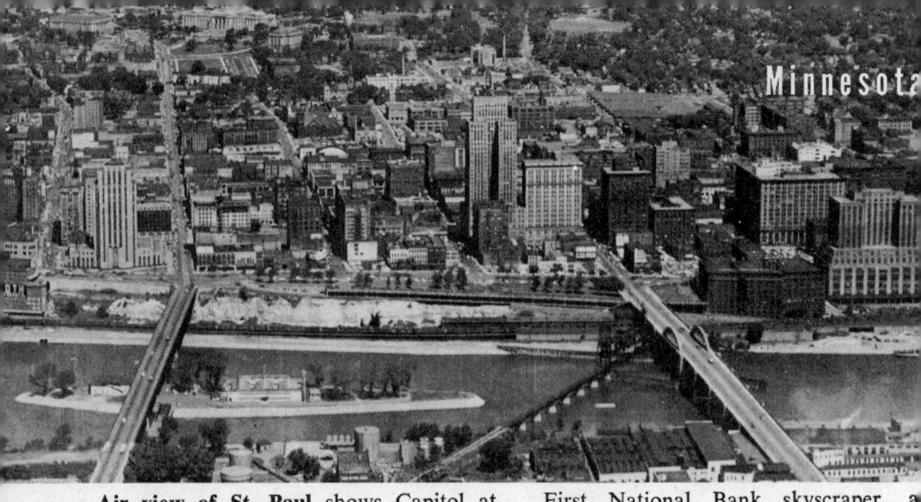

Air view of St. Paul shows Capitol at upper left, main business section with First National Bank skyscraper, a three of many bridges across Mississip

Girl scouts paddle huge "war canoe" near their camp on Northern Minnesota lake.

Giant statues of Paul Bunyan and Blue Ox stand on shore of Lake Bemid

Falls of Minnehaha, immortalized in poem by Longfellow, are in Minneapolis park.

Kensington Runestone, shown in replic says Vikings came to Minnesota in 136

Photos: Kenneth M. Wright; center left, Bar Thomas; center right, Minnesota Division Publicity; bottom left, Northwest Orient Airli

THE PLAINS STATES

by SETH S. KING

he moment a traveler crosses the Missis-ppi River and heads west he begins to ıcounter the one dominant quality of ıe Plains States—space. Starting with the ›lling, compact corn fields and pasture ınds of Iowa, and extending beyond the Iissouri River to the great wheat plains ıd ranges of Nebraska, Kansas, and the akotas, his horizon broadens until it is most limitless.

From the rich black and green of the ɔrn country he moves into the grayer, ghter green and gold of the wheat lands ıd then to the brown ranges that stretch ear to the foot of the dark blue moun-ıins. From the great white barns and los of Iowa and Minnesota, past the ›wering grain elevators and sprawling :ed lots of eastern Nebraska and Kansas, ıe traveler crosses on to the Great Plains, 'here the small ranch houses and corrals re almost lost in the expanse of land.

In the Plains States, people earn their ving from the land; they do not merely ve on it. Because of this, the people ıange as the land changes.

In Iowa there is a tendency toward ɔnservatism. Here the people have been stablished for several generations, and ıey are more secure in the knowledge ıat theirs is one of the most consistently roductive farm areas in the world. Be-ond the Missouri, nature is more uncer-ıin. As the yearly rainfall diminishes, ıe gamble on livelihood or even on sur-ival increases. The people more often re imbued with a casual disregard for ›rmality and are generally sustained by persistent optimism. Still farther to the 'est, the land becomes rougher. It makes greater demand on the people there, nd they, like their pioneer fathers, take ride in having withstood the fierce winter

Six combines cut wide swath through the wheat of an enormous Plains States farm.

blizzards, the dust and the summer heat. They are marked by their independence.

The great sweep of plains from the Missouri westward to the Rockies is a relatively new country. But it is rich with the history of this nation's drive toward the Pacific. And most of its sections are still wild enough for a traveler to visual-ize, with ease, the wagon trains that once labored over the plains or the keel boats and war canoes that struggled up the rivers in search of a route to the Western Sea.

The great expanses of North and South Dakota beyond the Missouri can also be fascinating, if one looks across the un-broken rangeland and remembers that the wild Sioux Indians once came plunging over these same rolling hills in pursuit of buffalo or the white man.

ʰoto: Greater North Dakota Association

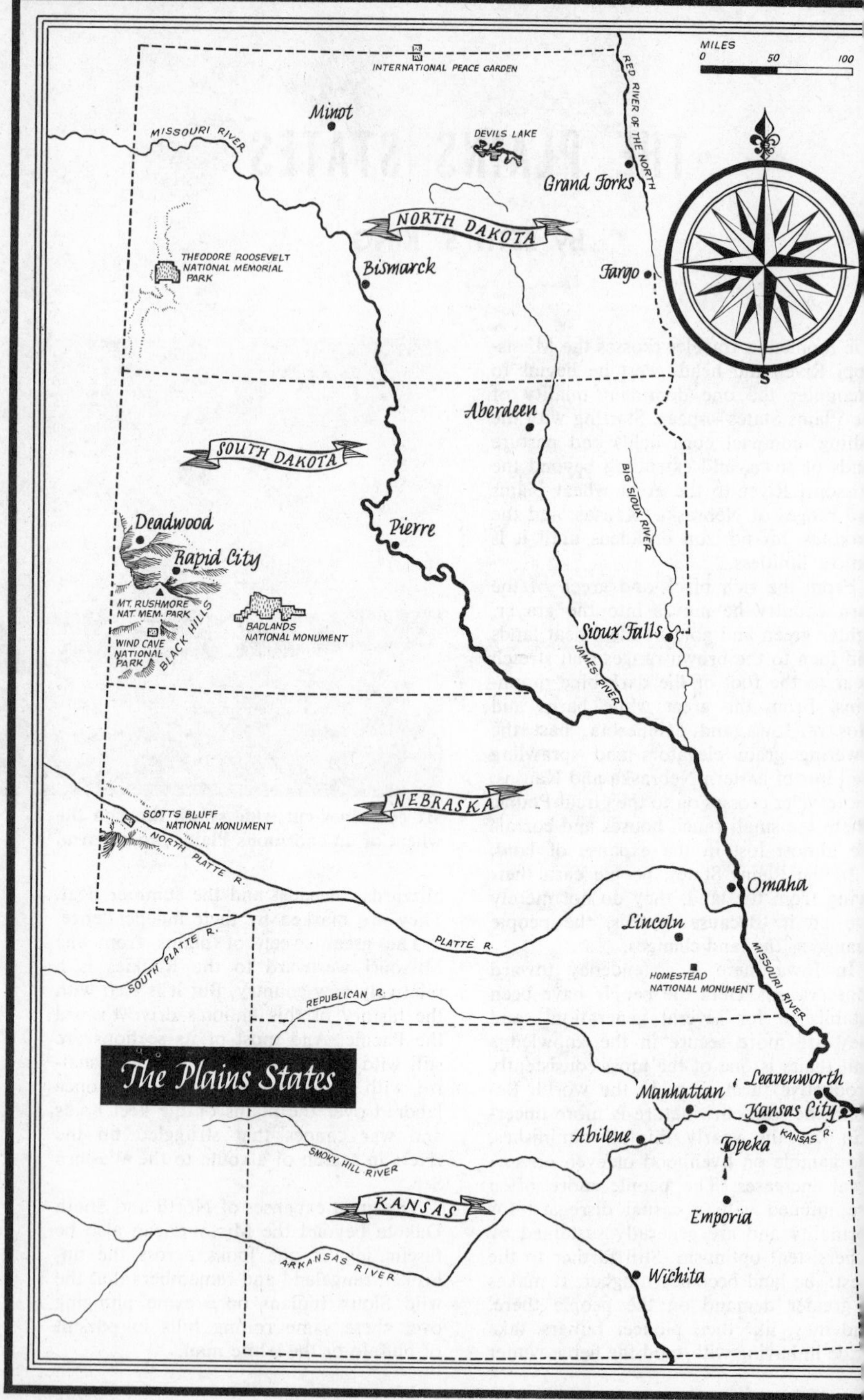
MILES
0
50
100
INTERNATIONAL PEACE GARDEN
Minot
MISSOURI RIVER
DEVILS LAKE
RED RIVER OF THE NORTH
Grand Forks
NORTH DAKOTA
THEODORE ROOSEVELT NATIONAL MEMORIAL PARK
Bismarck
Fargo
Aberdeen
SOUTH DAKOTA
BIG SIOUX RIVER
Deadwood
Pierre
Rapid City
MT. RUSHMORE NAT MEM. PARK
BLACK HILLS
BADLANDS NATIONAL MONUMENT
WIND CAVE NATIONAL PARK
Sioux Falls
JAMES RIVER
NEBRASKA
SCOTTS BLUFF NATIONAL MONUMENT
NORTH PLATTE R.
Omaha
Lincoln
PLATTE R.
SOUTH PLATTE R.
HOMESTEAD NATIONAL MONUMENT
MISSOURI RIVER
REPUBLICAN R.
Leavenworth
Manhattan
Kansas City
Abilene
KANSAS R.
Topeka
SMOKY HILL RIVER
KANSAS
Emporia
ARKANSAS RIVER
Wichita

The Plains States

NORTH DAKOTA HAS UNBOUNDED PLAINS, HILLS, COLORFUL BADLANDS

iders explore Theodore Roosevelt Na-
onal Memorial Park, in Badlands of the Little Missouri. Park honors the President who ranched here as a youth, 1883–86.

oto: Greater North Dakota Association

Logging camp near Little Missouri River was used to cut ties for building of the Northern Pacific Railway. Bunkhouse h rifle loopholes to ward off Indian rai

Combines in North Dakota wheat field: State leads all others in production of rye and durum wheat, is second in barle Most of state is crop and pasture lan

Photos: Greater North Dakota Assoc ation; Northwest Orient Airlir

his marker notes geographical center of orth America, at Rugby, North Dakota.

Ionument on Missouri River at Sanish onors the French explorer, La Verendrye.

Dil well rig towers above flat prairie f Beaver Lodge Field, south of Tioga.

North Dakota's 19-story State Capitol overlooks Bismarck and Missouri valley.

17 inches of water spill over gates of Baldhill Dam and its irrigation reservoir.

Fort McKeen blockhouse stands in Fort Abraham Lincoln State Park, at Mandan.

'hotos: Greater North
Dakota Association

These columnar cedars, known as "upside-down trees," are the only known growth of this species in the world. Nearby is Nor Dakota's famous Burning Coal Min

This cairn marks boundary between Canada, U.S. in International Peace Garden.

Lake adds loveliness to Peace Garde shared by Manitoba and North Dakot

Photos: Greater Nor Dakota Associati

OUTH DAKOTA IS SCENE OF FAMOUS LACK HILLS AND MOUNT RUSHMORE

he Dakota Indians named this colorful nd deeply eroded country *makosica*, or "bad land." Now a National Monument, the Badlands is labyrinth of odd shapes.

hoto: Alfred E. Reichenberger

The Badlands has 640,000 acres of jagged peaks, deep canyons. Once an ocean bed,

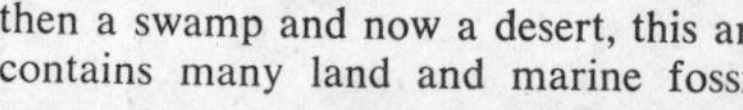

then a swamp and now a desert, this ar contains many land and marine fossi

Harney Peak, 7,242 feet, is highest in the Black Hills and highest in state.

Sylvan Lake, called by Indians "Tear i Mountains," is 6,300 feet above sea leve

Photos: Publicity Department, Sou
Dakota State Highway Commissic

he herd of buffalo at pasture in Custer tate Park numbers close to a thousand. Calvin Coolidge used Game Lodge in the park as his Summer White House in 1927.

Mount Rushmore National Memorial has giant heads of Washington, Jefferson, Theodore Roosevelt, Lincoln, sculptured by Gutzon Borglum and his son, Lincoln.

Photos: Grant M. Haist; top, Publicity Department, South Dakota State Highway Commission

South Dakota

Highway through Custer Park takes you past these impressive "Cathedral Spires."

South Dakota State Capitol is at Pier where the Bad and Missouri rivers jo

Soldiers' & Sailors' World War Memorial is another point of interest in Pierre.

Homestake, in town of Lead, is large gold mine in U.S., discovered in 187

Wind Cave has formations quite unlike those in any other National Park cave.

Dinosaur Park is museum of prehistori creatures at the state School of Mine

Photos: Publicity Department, Sou Dakota State Highway Commissic

"CORNHUSKER STATE" OF NEBRASKA MERGES MIDDLE WEST WITH WEST

Nebraska is one of the country's highest-ranking states in growing wheat, corn, rye, hay. The sand hills areas raise much livestock. Most of land is farmed.

Photo: Burlington Route

Mitchell Pass, near Scottsbluff, is one of the landmarks of the old Oregon Trail.

Ruts worn by covered wagons of the pi neers moving westward can still be see

Nebraska's State House, Lincoln, towers 400 feet, is topped by symbolic "Sower."

Graduates of the University of Nebrask parade on the orderly campus at Lincoln

Photos: Division o
Nebraska Resource

Beef cattle judging at Nebraska State Fair: The huge 287-acre Fairgrounds at Lincoln attract thousands of visitors to Fair held each September since 1900.

Union Stockyards, Omaha: Largest city in state, Omaha is a leading meat-packing and stockyard center, and it leads all the world's cities in butter production.

Kingsley Dam forms Lake McConaughy, with storage capacity of two million acre-feet of water for irrigation. It is one of largest earth-filled dams in U.S.

Photos: Division of Nebraska Resources

Nebraska

The Burlington "Hump" on the western outskirts of Lincoln is considered one of

nation's finest freight assembly yards. It is a marvel of modern traffic control.

J. Sterling Morton, who instituted Arbor Day, lived in this Nebraska City mansion.

Joslyn Memorial Art Museum, Omaha, has Early Renaissance, other exhibits.

Soldier Creek winds through the 36,000-acre Fort Robinson Military Reservation.

Homestead National Monument is site o first land claimed under Homestead Law

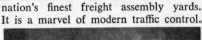

Photos: Division c
Nebraska Resource

KANSAS, GRASS PRAIRIE AND HIGH PLAINS, IS GEOGRAPHICAL CENTER OF U.S.A.

ansas produces most hard winter wheat, ›out 20% of nation's supply. 48 million acres are in farm and range land. State slopes from 4,000 feet in west to 750.

oto: Kansas Industrial
›velopment Commission

Kansas

Monument Rocks, sometimes known as "the Kansas pyramids," rise abruptly from the High Plains, in valley of Smoky H River. At north end is "Kansas sphinx

This house at Abilene was the boyhood home of President Dwight D. Eisenhower.

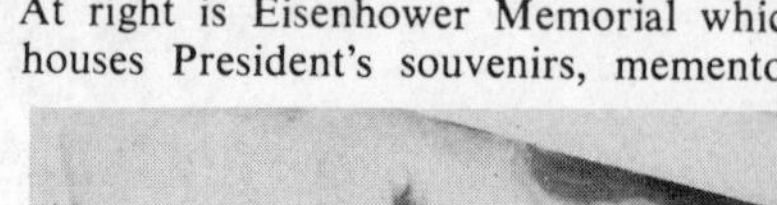

At right is Eisenhower Memorial whic houses President's souvenirs, memento

William Allen White made little *Emporia Gazette* a nationally respected newspaper.

State Capitol at Topeka contains striki John Brown mural by John Steuart Curr

Photos: Kansas Industr Development Commiss

Kansas State College, originally Bluemont College, has its campus at Manhattan.

Design of the Kansas Capitol is based on that of the Capitol at Washington.

Scott County Lake is typical of meager atural bodies of water in the state.

World's largest municipal free swimming pool, 337 x 218 feet, is at Garden City.

atton Hall, Fort Riley: This is only valry school maintained by U. S. Army.

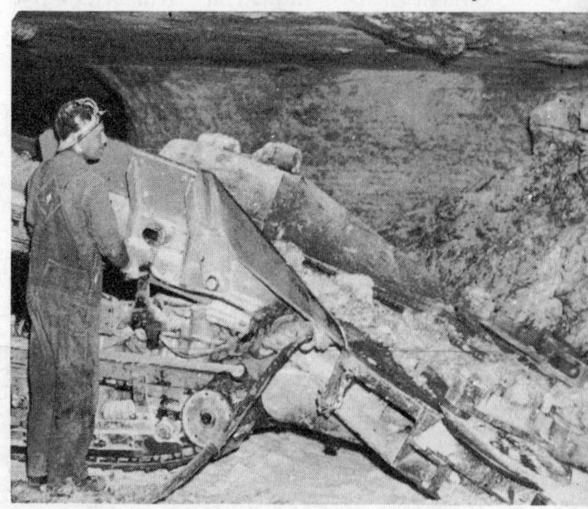

Salt mining, Lyons: Minerals are second in importance to agriculture in Kansas.

otos: Kansas Industrial
velopment Commission

Kansas

Three Kansas landmarks: Campanile at the University of Kansas, in Lawrence. Cowboy statue in Boothill Park, Dodg City. Madonna of Trail, Council Grove

Wyandotte County Lake and Park are in outskirts of industrial Kansas City.

Indian burial pit is point of interes near the flour-milling city of Salina

Dodge City is keen for sporting events, motorcycle races, dog and horse races.

At right is cairn near Lebanon markin geographic center of the United State

Photos: Kansas Industri Development Commissi

THE ROCKY MOUNTAINS

by MARSHALL SPRAGUE

I regained my health a dozen years ago in the Rockies and perhaps that is why I can't imagine enjoying life unless I'm a mile or so up in the air with my pulse clipping along at 90 or 100 to the minute. I am nuts about the Rockies and about the altitude which gives a special quality to this whole vast beautiful region from Colorado to the Sierras, from New Mexico to Montana.

Life is simpler, for one thing. The mountains are majestic, simple forms, easy on the eye and mind. It rarely rains so we have no dank vegetation to worry about or many bugs or varieties of birds. We don't have to garden or go swimming or build gutters around our houses if we don't want to. The river systems are so few that my own town of Colorado Springs names its principal streets after them and my children can name every river and most of the creeks between here and Spokane. Though our cities are growing to beat the band, they are not crowded in the eastern sense and we don't ever think they will be unless someone invents a machine to manufacture water.

The scarcity of people makes mountain society more relaxed than sea-level society or middle west society. I don't think Rocky Mountain dwellers are kinder or more generous or more hospitable or more honest than New Yorkers. But they are easier to know on brief acquaintance, less suspicious of motives, less reserved, less jumpy. I am told that bear and buffalo never fled from the first hunters out here because it did not occur to them that anyone would want to harm them. Mountaineers are a bit like that today. I notice often how Broadway plays depicting big-city tension—like "Season in the Sun" or "Light Up the Sky" bewilder audiences in Denver or Colorado Springs. Such tension is unfamiliar to them.

We tend to take things easy. Nobody runs for a bus because if he does, he'll have to spend the rest of the day catching his breath. Sports are on the reflective side. We fish for trout in the clear, blue, cold, rippling rivers, some of which we can jump across. We ride horses in the vast clean parks, liking the smell of horses and sage and the look of the sky bluing deeply at the edges. We explore old mining roads in jeeps and we climb mountains which sounds hard but isn't —not the slow way we do it. We picnic a lot. Many towns out this way own pleasant picnic grounds in the hills.

I'll tell you frankly, though, I'd stay East for eating. In season our lettuce, celery, cantaloupe and peas are superb, but beef is seldom first rate because this is where cattle are grown, not fattened. Chickens and pork are so-so, fresh eggs a gamble. Naturally under these conditions good chefs are rare. They just won't stay around and be unhappy working with inferior materials.

People seem to get fresh ideas in the mountains. Every summer a remarkable industrialist named Walter Paepke finances a kind of think center called The Institute for Humanistic Studies in the mining town of Aspen, Colorado, beneath the Elk Mountains. Other industrialists come out for weeks to sit around and talk to each other and to professional thinkers and to hear good music in a big orange tent. They claim the process lets them see their particular industry in relation to what it can do for all humanity. When they return home, everyone in their industry is apt to be better off because of what Aspen did to them.

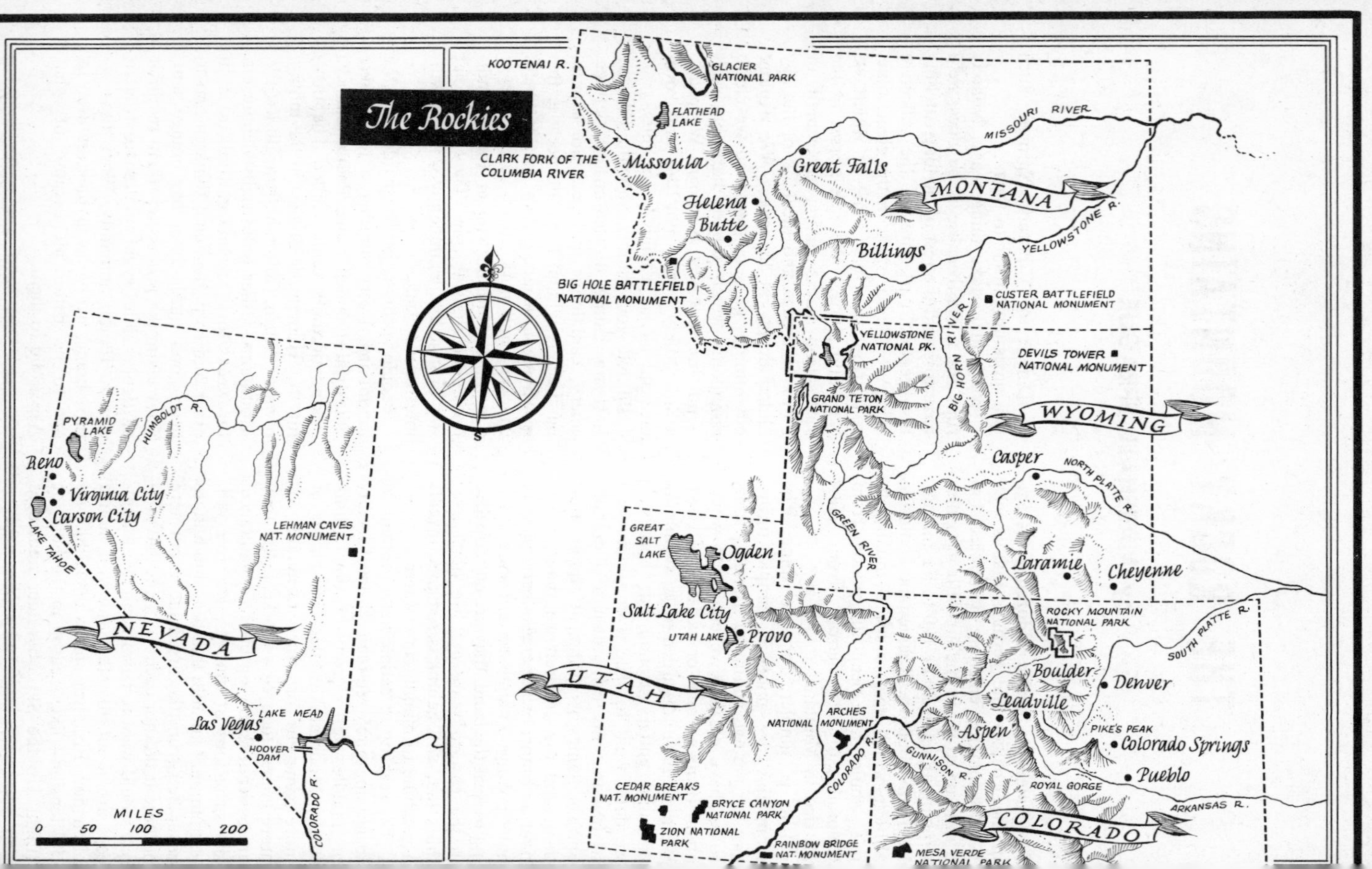

The Rockies
KOOTENAI R.
GLACIER NATIONAL PARK
FLATHEAD LAKE
CLARK FORK OF THE COLUMBIA RIVER
Missoula
Great Falls
MISSOURI RIVER
MONTANA
YELLOWSTONE R.
Helena
Butte
Billings
BIG HOLE BATTLEFIELD NATIONAL MONUMENT
CUSTER BATTLEFIELD NATIONAL MONUMENT
YELLOWSTONE NATIONAL PK.
BIG HORN RIVER
DEVILS TOWER NATIONAL MONUMENT
GRAND TETON NATIONAL PARK
WYOMING
Casper
NORTH PLATTE R.
GREEN RIVER
Laramie
Cheyenne
S
PYRAMID LAKE
HUMBOLDT R.
Reno
Virginia City
Carson City
LAKE TAHOE
LEHMAN CAVES NAT. MONUMENT
NEVADA
LAKE MEAD
Las Vegas
HOOVER DAM
COLORADO R.
MILES
0 50 100 200
GREAT SALT LAKE
Ogden
Salt Lake City
UTAH LAKE
Provo
UTAH
ROCKY MOUNTAIN NATIONAL PARK
SOUTH PLATTE R.
Boulder
Denver
Leadville
Aspen
ARCHES NATIONAL MONUMENT
PIKE'S PEAK
Colorado Springs
GUNNISON R.
ROYAL GORGE
Pueblo
COLORADO R.
CEDAR BREAKS NAT. MONUMENT
BRYCE CANYON NATIONAL PARK
ZION NATIONAL PARK
ARKANSAS R.
COLORADO
RAINBOW BRIDGE NAT. MONUMENT
MESA VERDE NATIONAL PARK

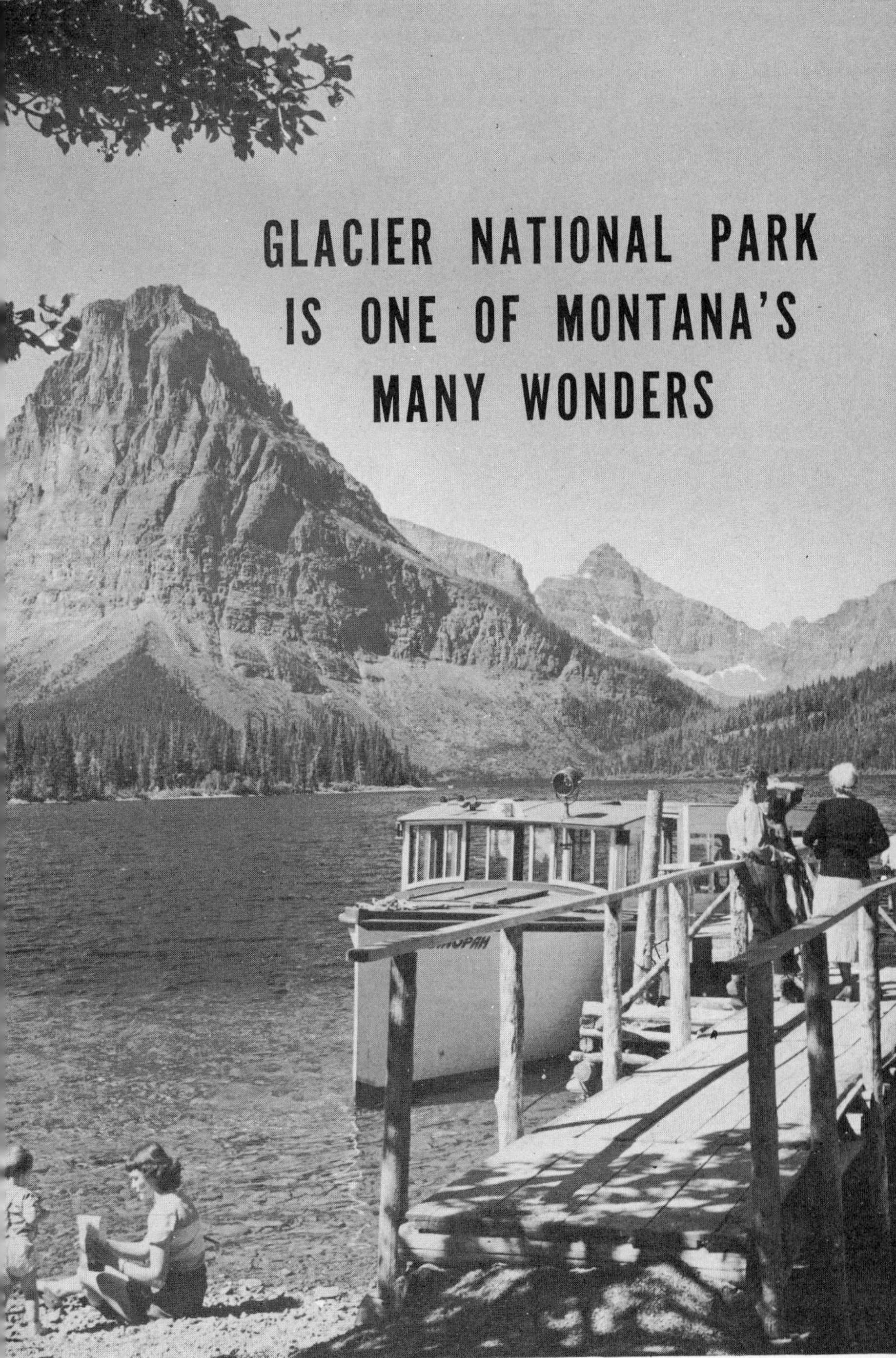
GLACIER NATIONAL PARK
IS ONE OF MONTANA'S
MANY WONDERS

Glacier National Park is magnificent glacier-carved region astride Continental Divide. Two Medicine Lake is one of 200 lakes, set against the spectacular peaks.

Photo: Great Northern Railway

St. Mary Lake's dark blue waters mirror great peaks, some over 9,500 feet high.

Lake McDonald, largest lake in Glaci National Park, is 10 miles long and ov

Glacier Park Hotel adjoins the Great Northern Railway station at easterly entrance to the park. There are fo hotels and three chalets for visito

a mile wide. Because of its depth, up to 437 feet, it is frequently ice-free all winter, though the banks may be deep with snow. Fly-fishing is good here.

Trails in Glacier National Park total some 900 miles, and trail tours are very popular. Others prefer hiking, climbing, auto tours, fishing, or just plain looking.

Photos: Top, Glacier National Park, by Hileman; bottom, Great Northern Railway

Montana's Capitol, at Helena, is viewed from "Last Chancer," popular tour train

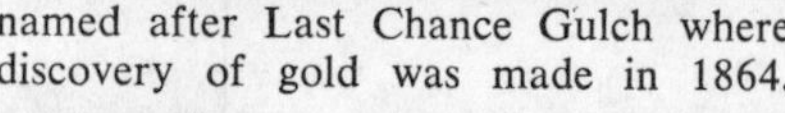

named after Last Chance Gulch where discovery of gold was made in 1864.

Algeria Shrine Temple and nearby Hill Park are two points of interest in Helena.

St. Helena Roman Catholic Cathedral is modeled after one at Cologne, Germany.

Photos: Dorothy Helton, Independent Record Staff, Helena

Lewis and Clark National Forest, named for the leaders of the epic expedition, is one of 11 national forests in Montana. Four trail riders follow the Chinese Wall.

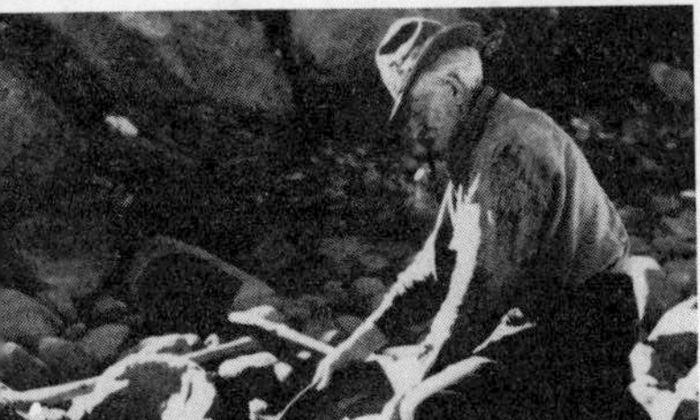

Prospectors still pan for gold, convinced that sooner or later they'll strike it rich.

Midland Empire Fair, at Billings, features rodeo in which ranking riders compete.

Hungry Horse Dam forms a 30-mile-long reservoir south of Glacier National Park.

Visitors to Lewis and Clark Cavern are awed by the 26-foot Empire State Column.

Photos: Montana Highway Commission; top, U. S. Forest Service; center right, bottom left, Northwest Orient Airlines.

Winter scene near Billings: Montana has every advantage for winter sports— plenty of snow and clear, cold weather; hilly country; people with skiing traditions.

Sheep grazing: Montana ranks high in production of wool from flocks like this.

Cowboys separate calves from cows. Chief livestock markets are Miles City, Billings.

Photos: Burlington Route; top, Northwest Orient Airlines

tte, second largest city in state, is own as "richest hill on earth," pro-

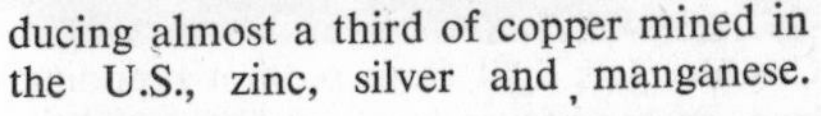

ducing almost a third of copper mined in the U.S., zinc, silver and manganese.

are albino buffalo is one of herd of 00 bison on the National Bison Range.

University Hall is center of campus at Montana State University, at Missoula.

uster Battlefield National Monument arks "Last Stand" made by Col. George Armstrong Custer and his 263 soldiers before massacre by Sioux and Cheyennes.

otos: Montana Highway Commis- on; center row, E. N. Harrison

Montana

Cowboy gets light from red-hot branding iron, on one of state's many dude ranches.

Native blackspot trout and Dolly Vard abound in larger streams, northwest lak

In Virginia City, rejuvenated gold camp town, actors re-enact stage-coach robbery.

Indian pow-wow on Flathead Reservatic features performance of old ceremonie

Dark soils of north and east prairies make state a major producer of wheat.

John Lewis Clark, Indian sculptor, carve miniature wild animals of native woods

Photos: top, Northwest Orient Airlines; cente Montana Highway Commission, E. N. Harrison; bottom Ray J. Manley, Charles W. Herbert (Western Ways

YELLOWSTONE PARK HEADS WYOMING'S LIST OF NATURE'S MARVELS

llowstone National Park is largest and lest of our national parks, established 1872. Best-known geyser is Old Faithful which spouts 140 feet every 65 minutes.

to: Willard Luce

Muddy "paint pots" boil and hiss on the shore of Yellowstone Lake, largest lake in North America above 7,500 feet elev tion. It spreads over 138 square mil

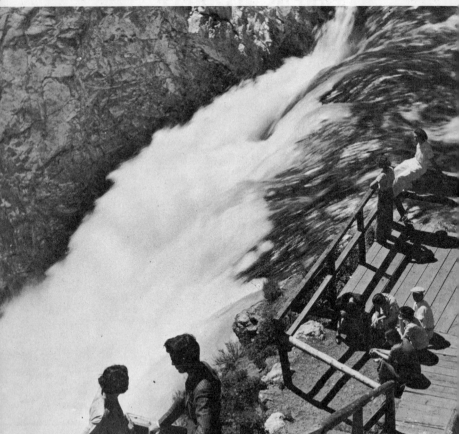

Upper Falls of the Yellowstone may be seen from two platforms, one at the head and one halfway down the side of t 112-foot cataract in its 50-foot chann

Photos: Bill Sears (Western Wa bottom, Northern Pacific Railw

reat columns of steam rise from 18 or ıore geysers in Norris Geyser Basin, named after Philetus W. Norris, one of the early superintendents of the park.

wer Falls of the Yellowstone, plunging ·r 300 feet, is park's most spectacular sight. Below the falls is Grand Canyon of the Yellowstone in 1,000-foot gorge.

tos: Bill Sears (Western ʋs); bottom, Willard Luce

The Church of the Transfiguration, built of logs, has only one room. It nestles against the Grand Teton Mountains, nc far from Jackson Hole and Jackson Lake

Picture window behind the altar in Church of the Transfiguration frames magnificent view of the sharp, ragged peaks of t Teton Range, 22 of them over 10,000 fe

Photos: Grant M. Ha
bottom, Willard L

nor's Flatboat Ferry crosses Snake ver at Moose, in shadow of the Grand Tetons. It started operation in 1892, and was authentically restored in 1949.

ny Lake reflects the blue-green woods l cathedral spires of Teton Mountains.

This twisted aspen tree is favorite of camera fans in Grand Teton National Park.

tos: Willard Luce; bottom left, Grant M. Haist

Below Jackson, the Snake River flows through forested hills, in its twisting, winding course. The channel is known the Grand Canyon of the Snake Riv

Rugged mountain scenery greets visitors along the Cody Road to Yellowstone Park.

Devils Tower was first National Mo ment, named by Theodore Roosevelt, 19

Photos: Willard Luce; Burlin Route; Wyoming Travel Commis

ith 3½ million sheep and lambs, Wyo-ng ranks next to Texas in the production of mutton, wool. State's 33 million acres of farmland are mostly for sheep, cattle.

eed demons of the West: This unusual nera shot of a group of fast-scurrying antelope was made from low-flying plane. They make long migrations, seeking food.

ere are more than 30,000 elk in the te, divided into several herds. Over 10,000 are fed hay each winter in Teton Forest Game Sanctuary, Jackson Hole.

:os: Charles J. Belden

Wyoming

Black and brown bears enjoy Yellowstone Park almost as much as human visitors do.

Teton Mountains edging Jackson L give it a setting of Alpine lovelin

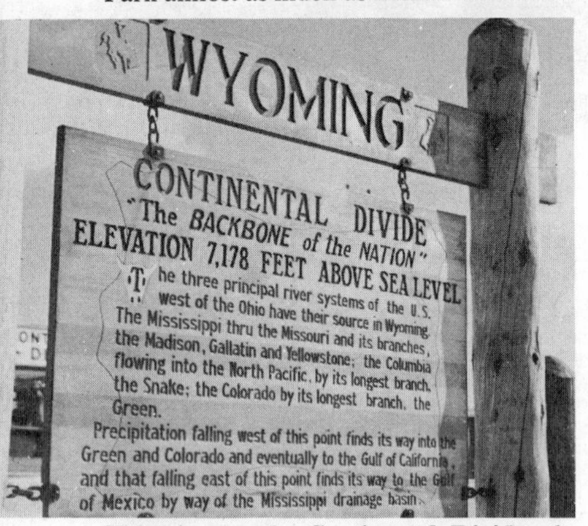

This sign marks Continental Divide, the 7,178-foot-high "backbone of the nation."

Climax of most Wyoming rodeos is "w race, with horses never before ridc

Mount Moran: Wyoming's great ranges include Bighorn Mountains, Absaroka Range in the east, peaks of Yellowst Park in northwest, and Tetons in w

Photos: Grant M. Haist; top right, center left, Alfre Reichenberger; center right, Union Pacific Railroad

OLORADO'S RUGGED BEAUTY BOASTS 51 PEAKS OVER 14,000 FEET HIGH

orado has highest average altitude of state, 6,800 feet, with Continental Divide of the Rocky Mountains running across the state from north to south.

o: Konstantin Kostich

Colorado National Monument is 18,000-acre wonderland. These are "coke ovens."

Rocky Mountain National Park has square miles of mountains and la

Mesa Verde National Park preserves the remarkable homes of the Cliff Dwellers.

Black Canyon of the Gunnison Nati Monument includes 10 miles of go

Photos: D. L. Hopwood; Burlington Route; Wi Luce; Colorado Advertising & Publicity Depart

:s Peak, 14,110 feet, may be climbed :ar, or by cog railroad from Manitou Springs. Auto race to the top is held annually on winding Pikes Peak Highway.

: Colorado Advertis- Publicity Department

Colorado

Statue of Broncho Buster in Denver's Civic Center typifies life of cowboys.

Red Rocks Amphitheater, Denver M‹ tain Parks, has a capacity of 10,‹

View from Civic Center shows how near Denver, the "Mile High City," is to the Rockies. City and County Building, ab faces the State Capitol across the Ce

Balanced Rock is one of natural marvels in Garden of the Gods, Manitou Springs.

Mushroom Park is another of many w rock formations in Garden of the G

Photos: D. L. Hopwood; top G. A. Reims; center, Burlington R

ere are plenty of thrills and spills at lorado rodeos throughout the summer.

In winter, skiing is favorite sport at Aspen, Winter Park, Berthoud Pass, etc.

yal Gorge, or Grand Canyon of the kansas, has sheer 1,000-foot walls.

Royal Gorge Suspension Bridge, carrying highway across, is highest in the world.

os: Glenn U. Nichols; Chas. Grover; D. L. Hopwood

About 7 million acres of the state's Great Plains area is devoted to wheat raising.

Some 800 descendants of Colorado's (numerous Indians live on one reserva'

Great Sand Dunes, named as a National Monumeht, 1932, cover 80 square miles. The mounds, constantly changing, c rise to heights of more than 1,500

Red Rock Lake, with Indian Peaks in the background, is in the Roosevelt National Forest. State has 20 million acres forest and many fine trails for hil

Photos: D. L. Hopwood; top right, Alf Reichenberger; bottom, U. S. Forest Se

rkey ranch: Raising of poultry, cattle, gs and horses is important activity.

Quarries yield granite, marble, limestone, sandstone, lava, other building stones.

osaur National Monument has skeletal ains of dinosaurs, prehistoric reptiles.

Wheeler National Monument has striking varicolored configurations of sandstone.

s: top left, Konstantin Kostich; ado Advertising & Publicity Deent; bottom right, D. L. Hopwood

Colorado

Estes Park is mountain playground and resort on eastern side of Rocky Mountain National Park. It is in lovely va near Longs Peak, other lofty mounta

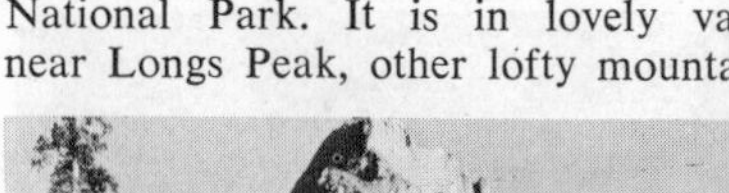

Grand Lake is extremely deep; in places the lake bottom has never been sounded.

Crater Lake mirrors Lone Eagle P State has 1,500 peaks over 10,000

Photos: D. L. Hopw
top, Konstantin Ko

UTAH OUTRANKS ALL STATES IN WONDERS OF NATURE

This natural bridge is one of best known landmarks of Bryce Canyon National Park. Over 70% of Utah's beautiful land is in U.S. ownership, as parks and forests.

Photo: Willard Luce

Bryce Canyon National Park has 100,000 visitors a year to view amazing area the Piaute Indians called "red rocks standing like men in a bowl shaped canyon."

Bryce is entered at rim of the canyon, with trails leading down to the floor.

Almost every conceivable shape is found in Bryce, and some sixty different tints.

Photos: National Park Service; Grant M. Haist; Willard Luce

Zion National Park is noted for scenic grandeur. This is First Patriarch Peak.

Grand Arch Lookout views Mt. Carmel highway, climbing 800 feet in 3 miles.

The Great White Throne is best-known of the monoliths in Zion National Park.

Checkerboard Mesa shows unusual result of nature's action on porous sandstone.

Photos: Willard Luce

Landscape Arch, 292 feet, is considered longest natural span in the world. It is located in Devils Garden section of Arches National Monument, near Moab.

The Double Arch, sometimes called the "jughandles," is in The Windows section.

Delicate Arch, alone and sharp against sky, is one of most popular with visitors.

Photos: Willard Luce

If Millet had been American, says Henri Cartier-Bresson, he would have painted

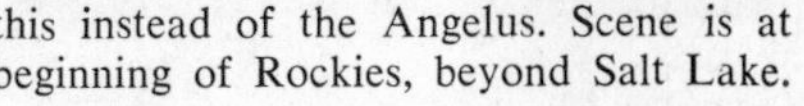

this instead of the Angelus. Scene is at beginning of Rockies, beyond Salt Lake.

Hackberry Canyon Ruins show beautiful stone work of Hovenweep Monument.

Point Supreme overlooks Cedar Breaks National Monument, surpassing Bryce.

Photos: Henri Cartier-Bresson (Magnum); bottom, Willard Luce

Utah SALT LAKE CITY

Sailing is one of principal recreational activities on Great Salt Lake, largest

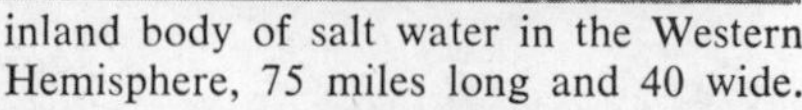

inland body of salt water in the Western Hemisphere, 75 miles long and 40 wide.

Impressive monument marks spot where Brigham Young said, "This is the place."

State Capitol building, Salt Lake City, is seen from gardens of the Hotel Utah.

Mormon Temple took 40 years to build, with granite hauled 28 miles by oxen.

City and County building, Salt Lake City, served as the capitol from 1894 to 1915.

Photos: Willard Luce

Newly-completed Pioneer Memorial Museum is near Capitol, in Wasatch foothills.

Guide tells tourists, at Seagull Monument, how gulls saved starving pioneers.

The Lion House was home of Brigham Young, Mormon leader, and many wives.

This little cabin, preserved on Temple Square, was one of first built by settlers.

Photos: Willard Luce

Rainbow Bridge National Monument was established by President Taft in 1910. It includes 160 acres around the great arch, 308 feet high and 275 feet across.

The Narrows is 18-foot cleft in Capitol Gorge, Capitol Reef National Monument.

Utah Copper Mine, near Bingham Canyon, is world's largest open pit copper mine.

Photos: Willard Luce; top, Ray Manley (Western Ways)

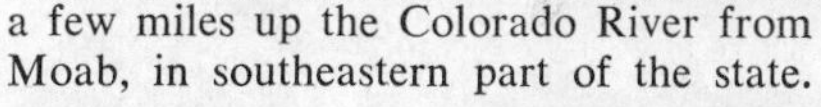

emnant of old movie set stands beneath ıpressive butte in Professor Valley a few miles up the Colorado River from Moab, in southeastern part of the state.

ıese mountain meadows are below timrline of 12,008-foot Mount Timpanogos.

Mile-long zigzag trail leads to entrance of Timpanogos Cave National Monument.

ıtos: Willard Luce

Scenic panorama is enjoyed by visitors to Dixie National Forest as they stand on Strawberry Point and look across Vi gin River country to Zion National Par

Sipapu Natural Bridge is the largest and most impressive of the three water-carved bridges comprising Natural Bridg National Monument, in southeastern Uta

Photos: U. S. For Service; Willard Lu

NEVADA MATCHES 24-HOUR GAMBLING AND GREAT SCENIC BEAUTY

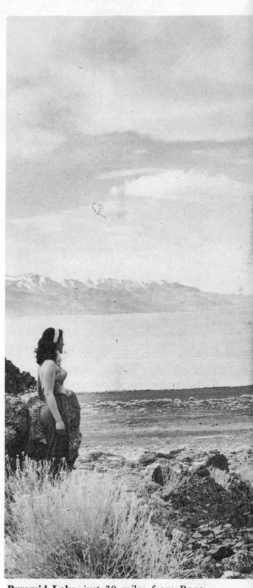

remont Street, Las Vegas, glories in ancing dice, spinning wheels of fortune.

Pyramid Lake, just 30 miles from Reno, is beautiful blue gem set in the desert.

otos: TWA Trans World Aires; Reno Chamber of Commerce

Famous Reno arch across Virginia Street displays slogan that the city tries hard to live up to. Beyond arch are princi hotels, clubs, places of entertainme

Spectacular sign identifies Harolds Club, nationally known gaming establishment.

Tax on gambling helped build this ne modern $3 million high school in Ren

In this pastoral Reno park, you wouldn't think you were in Nevada's largest city.

University of Nevada has outstandi school of mines and school of journalis

Photos: Reno Cha ber of Comme

Roulette is one popular form of gambling in Reno and Las Vegas, but there are also slot machines, poker games, many others. Players—win or lose—are seldom gay.

Photo: Henri Cartier-Bresson (Magnum)

Virginia City, "richest hill on earth" in 1800's, is perched high on slopes of Sun Mountain. It is now having boom o tourists re-living the old bonanza days

Double chair lift at new Reno Ski Bowl carries skiers to height of 9,600 feet.

The Parachutes are interesting formation in Lehman Caves National Monumen

Photos: Henri Cartier-Bresson (Magnum
Reno Chamber of Commerce; Willard Lu

Horseback riding is enjoyed at many guest ranches near Reno and Las Vegas.

Lake Tahoe, 40 minutes drive from Reno, is beautiful vacation setting in mountains.

Cathedral Gorge, state park in eastern Nevada, has spectacular stone steeples.

About 87% of Nevada's land is Federally owned, highest percentage of any state.

State Capitol is at Carson City, named for Kit Carson, 24 miles south of Reno.

Among the Indian tribes in Nevada were the Paiutes, Washoes and Shoshoneans.

Photos: Reno Chamber of Commerce; center, Willard Luce; bottom left, Nevada State Highway Department

Nevada

Hoover Dam, on Colorado River, is used for flood control, irrigation and hydro- electric power. It forms 115-mile Lak Mead, the largest reservoir in the worl

Elephant Rock is formation in the Valley of Fire, Lake Mead Recreational Area.

Humboldt National Forest is part of fi million acres of forest reserves in stat

Photos: Belnap Photo Services, National Highway Association; Willard Luce; U. S. Forest Servi

THE SOUTHWEST

by GLADWIN HILL

A motorist driving across the plateau of northern Arizona recently halted to secure a rattling trunk-latch. As he turned to climb back in the car, he was stopped in his tracks by a strange feeling. It took him several seconds to realize that he was experiencing, for the first time in months and perhaps years, absolute, uninterrupted silence.

Not only were there no people jabbering, automobiles honking, radios blaring, sirens screeching, trains roaring, or airplanes droning. There was not, with the low-lying vegetation, even the sounding harp for random breezes that punctuate the remotest forests of the world. There was only silence.

Yet it was an eloquent silence. It went a long way toward explaining the impassiveness, the contentment even in privation, of the Navajo, systematically living a mile or more from his neighbor on that plateau. It explained generations of cowboys, with their cheerfully lonesome ballads. It explained why a half million people have vied with the rigors of nature to achieve the peace of the Arizona desert; why thousands of others choose to dwell on the isolated farms and ranches of New Mexico and west Texas.

"The great open spaces" are what the Southwest is celebrated for. But it's the quiet and serenity that give the distances meaning for humankind.

The wail of a midnight juke box at a crossroads filling station in New Mexico, the hearty greeting of a prospector or rancher as he clumps into the solitary eat-joint of a sagebrush town, seem to reverberate more through the cosmos than the clangor of millions in the world's cities.

Time moves at a different pace. Through the clear night air of the desert, the stars speak silently of their incomprehensible antiquity. Down the mile-deep gorge of Grand Canyon lie, layer upon layer, the ashes of a billion years. The seasons roll, some wet, some dry. In the highlands, the winter snows swirl in. On the plains, the tumbleweeds race erratically before the winds. Year in and year out, the sun bakes down, on scattered cottonwoods and live-oaks, on pueblos, shacks, hamlets and towns.

Here the apposition between nature and men, and between men and other men, is plainest. The Indians, with their varied visages and customs, bespeak the mingling of migrations yet untraced, from as far away as Asia. In little towns along the Rio Grande are relics of the Spanish explorers who trod these selfsame routes long before the Pilgrims landed. For every modern, busy city like Phoenix, Albuquerque, and Amarillo, dozens of places like Tombstone and Cimarron provide living links with the cattle-trail and mining-boom days of the 19th century.

The visitor here is not taken for granted as he would be in Cincinnati or Dallas. He gets the same incisive once-over that met passengers alighting from the stagecoaches. Is he a city slicker, a card-sharp, a gold-brick salesman—or someone adaptable to the Southwest community? The wise guy is quickly cut down to size; the condescending remark boomerangs.

The spirit of the region—its great open spaces, its solitude, its individuality—is poignantly reflected in one of its commonest mannerisms: greetings are effusive, farewells laconic—in the tacit wish that the absence will be short.

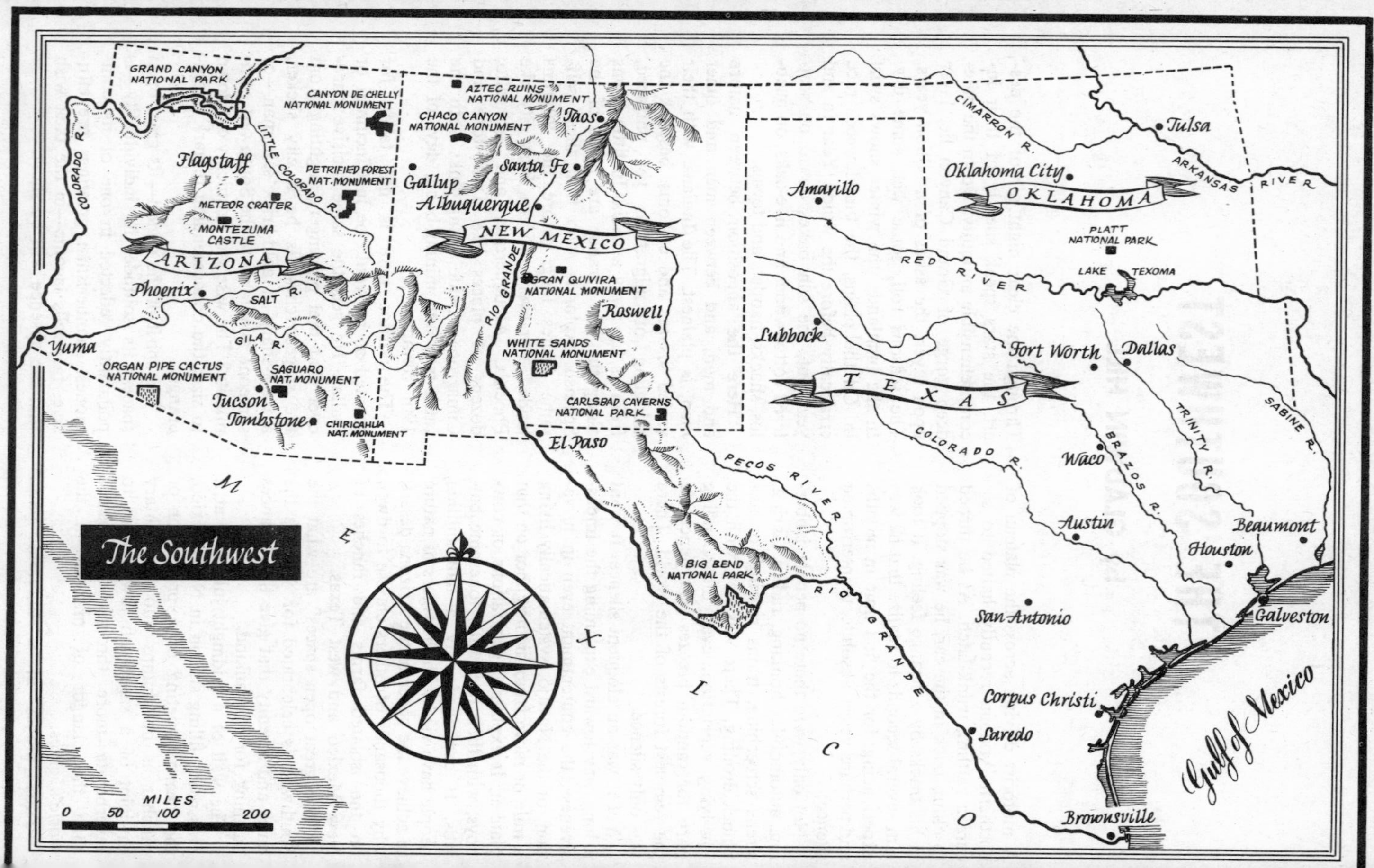
The Southwest
GRAND CANYON NATIONAL PARK
CANYON DE CHELLY NATIONAL MONUMENT
AZTEC RUINS NATIONAL MONUMENT
CHACO CANYON NATIONAL MONUMENT
Taos
Santa Fe
Gallup
Albuquerque
PETRIFIED FOREST NAT. MONUMENT
Flagstaff
METEOR CRATER
MONTEZUMA CASTLE
LITTLE COLORADO R.
COLORADO R.
ARIZONA
NEW MEXICO
Phoenix
SALT R.
GILA R.
Yuma
ORGAN PIPE CACTUS NATIONAL MONUMENT
SAGUARO NAT. MONUMENT
Tucson
Tombstone
CHIRICAHUA NAT. MONUMENT
RIO GRANDE
GRAN QUIVIRA NATIONAL MONUMENT
Roswell
WHITE SANDS NATIONAL MONUMENT
CARLSBAD CAVERNS NATIONAL PARK
El Paso
Amarillo
Lubbock
CIMARRON R.
Tulsa
ARKANSAS RIVER
Oklahoma City
OKLAHOMA
PLATT NATIONAL PARK
RED RIVER
LAKE TEXOMA
Fort Worth
Dallas
TEXAS
SABINE R.
TRINITY R.
BRAZOS R.
COLORADO R.
Waco
PECOS RIVER
Austin
Beaumont
Houston
Galveston
BIG BEND NATIONAL PARK
San Antonio
Corpus Christi
Laredo
Brownsville
Gulf of Mexico
MEXICO
MILES
0 50 100 200

GRAND CANYON IS TOP SCENIC LURE OF ARIZONA'S SUNLAND

Grand Canyon of the Colorado is by all odds the greatest single spectacle in America. It cuts a 217-mile gash across Northern Arizona, 4 to 18 miles in width.

Photo: Union Pacific Railroad

In Monument Valley, giant rock buttes stick up 1200 feet from the valley floor, near the border between Arizona and Utah. Valley also has many sand dunes.

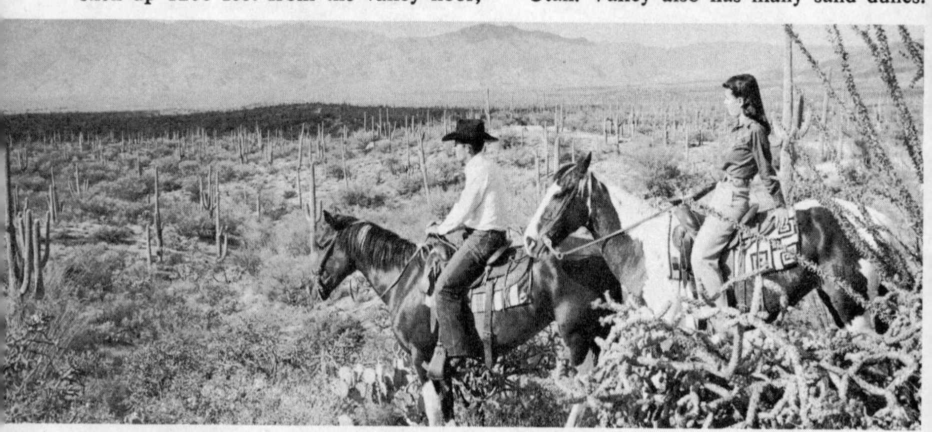

Saguaro National Monument preserves the giant cactus that serves as a natural storage tank for meager desert rainfall. Largest specimens grow to 50-foot height.

Organ Pipe Cactus National Monument has 20-foot organ-pipe cacti, other species.

Chiricahua National Monument outdoes all others in grotesqueness of its rocks.

Photos: Ray Manley, bottom left, Charles W. Herbert (Western Ways); bottom right, Willard Luce

Mount Lemmon Highway has mantle of snow, found only on the higher mountain slopes. Arizona is noted for its many days of sunshine, about 80% of the year.

Montezuma Castle National Monument has remarkable Indian cliff dwellings.

White House, niched into towering walls of Canyon de Chelly, is 900 years old.

Photos: top, Bill Sears, bottom right, Ray Manley (Western Ways); bottom left, TWA Trans World Airlines

Vast areas of semi-arid land, suitable only for grazing, make stock-raising an important industry. State has more than a million head of cattle, even more sheep.

One of a cowboy's duties is to locate a stray calf, bring it home to the ranch.

Cow hand demonstrates roping of calf so it can be branded with Empire mark.

Photos: Balestrero, bottom left, Ray Manley (Western Ways)

At Desert Willow Ranch, dudes on winter vacation are given a lesson on proper way to saddle a horse for trail riding. Visitors find crisp desert air invigorating.

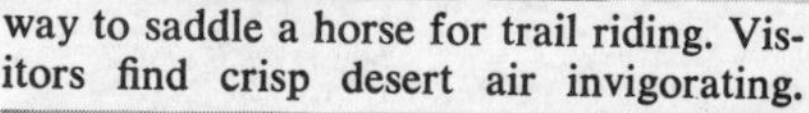

Coffee tastes extra special when it is made from sparkling mountain stream water.

Note rubber tires on this modern chuck wagon, vital equipment on working ranch.

Chuck wagon keeps ahead of moving herd, provides warm chow at mealtime.

Dudes from Flying V Ranch enjoy evening chow in Santa Catalina Mountains.

Photos: Ray Manley (Western Ways)

Arizona's capital, Phoenix, is lively, friendly city, protected on the north by the Phoenix Mountains. At top right is odd silhouette of Camelback Mountain.

Camelback Inn is one of elegant Phoenix resorts where life centers around pool.

Phoenix South Mountain Park has ancient writings on stone, and á small gold mine.

Photos: Phoenix Chamber of Commerce

ucson ranks next to Phoenix in size, and ıares its mild, warm dry climate. Both have much business and industry, but are best known as tourist, health resorts.

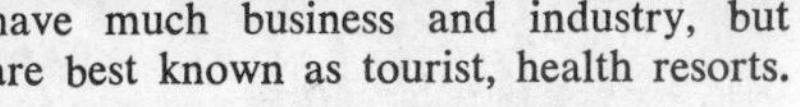

iesta and rodeo take place at Tucson February, at height of winter season.

Ted DeGrazia, one of Southwest's leading artists, teaches at his school in Tucson.

ıotos: Ray Manley, bottom
ft, Koonce (Western Ways)

Arizona

San Xavier del Bac Mission, consecrated 1797, is considered finest mission architecture in Southwest. This is the mission' famous Arizona Boys Chorus at practic

Hopi corn-grinding dance: The Indians of Arizona are divided into more than 30 tribes, the Navajo, Apache, Hopi, Pim Papago, Mojave, Yuma and many other

Tony Whitecloud performs hoop dance at the annual Indian Powwow at Flagstaff.

Navajo woman demonstrates first step preparing to weave intricate rug desi

Photos: Ray Manley (Western Wa center, Phoenix Chamber of Comme

Apache Indians take part in Flagstaff Powwow Parade. Indian reservations are near this city, which is sheltered by San Francisco Peaks and Elden Mountain.

Tombstone is old mining town which was big boom city of 7,000 in the 1880's, when some of biggest gold mines in state were active. Helldorado Days enact past.

Hoover Dam, shown in different view on page 292, is shared by Northwest Arizona and Southeast Nevada. Called Boulder Dam, 1933–47, it was re-named Hoover.

Photos: Ray Manley, center, Tommy Lark (Western Ways)

Baldwins Crossing has beautiful red rock in the background. This is popular spot with movie makers who find Arizon fine for shooting with 80% sunny day

Meteor Crater is 600-foot-deep depression believed caused by meteor striking earth.

Painted Desert is large arid area note for the great variety of its color effect

Photos: Valdis Avots; bottom, Frashers Inc., Petrifi Forest National Park, and National Highway 66 Associati

CARLSBAD CAVERNS IS TOP ATTRACTION IN NEW MEXICO

argantuan stalagmites and bewildering riety of other formations are seen in Hall of the Giants in Carlsbad Caverns National Park, an underground fairyland.

oto: New Mexico
ate Tourist Bureau

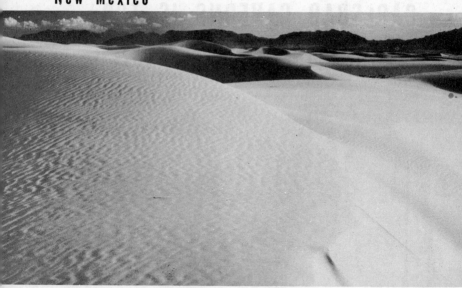

White Sands National Monument has some 176,000 acres of vast, shifting dunes, stretching to the skyline. The dunes a not true sand, but nearly pure gypsu

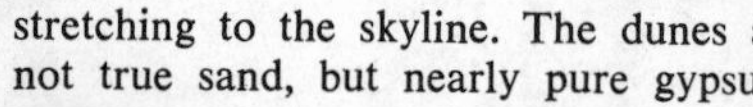

El Morro National Monument preserves rock with 17th century Spanish writings.

Pueblo Bonito is largest of old rui in Chaco Canyon National Monume

Photos: New Mex State Tourist Bure

ter-tribal Indian Ceremonial, held each ar at Gallup, draws Indians from 31 tribes in the Southwest. They parade in covered wagons, dance and powwow.

avajo rugs are woven on a crude loom at rests on side of the Indian dwelling.

Beautifully costumed Indian women parade with burdens carried on their heads.

otos: New Mexico ate Tourist Bureau

New Mexico

Organ Mountains, northeast of Las Cruces: New Mexico varies from 2,876 above sea level to 13,306 feet, a variatic caused by great shiftings of earth's crus

Library at the University of New Mexico, Albuquerque, is constructed in pueblo style architecture and is one of mo beautiful buildings on 315-acre campu

Photos: New Mex
State Tourist Bure

State Capitol in Santa Fe: Distinctive new building was completed in 1953. With Palace of Governors, below, state has nation's newest and oldest capitols.

Cathedral of St. Francis was built in 1869 to serve needs of Spanish residents.

Fiesta in Santa Fe is held annually over the three-day Labor Day weekend.

This is America's oldest public building, Palace of the Governors, Santa Fe. It was constructed of adobe, in 1610, and served as State Capitol nearly 300 years.

Photos: New Mexico State Tourist Bureau; center right, TWA Trans World Airlines

New Mexico

Mission Church at Pecos Pueblo, now in ruins, was one of largest in the state.

Mission Ranchos de Taos has twin bell towers and crosses, beautiful entry door.

Taos Pueblo is spectacular Indian village, with primitive cubist skyscrapers. It is at foot of the majestic Sangre de Cristo mountain range, in northern part of state.

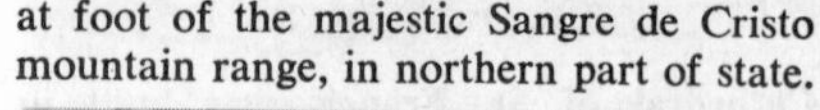

Replica of cliff house is seen in Frijoles Canyon, Bandelier National Monument.

Acoma Mission is unique church in Sky City, Indian pueblo 400 feet above plain.

Photos: New Mexico State Tourist Bureau

TEXAS IS A WORLD OF ITS OWN

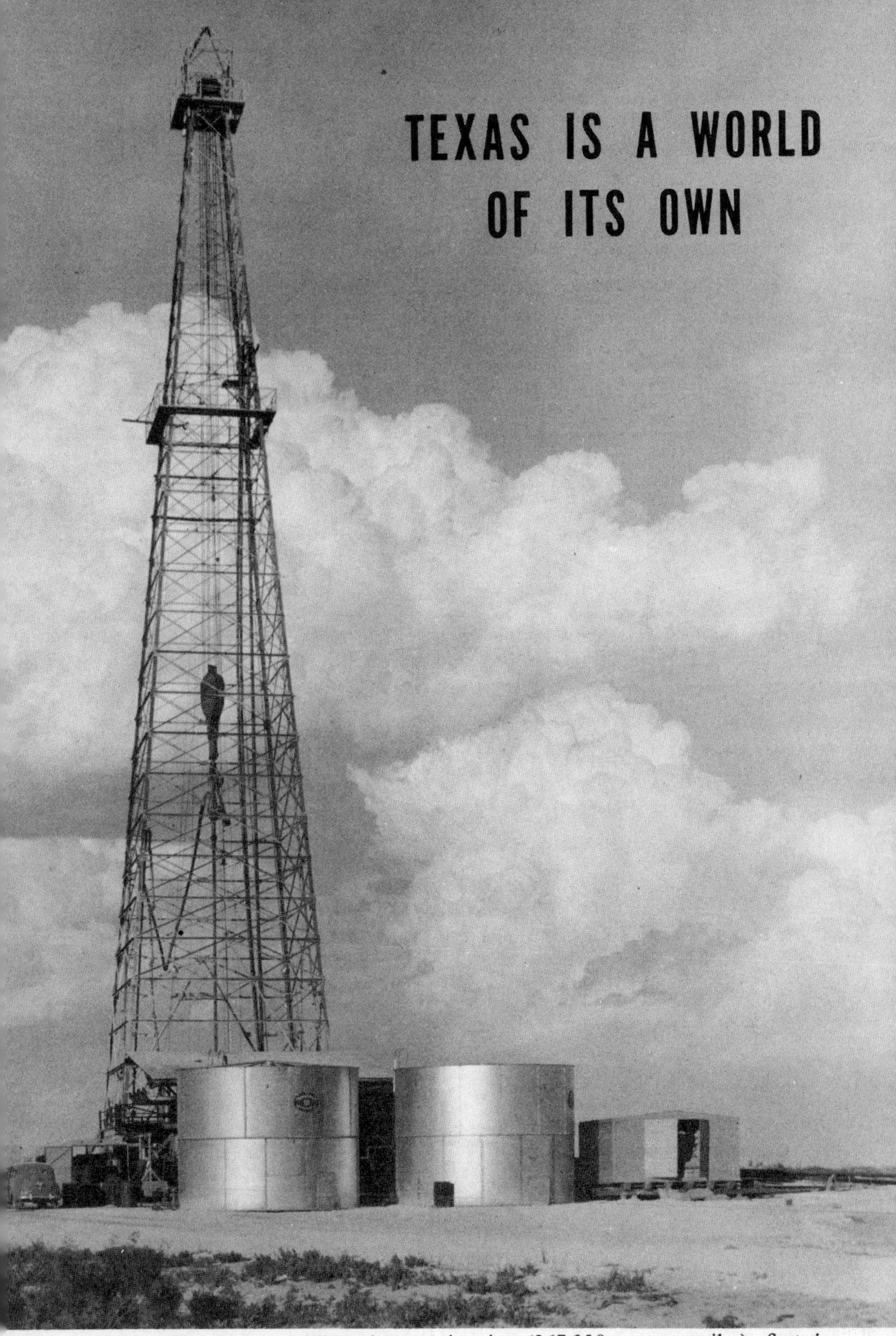

One of the world's largest drilling rigs, this typifies the bigness of Texas, great in size (267,339 square miles), first in oil production and in many farm products.

Photo: Shell Oil Company

Houston is the largest city in the Lone Star State, big manufacturing center and one of greatest U.S. ports, with 50-mile canal to Gulf. Shamrock Hotel is at left.

Shamrock, in Eastern Panhandle section, is home of the annual St. Patrick's Day celebration, and of the Eastern Panhandle Livestock Show fourth week in February.

Photos: Braniff International Airways; National Highway 66 Association

Texas State Capitol, at Austin, has 18 acres of floor space and some 500 rooms. Built of native red granite, it is 308 ft. high, topping most other state capitols.

State Fair of Texas, held at Dallas in October, is largest of its kind in the nation, drawing over 2½ million attendance. In background is Hall of State Building.

Photos: Texas Highway Department; Braniff International Airways

Corpus Christi Bay and skyline of city: Sheltered from Gulf of Mexico by Mustang Island, Corpus Christi is shipping center and all-year-round playground.

Alabama-Cooshatti Indians, only remaining tribe in Texas, live near Livingston.

Arthur's, in Dallas, is one of the state's distinguished places for excellent food.

Galveston's long beach for surf bathing, good climate, facilities for fishing and boating, attractive subtropical plants, all combine to make it tourist playground.

Photos: Texas Highway Department; center right, Arthur's

San Antonio River flows through lovely park in downtown San Antonio. One of oldest Texas cities, and third largest, it has interesting past, colorful present.

The Alamo, where heroic defenders died, is one of best-known U.S. historic shrines.

Spanish Governors' Palace, San Antonio, was used during Spanish rule of Texas.

Photos: Texas Highway Department

Texas

570-foot San Jacinto Monument commemorates battle for Texas freedom.

McDonald Observatory, located in Davis Mountains, is third largest in the world.

Indian Lodge is tourist resort in Davis Mountains, towering to 7,000-foot peaks.

Spring roundup is like a three ring circus —you have to be quick to see everything. This typical scene is near Vernon, which has one livestock pasture of 200,000 acres.

Photos: Texas Highway Department

Iission San José is the most complete of ıe four Spanish missions standing in

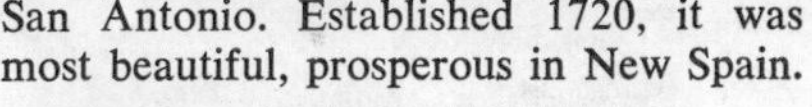

San Antonio. Established 1720, it was most beautiful, prosperous in New Spain.

Church of Our Lady of Mount Carmel is eproduction of mission founded in 1681.

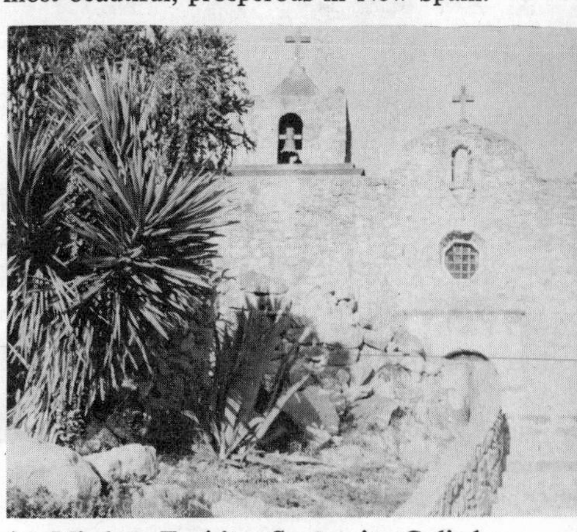

At Mission Espíritu Santo, in Goliad, excavators found ancient Indian homes.

ıotos: Texas Highway Department; ottom left, Ray Manley (Western Ways)

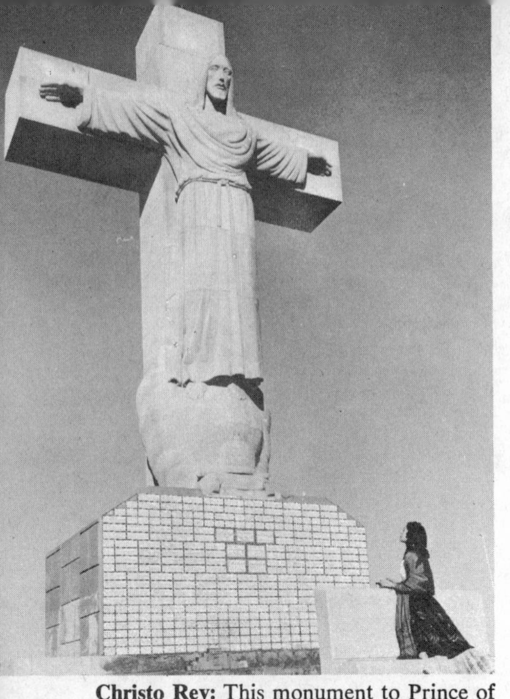

Christo Rey: This monument to Prince of Peace is on summit in northwest El Paso.

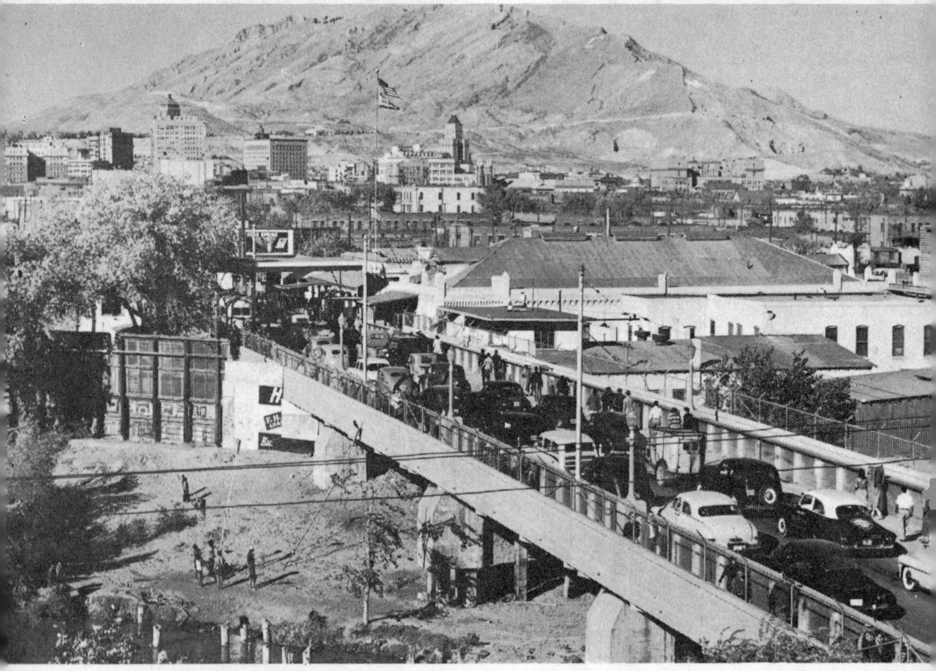

Purchasing colorful and serviceable boo is vital shopping-day task for cowboy.

Historic field piece stands near first c the Hilton Hotels, in downtown El Pas

International bridge crosses Rio Grande from Juarez, Mexico, to El Paso, the city that stands at westernmost tip of Texa Name means "the Pass" through hill

Photos: Ray Manley, top rig
C. W. Herbert (Western Wa

OKLAHOMA POSSESSES GREAT RICHES, GREAT CAPACITY TO ENJOY THEM

Oklahoma City, capital of the state, has symbols of its wealth—a row of oil wells —right on the State House grounds. City was settled in one day, by homesteaders.

Photo: Oklahoma City Chamber of Commerce and National Highway 66 Association

Turner Falls, in the Arbuckle Mountains near Davis, is one of the scenic spots of

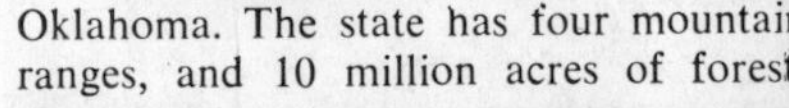
Oklahoma. The state has four mountai ranges, and 10 million acres of forest

Platt National Park, near Sulphur, in the southern part of state, has streams, springs, waterfalls, swimming holes. I was once part of old Indian Territory

Photos: Charles J. Belden; National Par Service; Oklahoma Planning & Resources Boar

Oklahoma Agricultural and Mechanical College, at Stillwater, was founded 1890. It has $50 million in buildings, equipment, 4,976 acres of land, 8,800 students.

University of Oklahoma, at Norman, has enrollment of 8,000, and 2,471 acres of land. University of Oklahoma Press is noted for success of regional publishing.

Will Rogers Memorial at Claremore honors the Oklahoma humorist-philosopher.

Indian population is largest of any state, comprising members of some thirty tribes.

Photos: Oklahoma Planning & Resources Board; bottom, Claremore Chamber of Commerce; El Reno Chamber of Commerce, and National Highway 66 Association

Lake Texoma, shared by Oklahoma, Texas, is one of our biggest playgrounds.

Cimarron and many other rivers in the state provide abundant fishing streams.

Devils Den is quiet spot created by some angry upheaval of the earth's crust centuries ago. Now it's ideal for rock-clambering and just plain contemplation

Lake o' the Cherokees is formed by huge multiple-arch Grand River Dam, built in 1938–41, and also called the Pensacola Dam. The lake covers 85 square miles

Photos: Oklahoma Planning & Resources Board

CALIFORNIA—THE GOLDEN GATE

by LAWRENCE E. DAVIES

ORLD'S GREATEST BRIDGE SPANS GOLDEN GATE AT SAN FRANCISCO.

visitor stood in a crowd of 10,000 in he "Wall Street of the West" not long go watching a ceremony. The financial istrict of San Francisco had been driven o distraction for four months by the teady, nerve-fraying pounding of a pile river while it sank supports for a new kyscraper. Now the job was done, the uge hammer silenced, and San Fran-isco, true to form, brought out pall-earers, wreaths and eulogists and even ut the symbolic remains of Alfred the ile driver on a trans-Pacific liner for urial at sea. The visitor thought he had aptured the spirit of this metropolis uilt on a dozen hills. This spirit is an lusive thing, but fun-loving tolerance urely is an ingredient.

The town shows a maturity greater han that of many older ones. It has tability, based on the knowledge that neither earthquake nor seven disastrous fires could down its spirit. Withal, it has never been afraid to be exuberant.

Fog may account for some of San Francisco's character. The relentless bil-lowing of the fog inward through the mile-wide Golden Gate, sometimes leav-ing the tips of the Golden Gate Bridge towers hanging like ghostly spires, is a fascinating sight almost every afternoon from mid-June through August.

Lake Tahoe, nestling 7,000 feet high in the Sierras, vineyards and wine cel-lars, natural wonders like Yosemite, all contribute to the character and spirit of the region. But nothing, in the opinion of this adopted Far Westerner, is more awe-inspiring, more majestic, more likely to instill a sense of humility, than a cathe-dral-like grove of giant redwoods, "na-ture's oldest living things."

hoto: Californians Inc.

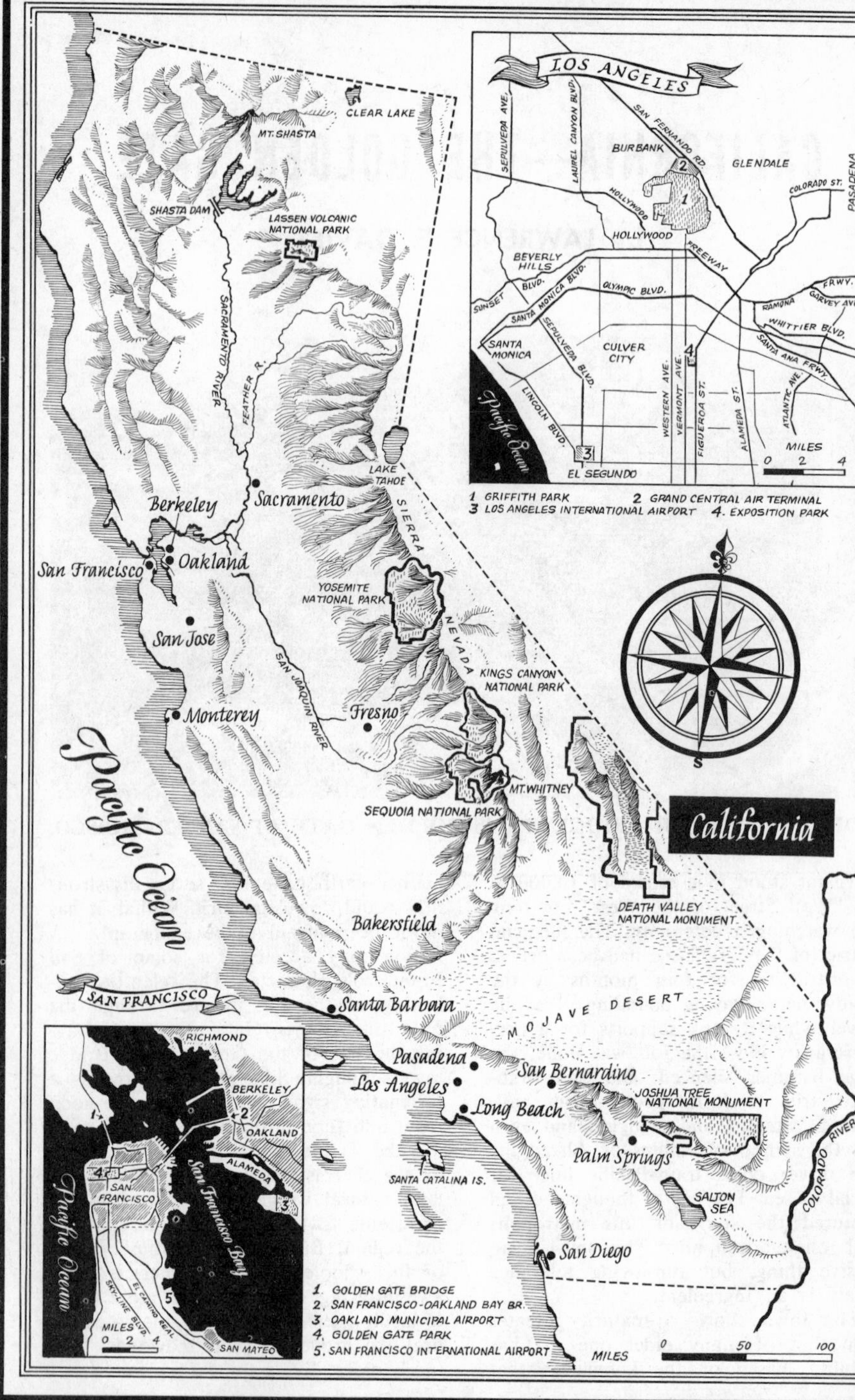

California
Pacific Ocean
CLEAR LAKE
MT. SHASTA
SHASTA DAM
LASSEN VOLCANIC NATIONAL PARK
SACRAMENTO RIVER
FEATHER R.
LAKE TAHOE
Sacramento
Berkeley
Oakland
San Francisco
San Jose
Monterey
SIERRA
NEVADA
YOSEMITE NATIONAL PARK
SAN JOAQUIN RIVER
KINGS CANYON NATIONAL PARK
Fresno
MT. WHITNEY
SEQUOIA NATIONAL PARK
DEATH VALLEY NATIONAL MONUMENT
Bakersfield
Santa Barbara
MOJAVE DESERT
Pasadena
Los Angeles
San Bernardino
Long Beach
JOSHUA TREE NATIONAL MONUMENT
Palm Springs
SANTA CATALINA IS.
SALTON SEA
COLORADO RIVER
San Diego
MILES
0
50
100
LOS ANGELES
SEPULVEDA AVE.
LAUREL CANYON BLVD.
SAN FERNANDO RD.
BURBANK
GLENDALE
PASADENA
COLORADO ST.
HOLLYWOOD
FREEWAY
BEVERLY HILLS
SUNSET
BLVD.
SANTA MONICA BLVD.
OLYMPIC BLVD.
RAMONA
GARVEY AVE.
FRWY.
WHITTIER BLVD.
SANTA ANA FRWY.
SANTA MONICA
SEPULVEDA BLVD.
CULVER CITY
LINCOLN BLVD.
WESTERN AVE.
VERMONT AVE.
FIGUEROA ST.
ALAMEDA ST.
ATLANTIC AVE.
Pacific Ocean
EL SEGUNDO
MILES
0 2 4
1 GRIFFITH PARK
2 GRAND CENTRAL AIR TERMINAL
3 LOS ANGELES INTERNATIONAL AIRPORT
4. EXPOSITION PARK
S
SAN FRANCISCO
RICHMOND
BERKELEY
OAKLAND
ALAMEDA
SAN FRANCISCO
San Francisco Bay
Pacific Ocean
SKY-LINE BLVD.
EL CAMINO REAL
SAN MATEO
MILES
0 2 4
1. GOLDEN GATE BRIDGE
2. SAN FRANCISCO-OAKLAND BAY BR.
3. OAKLAND MUNICIPAL AIRPORT
4. GOLDEN GATE PARK
5. SAN FRANCISCO INTERNATIONAL AIRPORT

YOSEMITE PARK HEADS THE NATURAL WONDERS OF NORTHERN CALIFORNIA

Yosemite National Park is a peaceful empire of 1,189 square miles, with giant sequoias, tumbling waterfalls, and lakes which reflect the spectacular mountains.

Photo: Konstantin Kostich

Yosemite Valley is in the heart of the great national park's scenic marvels, with Half Dome looming ahead. Park lies on western slope of the Sierra Nevada.

Ski-tow at Yosemite is sort of uphill sled. National parks and many other places provide Californians with tobogganing, snowshoeing, skiing, sleighing, ice-skating.

Photos: Southern Pacific Lines; Konstantin Kostich

Yosemite Fall first leaps a sheer 1,430 feet and then, after a series of cascades, plunges another 320. Park has five great falls, one 10 times height of Niagara.

Photo: United Air Lines

San Francisco, with its roller-coaster streets, ranks with Paris and Rome as one of world's greatly loved cities. Cab cars have won fight to keep clangin

Photo: Henri Cartier-Bresson (Magnu

Top of the Mark" is the many-windowed ntage point where San Franciscans and visitors meet for cocktails while they watch the great city spread out below.

ark Hopkins Hotel is built on Nob Hill, here railroad-builder's mansion stood.

Ferry Building, foot of Market Street, is less active because of Bay Bridge.

hotos: Henri Cartier-Bresson (Magnum); bottom left, oulin Studios; right, Redwood Empire Association

Golden Gate Bridge, connecting San Francisco with communities to the north, was completed in 1937 at cost of $35½ million. Main central span, 4,200 fe

Fisherman's Wharf is landing point for San Francisco's many Italian fishermen. Visitors love brightly painted fishin boats, and many fine seafood restaurants

n length, is the longest single span in he world. The bridge carries 6 lanes for auto traffic, has 2 sidewalks. Clearance above San Francisco Bay is 220 feet.

Sidewalk stands on Wharf cook freshly caught crabs in steaming iron cauldrons.

San Francisco's Chinatown is an exotic city-within-a-city of more than 20,000.

Photos: TWA Trans World Airlines; bottom, Redwood Empire Association

San Francisco-Oakland Bay Bridge was opened to traffic in 1936. It is double-decked, with six traffic lanes for auto on the upper level, and three truck lanes

Mission Dolores, in downtown San Francisco, was founded on June 29, 1776.

Trader Vic's, with main restaurant i San Francisco and one in Oakland, i

d two interurban tracks on the lower. ıe bridge is illuminated at night with yellow sodium vapor lights, the rays of which can penetrate the frequent fogs.

ıe of bay area's many notable eating ıces. Vic's has South Seas atmosphere.

Unique cable cars were doomed to oblivion, but aroused public saved many.

ıotos: Strohmeyer Photographs; bottom left, Californians Inc.; ıter, Trader Vic's; San Francisco Chamber of Commerce

Union Square, San Francisco: At left is St. Francis Hotel, one of best known. Beneath square is four-level garage wi capacity for more than 1,700 automobile

San Francisco meets the Pacific on long white beach extending over 3½ miles.

Outdoor flower stands are to Union Squa what cafés are to Champs-Elysé

Photos: Californians Inc.; bott right, Redwood Empire Associat

her Gate is famed entrance to the iversity of California at Berkeley.

Campanile's high lookout gives splendid view of San Francisco and whole bay area.

ader Vic's in Oakland is even more uth Seas than San Francisco version.

Hoover Tower, at Stanford University, houses library on war, revolution, peace.

tos: Californians Inc.;
tom left, Trader Vic's

Lake Tahoe, shared by Nevada, California, is of glacial origin and covers nearly 200 square miles. Mark Twain called "fairest picture the whole earth affords.

Sutter's Fort, in California's capital city of Sacramento, contains authentic exhibits showing life in the early day and during the hectic Gold Rush perio

Photos: Southern Pacific Line
Sacramento Chamber of Commer

assen Peak is the only recently active olcano in the United States. Violent eruptions occurred in 1914 and 1915, after sixty-five years of inactivity.

oto: National Park Service

This is the rugged coast along Del Norte County, near boundary of Oregon. Area from San Francisco north to the Orego border is known as the Redwood Empir

In Eldorado National Forest, a "shovel" loader places huge logs on truck. Except for its valuable redwoods, Califor must import much of the lumber it nee

Photos: Redwood Empire As ciation; U. S. Forest Serv

ɪese Giant Sequoias in Mariposa Grove, ɔsemite National Park, are probably the oldest living things in the world. Ring counts show some to be 4,000 years old.

ɔto: Ralph H. Anderson, ɪtional Park Service

The Napa, Livermore and Sonoma valleys produce grapes for table use, raisins and wine. California farms are outstan ing in use of irrigation, modern metho

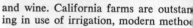

California wineries make about 90% of the country's domestic wines, brandies.

Blossomtime in Santa Clara Valley: I called "Valley of the heart's delight

Photos: Redwood Empire Association; bo tom right, San Jose Chamber of Commer

SOUTHERN CALIFORNIA

by GLADWIN HILL

There is an exotic Oriental dish with some name like mooey-mooey composed of so many ingredients it is said that no two people have ever agreed on what it tasted like.

The same quality is shared, for similar reasons, by Southern California. The "S" in Southern California, incidentally, is always capitalized—in Southern California. It is climatically and culturally quite different from northern California (spelled with a small "n"), which bears it approximately the same relationship as Albany does to New York City: the legislature meets there.

At first blush, Southern California is a bewildering melange: a land of forested mountains, barren deserts, shimmering seashore . . . of Indians and atomic scientists . . . and the Mexican "wetbacks." People from every state in the union, who annually hold Iowa picnics and New England picnics . . . but who concur that they never had it so good.

Southern California is a melting pot which has not yet come to heat. The population is stratified not economically or socially, but chronologically. There are the Spanish-named Old Families. There are the descendants of the 19th-century pioneers. There are the folks from the big influx of the 1920's, living in an increasingly imaginary world of orange-groves and annuities in 100-cent dollars. There are the Okies of the 1930's—many now prospering entrepreneurs. There are the industrial immigrants of World War II, who hurtled from Alabama's cotton patches to suede shoes in half a decade. And there are the "vets"—the nation's biggest concentration of them—who formed the nucleus of the continuing post-war migration.

The keynote, the strand running through all these diverse elements, is "living." "California living" has become a tag associated with everything from clothes to condiments. It derives primarily from *Southern* California and its bland climate, which encourages people in a thousand pastimes, from skiing to skin-diving, from sun-bathing to salad-making.

The swimming pool is Southern California's trade-mark, not as a badge of affluence (they cost less than a car), but as a symbol of people's defiant devotion, in the frenetic atomic era, to something more than the humdrum business of Making Ends Meet. An even more universal symbol, no longer exclusive to the region but indigenous to it, is the patio. You may stage barbecues in it, or just sit in it, or just have it. The point is that you're proclaiming that there's more to life than four walls and a roof.

"California living" takes many forms, some of them ridiculous. It connotes Pasadena's palm-shaded New England-style houses, their roofs determinedly peaked (by transplanted New Englanders) to shed completely non-existent snows.

It connotes the paradox of the Cadillac, the badge of "arrival" on the one hand in the Hollywood movie colony, and on the other along Central Avenue, Los Angeles' Harlem . . . and in many cases the pickup truck of the large-scale cotton grower, who counts his holdings in square miles.

It isn't the people who are crazy. It's the pattern. The common trait of Southern Californians is that they're all converts. "You may not like it at first," they advise visitors. "But after you've been here a while—" Once the visitor finds some kind of niche in the pattern, he's set. And pretty soon, he's saying: "You may not like it at first, but—"

SOUTHERN CALIFORNIA MEANS HOLLYWOOD, ORANGE GROVES, COAST AND DESERT RESORTS

Palm Springs, in the desert 70 miles southeast of Los Angeles, is an opulent resort that is said to have the world's highest per capita count of swimming pools.

Photos: Charles W. Herbert (Western Ways)

Hollywood is center of world's movie industry. Hollywood Boulevard becomes "Santa Claus Lane" at Christmas and is gaily festooned, brilliantly floodlighted.

Grauman's Chinese Theater is noted for glamorous movie premieres and for the concrete slabs bearing hand and foot prints and messages from celebrities.

Photos: Hollywood Citizen-News; Hollywood Chamber of Commerce

Wilshire Boulevard, famous Los Angeles thoroughfare, sweeps through MacArthur Park and on to the Miracle Mile section with spectacular shops, hotels, offices.

New Chinatown is Los Angeles center for curio shops and Oriental restaurants.

Union Station, in modified mission architecture, has 135-foot clock tower.

Photos: TWA Trans World Airlines; Konstantin Kostich; All Year Club of Southern California

Biltmore Hotel is on edge of Pershing Square in heart of downtown Los Angeles. A multi-level garage has recently been constructed beneath the palm-lined park.

Guests at Beverly Wilshire enjoy lunch beside the big "Copa Club" swimming pool. Fashion shows, fencing exhibitions are among events attracting crowds to hotel.

Photos: Southern Pacific; Ann Clark, Beverly Wilshire

The famous Rose Bowl, at Pasadena, is packed with nearly 100,000 fans on each New Year's Day to see the keen rivalry of the annual Rose Bowl football game.

Santa Anita Race Track, with mountains as backdrop, is one of handsomest. Mid-winter racing events attract throngs to $1 million plant with stands for 30,000.

Photos: Pasadena Tournament of Roses Association; All Year Club of Southern California

Redlands, named for red soil of region, is packing and distributing center for wide citrus growing area. It is protected on the north by San Bernardino Mountains.

Lake Arrowhead, a mile high in the San Bernardino Mountains, is reached by scenic Rim of the World Drive, a 100-mile loop from San Bernardino and return.

Photos: Redlands Chamber of Commerce; TWA Trans World Airlines

Walt Disney's Magic Kingdom of Disneyland, at Anaheim, California, is newest amusement park for young and old. This is the "Turn of the Century" Main Street.

A "real" pirates' galleon sits at anchor in Disneyland courtyard, sails a-billow.

Lifelike alligators "threaten" the sight-seeing boat on the river at Disneyland.

Disneyland from the air: On left are Adventureland and Frontierland, at top center is Fantasyland and on the right, Tomorrowland. Entrance is at bottom.

Frontierland revives America's past in a busy transportation center of early days.

"Mark Twain" is authentically re-created paddle wheeler that carries 300 people.

Photos: Disneyland, Inc.

Southern California SAN DIEGO AREA

San Diego has one of the finest natural harbors in the U.S., attracting naval, 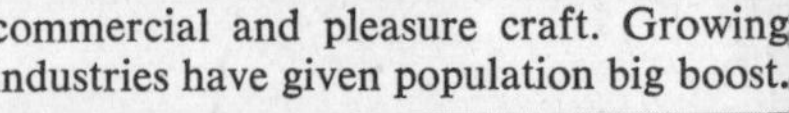 commercial and pleasure craft. Growing industries have given population big boost.

Serra Museum, of Spanish mission design, honors days of Father Junípero Serra.

Tower of California Building, in Balbo[a] Park, is outstanding San Diego landmark

Photos: TWA Trans World Airlines; Sa[n] Diego Convention and Tourist Burea[u]

La Jolla, just north of San Diego, has lovely homes on cliffs overlooking the sea.

Alligator Head, secluded sandy cove, is La Jolla's most popular spot for bathing.

The coves, headlands and flower-covered paths of Laguna Beach have served as inspiration for many landscape painters. The town has many rustic homes and shops.

Photos: San Diego Convention and Tourist Bureau; bottom, All Year Club of Southern California

Rodeo Parade at Palm Springs attracts gay-costumed riders from ranches for many miles around. Other events includ golf and tennis tournaments, circus week

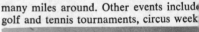

Youthful rider shows her skill in parade that passes along Palm Springs main street.

Young horse, too, puts on his best manne for event sponsored by Mounted Polic

Photos: A. Milton Runy

Palm Springs Tennis Club is a beautiful oasis in the desert Its swimming pool is one of well over 1,000 in Palm Springs, probably world's highest per-person count.

Photo: Charles W. Herbert (Western Ways)

Palisade Glaciers, near Big Pine, are the southernmost of the Northern Hemisphere. The gleaming "living ice" is two miles long, a mile wide, deeply crevassed.

Photo: American Airlines

General Sherman Tree, Sequoia-King's Canyon National Park, is *Sequoia gigantea.*

Sierra Nevada Mountains form eastern boundary of King's Canyon National Park.

Close-up of comely lass in Giant Joshua Tree: These desert lilies often grow 30 feet high and 3 feet thick. A forest of them covers desert area near Palmdale.

Photos: Southern Pacific; Ansel Adams; All Year Club of Southern California

Santa Barbara, founded 1786, is called "Queen of the Missions." It is the only California mission whose altar light ha never been extinguished since founding

Photo: Santa Barba Chamber of Commerc

Mission San Gabriel was founded in 1771 by the pioneer missionary, Junípero Serra.

Mission St. Charles Borromeo overlooks Carmel Bay. It has grave of Father Serra.

Mission Santa Ynez prospered in 1820, at which time it owned 12,000 head of cattle.

Mission San Diego de Alcalá was first of the 21 missions built by the Franciscans.

Photos: Southern Pacific; TWA Trans World Airlines; All Year Club of Southern California; United Air Lines

Southern California OIL AND AGRICULTURE

California ranks next to Texas in crude petroleum production. This is the valley

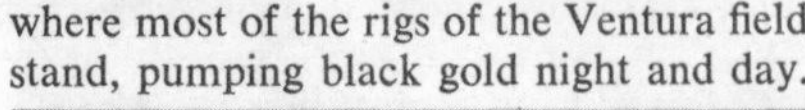

where most of the rigs of the Ventura field stand, pumping black gold night and day.

Typical pumping unit in the oil fields is this conventional rocker-arm type of pump.

Oilmen tackling a new field have to slice mountains, bulldoze roads, haul in rigs.

Photos: Shell Oil Company

Date clusters are covered with burlap or paper cones while the fruit is ripening.

Orange growing in California is world's most intensively-developed crop culture.

Abundance of water from melting snows of the Sierra Nevada, together with long hot summers, helps make the San Joaquin Valley vineyards a vast green garden.

Wine is stored in these huge barrels. Man on ladder uses "thief" to draw sample.

Cotton production centers on Alcalá, a quality variety that is in great demand.

Photos: All Year Club of Southern California; Wine Institute; Kern County Board of Trade

Cabrillo Boulevard, Santa Barbara: To the right is the municipal swimming pool and the Santa Barbara channel. To the left is the city and Santa Ynez Mountains.

Santa Barbara's white stucco courthouse resembles palace of a Spanish prelate.

Pigeons and swallows make their home in ruins of old Mission San Juan Capistrano.

Santa Catalina Island is 24 miles southwest of Los Angeles harbor. Avalon is the main center of this glamorous sport and resort showplace. Casino is at right.

Photos: Santa Barbara Chamber of Commerce; All Year Club of Southern California; Southern Pacific

THE NORTHWEST

by RICHARD L. NEUBERGER

Abundance is the dominant impression one gets of the Northwest. Everything is in profusion—trees, wildlife, water, flowered orchards, leaping salmon in the rivers. Even the vast interior desert of sagebrush is split by the mighty Columbia, champing in a deep lava gorge. Irrigation canals have wrested alfalfa fields and symmetrical panels of row crops from the choking grip of cactus and tumbleweed. At no other place in the land does so much annual rainfall descend from the skies as along the Northwest's timbered seacoast. This has produced majestic "rain forests" where Douglas fir giants scrape the heavens.

Seattle, Portland and Spokane are teeming cities, but essentially the realm seems untrammeled. On the Lolo Trail, sheer above Idaho's crystalline Lochsa River, stand rock cairns that helped to guide Lewis and Clark to Oregon, unchanged since the great explorers saw them 150 years ago. The Northwest is that much linked to its frontier beginnings. I have walked along the Lolo, knowing that my shoes were fitting into the bygone moccasin prints of the first of all westbound Americans.

Northwesterners are conscious of the region's hurtling rivers, which claw at granite cliffs with white-capped talons. In this one sprawling region lurks 42 per cent of all the undeveloped hydroelectric power in the United States. The Northwest has no other industrial fuel—no coal, no petroleum, no natural gas. If manufacturing payrolls are to ease the economic pressure on the forests of Oregon and Washington, this will come about only because of the generation of more low-cost water power. Already the rivers that tumble over concrete spillways are responsible for the major factories that dot the region.

Mount Rainier is framed by cave of snow.

The traveler, looking from his bus seat or Pullman berth, knows clearly when he has come to the Northwest. The trees are thicker, taller and more numerous. The peaks may not be intrinsically as high as those in the Rockies, but their cushion of snow is deeper, their glaciers more active. James Bryce said that nowhere else on the planet were sea and forest and upland so united in a single vernal panorama, and this is the Northwest's ultimate glory.

The Northwest's favorite legend is that of Paul Bunyan, the mighty lumberjack, who used a fir tree for a toothpick and measured the stuffing for his Christmas goose in metric tons. This tells a good deal about the region and its people. Northwesterners were radiant when Hell's Canyon on the Snake River turned out to be a few feet deeper than Grand Canyon on the Colorado River.

Photo: Kostantin Kostich

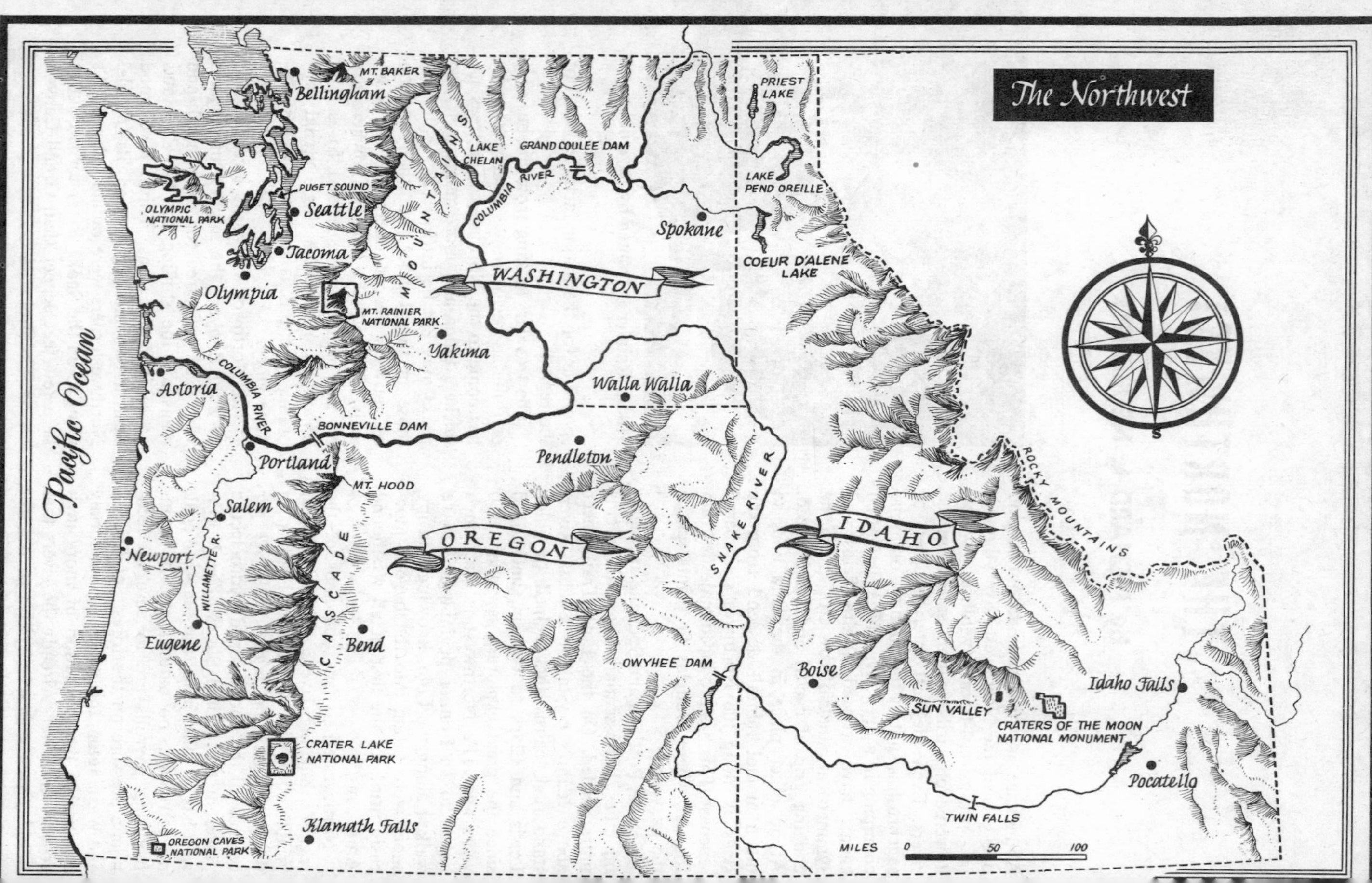
The Northwest
MT. BAKER
Bellingham
PRIEST LAKE
LAKE CHELAN
GRAND COULEE DAM
COLUMBIA RIVER
LAKE PEND OREILLE
PUGET SOUND
OLYMPIC NATIONAL PARK
Seattle
Spokane
Tacoma
COEUR D'ALENE LAKE
MOUNTAINS
WASHINGTON
Olympia
MT. RAINIER NATIONAL PARK
Yakima
Pacific Ocean
Astoria
COLUMBIA RIVER
Walla Walla
BONNEVILLE DAM
Pendleton
Portland
MT. HOOD
ROCKY MOUNTAINS
Salem
IDAHO
OREGON
SNAKE RIVER
Newport
WILLAMETTE R.
CASCADE
Eugene
Bend
OWYHEE DAM
Boise
Idaho Falls
SUN VALLEY
CRATERS OF THE MOON NATIONAL MONUMENT
CRATER LAKE NATIONAL PARK
Pocatello
TWIN FALLS
Klamath Falls
OREGON CAVES NATIONAL PARK
MILES 0 50 100
S

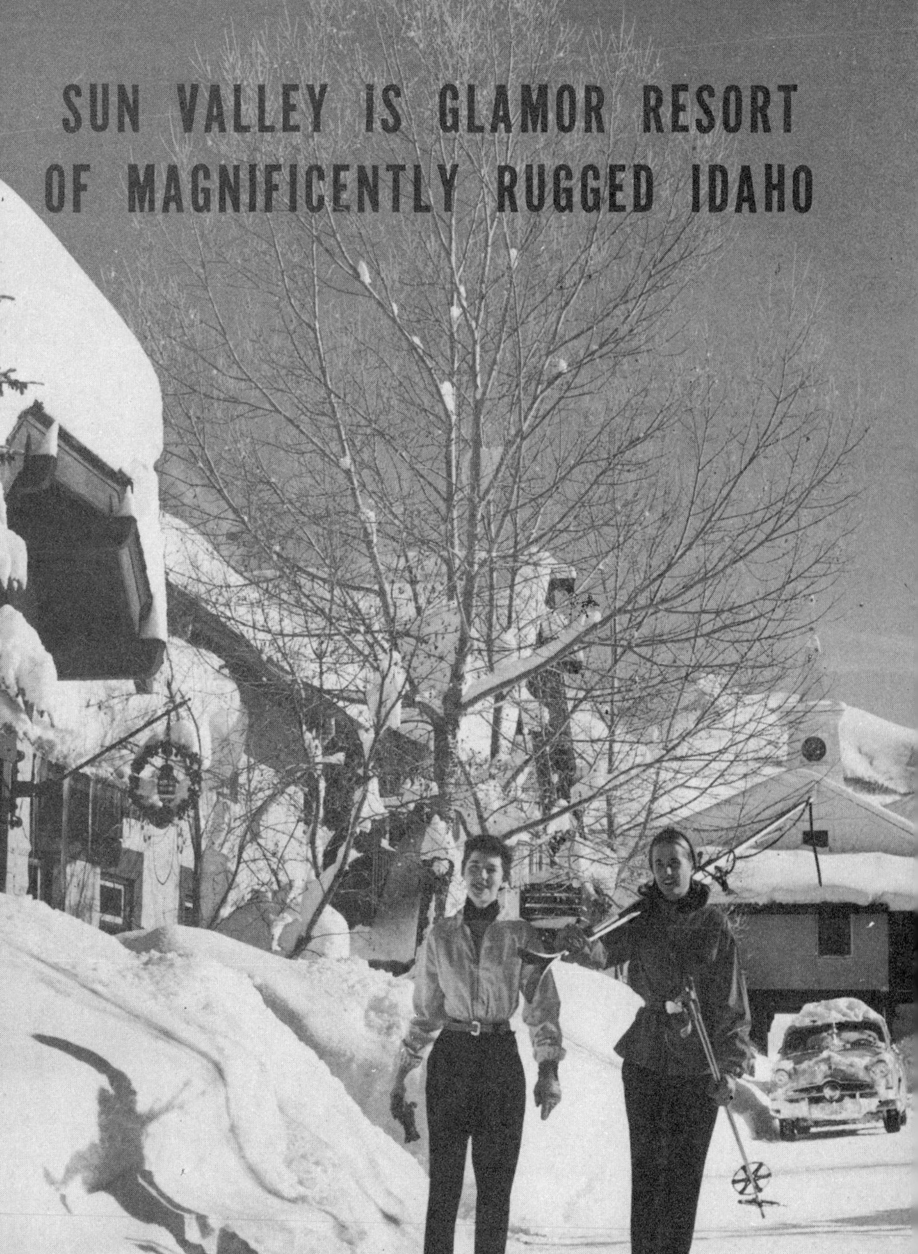

SUN VALLEY IS GLAMOR RESORT OF MAGNIFICENTLY RUGGED IDAHO

At Sun Valley, snow falls deep and powdery from early autumn on, the sun shines brilliantly, and the Sawtooth Mountains give protection from cold northern gales.

Photo: Sun Valley News Bureau

Sun Valley Lodge offers ice skating, the thrilling ski runs of Mount Baldy, milder slopes of Dollar and Half Dollar Mountains, even swimming in heated pools.

Photo: Sun Valley News Bureau

un Valley is year-round resort. Fishing or rainbow trout is favorite summer sport.

Boise is Idaho's capital and largest city, with its monumentally classic capitol.

Craters of the Moon National Monument: The splatter cones, terraces and weird piles of stone, caves and natural bridges resemble the moon seen through a telescope.

ndians say a dip before sunrise at Bath-ub Rock will restore youth to the aged.

Thousand Springs gush forth from the lava edges and plunge down into Snake River.

hotos: Willard Luce; top eft, Sun Valley News Bureau

Trail Riders explore the wilderness in Idaho's Primitive Area, a million-acre land of mountains and streams, plateaus an ridges, meadows, four National Forests

Shoshone Falls is largest of the Snake River waterfalls, a thousand feet across its horseshoe curve and 212 feet deep Irrigation dams make the flow irregula

Photos: Ross Madden (Western Ways); Willard Luc

CRATER LAKE AND CASCADE RANGE FEATURE OREGON'S RUGGED GRANDEUR

Mt. Hood loop, a wide, paved highway, encircles Oregon's highest peak, 11,245-ft. Mt. Hood is in the imposing Cascade Range. Rhododendrons grow on slopes.

Photo: Oregon State Highway Commission

Portland is Oregon's largest city with more than a half million in the urban area. This view is from Washington Park, with Mt. Hood in the distance, 50 miles away.

Known as "City of Roses," Portland has Rose Festival in June, with Floral Parade.

International rose test gardens cover a large acreage in city's Washington Park

Photo: Northwest Orient Airlines; bottom, Oregon State Highway Commission

'Joaquin Miller Chapel" is seen on the 'uided tour through famous Oregon Caves.

Pioneer figure atop Capitol at Salem symbolizes westward march of settlers.

Bachelor Butte is the predominant peak seen from Todd Lake and meadows, west of Bend. The lake is a favorite trout fishing spot in the central Oregon area.

Gladioli are an important flower crop n Grants Pass region, Josephine County.

Indian maiden displays her costume at the Pendleton Round-Up in eastern Oregon.

'hotos: Oregon State Highway Commission; top left, Northwest Orient Airlines

At Crater Lake National Park, visitors are looking toward Wizard Island, a small lava cone that rises 700 feet high out o the water of this mysterious blue lake

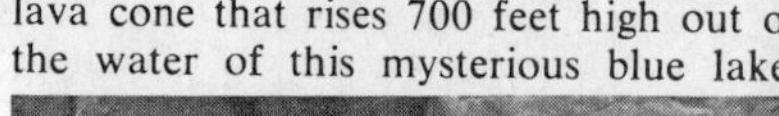

Astoria's fishing fleet waits for run of salmon to hit Columbia River or the coast.

Ancient Indian writings are found on roc cliffs of Picture Gorge, near Dayville

Photos: Oregon Stat Highway Commissio

ista House lookout, atop Crown Point, ves this view of Columbia River Gorge

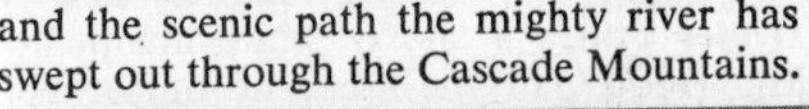

and the scenic path the mighty river has swept out through the Cascade Mountains.

onneville Dam, built 1933–43, is one f the Northwest's hydroelectric giants.

Fish ladders enable salmon to circumvent dam and swim upriver to spawning grounds.

Norwegian freighter docks at Coos Bay, one of coast's great lumber shipping ports.

Old fort at The Dalles displays many items pioneers brought in covered wagons.

Photos: Oregon State Highway Commission; top, Northwest Orient Airlines

Oregon

Winter brings a snowy white mantle to Mt. Hood and the trees at timberline.

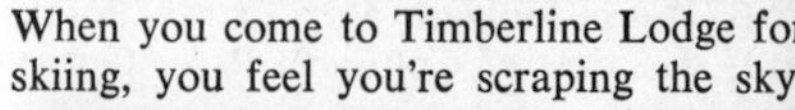

When you come to Timberline Lodge for skiing, you feel you're scraping the sky.

Oregon Caves Chateau is near entrance to the spectacular underground Marble Halls.

Baker's First National Bank displays a multimillion dollar collection of gold

Seal Rock State Park, south of Newport, is good place to view wild and colorful Oregon coast. Seals may frequently be seen on rocks beyond the breakers

Photos: Oregon State Highway Commission; top, Northwest Orient Airline

WASHINGTON'S BOLD FEATURES OFFER SOME OF WORLD'S LOVELIEST SCENES

Majestic Mount Rainier is the 14,408-ft. peak that the Indians called God. Clear water of Reflection Lake mirrors snow-crowned top of state's highest mountain.

Photo: Northern Pacific Railway

Hikers tackle the slopes of Mt. Rainier close to timberline. On a clear day you can see the Cascades billowing north to British Columbia, south toward California.

Olympic National Park includes nearly 850,000 acres, with most of the major peaks of the Olympic Mountains. This is Mt. Olympus, from Hurricane Ridge Road.

Photos: top, Northwest Orient Airlines; Washington State Advertising Commission

Seattle's crowded skyline testifies to ts importance as Washington's largest

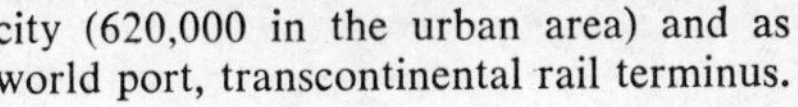

city (620,000 in the urban area) and as world port, transcontinental rail terminus.

Floating bridge is unique feature of Lake Washington, within Seattle city limits.

Government locks connect Puget Sound with Seattle's inland lakes and canals.

A young visitor to Washington studies the variety of boats docked at Westport, on sheltered Grays Harbor. Evergreen State has lakes, rivers, ocean, and inland sea.

Photos: Washington State Advertising Commission

Spokane is hub of the Inland Empire, the vast northwest area that produces wheat, apples, lumber. A pioneer trading post in 1872, it's now second city in the state.

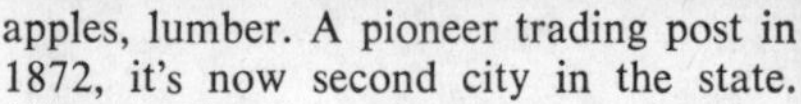

Mt. Spokane is center of 3,000-acre state park. This view shows Mt. Kit Carson.

Lookout on top of 5,878-ft. Mt. Spokane gives splendid view of eastern Washington.

Gold Creek in Chelan National Forest shows the rugged nature of this region.

Olympia, state capital of Washington, is the southernmost port of Puget Sound.

Photos: Washington State Advertising Commission; center left, Northwest Orient Airlines; bottom left, U. S. Forest Service

Grand Coulee Dam, finished 1942, is the largest concrete dam in the world. Water from reservoir flows to farms through a 4,000-mile system of irrigation ditches.

Toppenish is headquarters of the Yakima Indian Agency. This is July 4th pow-wow.

Fishing at Long Beach: This is claimed to be the longest in the world—28 miles.

Tacoma's Fort Nisqually, built by Hudson's Bay Company, was a trading post.

Apples from Yakima and Wenatchee, "Apple Capital of the World," are famous.

Photos: top, Northwest Orient Airlines; Washington State Advertising Commission

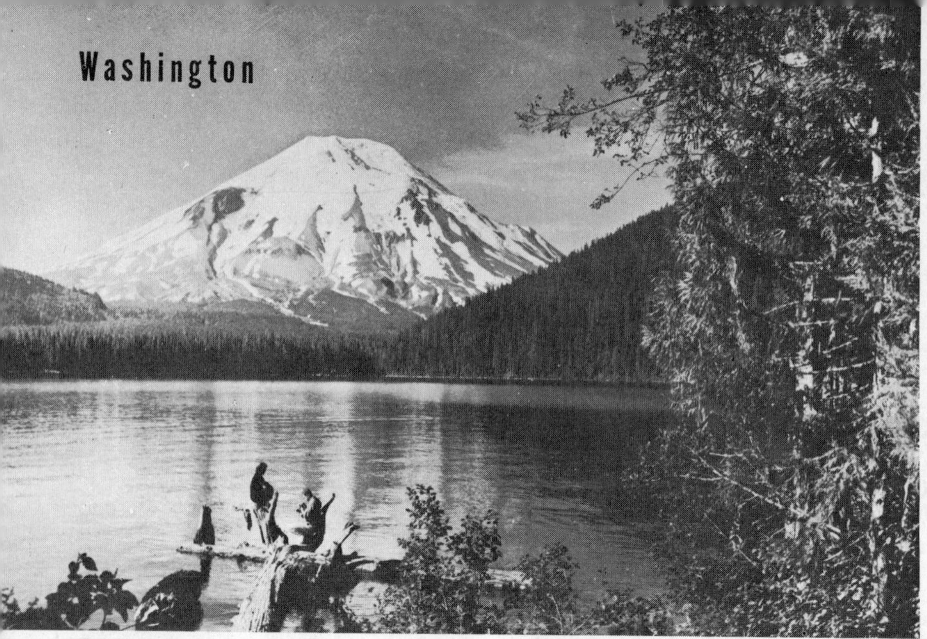

Washington

Spirit Lake, at foot of Mount St. Helens, is 44 miles from Castle Rock over a new highway. It has a Forest Service camping ground, excellent trout fishing, hunting.

Truck-trailers, trains and rivers bring Douglas fir and other woods to the mills.

Sheep graze in Gifford Pinchot National Forest, with Mount Adams in background.

This combine is working on pea harvest which now exceeds the value of wheat in many Washington counties. The state also raises barley, oats, potatoes, corn, hops.

Photos: U. S. Forest Service; center left, Washington State Advertising Commission; bottom, Northwest Orient Airlines

49TH AND 50TH STATES

by A. MILTON RUNYON

The creation of two new states so far away from their nearest neighbor states is an appropriate miracle for the jet age. Hawaii is in mid-Pacific, some two thousand miles from the American mainland. Alaska is in the land of the midnight sun, and even its southernmost city, Ketchikan, is about 550 miles north of Seattle. But thanks to modern jets, the senators and representatives from our newest states can get to Washington faster and more comfortably than many of the law-makers from the original thirteen states!

The two new states present a great contrast. Hawaii is a community of eight main islands and a dozen smaller ones, about equal in area to Connecticut and Rhode Island. But the 50th state is just a little more than *one per cent* of the area of her newest sister state. Alaska is more than twice as large as the tremendous state of Texas, and six times as large as Great Britain. The Aleutian Islands, like giant steppingstones, stretch far out into the Pacific Ocean, and the Panhandle runs nearly 400 miles down the coast of the continent to the southeast.

As to the population, the contrast runs somewhat the other way. Alaska has only a little over 200,000 inhabitants, about as many as Salt Lake City. Hawaii has three times as many people—some 600,000. Alaska's residents include many thousands of Eskimos and American Indians. Hawaii can boast of probably 12,000 citizens of pure Hawaiian stock. The others are of a dozen or more principal nationalities; they come from China, Japan, the mainland of Portugal and the Cape Verde Islands in the Atlantic, the Philippines, Korea, Puerto Rico, the American mainland.

Leis greet new arrivals in Hawaii.

Sugar is Hawaii's number one crop, with the pineapple industry occupying about one third as much land as the sugar plantations. There are nine pineapple canneries.

The newest big business of the "Aloha State" is tourism, with new hotels and faster transportation attracting new visitors all the time—for the lovely scenery, the tropical island color, and a climate where it's always spring.

The Klondike gold rush first brought world attention to Alaska. Mining has continued to be an important activity and Alaska has produced over 700 times its purchase price in gold alone. Fishing, largely salmon, ranks as the number one industry today. Fur trapping still provides a million and half dollars in revenue. And there is expanding use of forests and of hydroelectric power.

Alaska, with its comparatively warm summers, has a great deal to offer the tourist and the sportsman in search of dramatic scenery, unspoiled wilderness.

Photo: Pan American World Airways

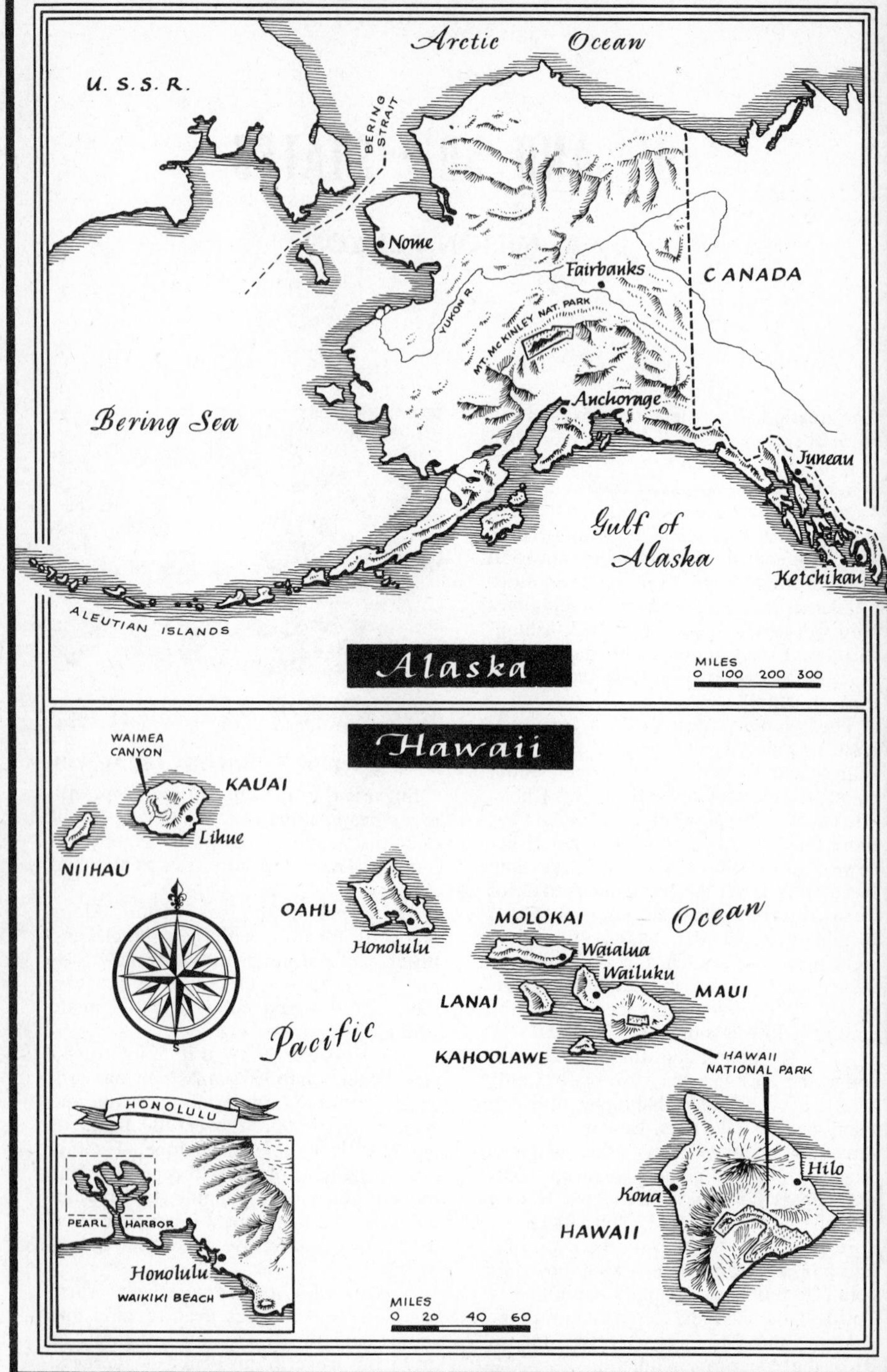
Arctic Ocean
U.S.S.R.
BERING STRAIT
Nome
Fairbanks
CANADA
YUKON R.
MT. McKINLEY NAT. PARK
Anchorage
Bering Sea
Juneau
Gulf of Alaska
Ketchikan
ALEUTIAN ISLANDS
Alaska
MILES
0 100 200 300
Hawaii
WAIMEA CANYON
KAUAI
Lihue
NIIHAU
OAHU
Honolulu
MOLOKAI
Ocean
Waialua
Wailuku
LANAI
MAUI
Pacific
KAHOOLAWE
HAWAII NATIONAL PARK
HONOLULU
Hilo
Kona
PEARL HARBOR
HAWAII
Honolulu
WAIKIKI BEACH
MILES
0 20 40 60

MILD CLIMATE, LOVELY BEACHES MAKE HAWAII TRUE GARDEN SPOT.

HAWAII IS OUR TROPICAL PARADISE

Ever since Captain Cook discovered the Hawaiian Islands in 1778, their magic has been known to the world—a land of mild climate the year round (the mean annual temperature is about 75°), of fine white sand beaches, of subtropical ocean waters, and of smiling, friendly citizens. It's wonderful to have as our 50th state!

Photo: Hawaii Visitors Bureau

Hawaii

The bi-annual transpacific yacht races are alternated with the local invitation series.

Fishing with thrownet is real art; needs sharp eye, quick coördination.

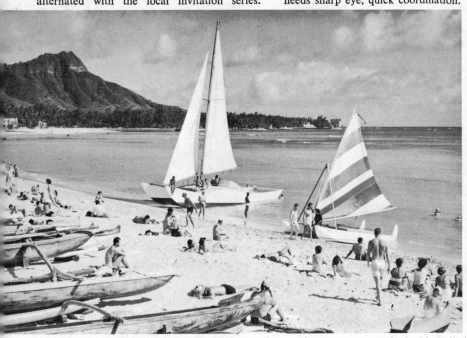

At famous Waikiki Beach, Honolulu, vacationists may go for exciting rides in outrigger canoes and double-hulled catamarans. Diamond Head is at the left.

Photos: Hawaii Visitors Bureau

Luxurious Royal Hawaiian Hotel is right at the edge of Waikiki beach, and so is

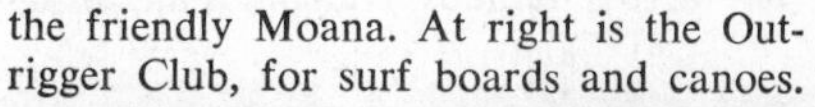

the friendly Moana. At right is the Outrigger Club, for surf boards and canoes.

Little island youngster, clad in bright Aloha shirt, makes friends with visitor.

During Aloha festival, Hawaiian enacts old ways, pounding poi in the old style.

Photos: Hawaii Visitors Bureau

A half-hour's drive from Honolulu's center, across famous Nuuanu Pali, brings you to beach area on windward side of Oahu, a splendid place for surf fishing.

Waimea Canyon, on the island of Kauai, is the "Grand Canyon" of Hawaii, cutting through the verdure of the lush, green island with gorges similar to Colorado's.

Photos: Hawaii Visitors Bureau

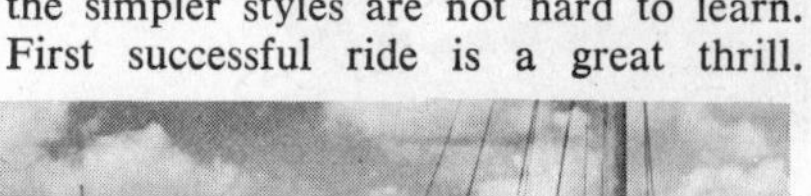

You won't be able to match the skill of these surfboard riders at first try, but the simpler styles are not hard to learn. First successful ride is a great thrill.

The Blow Hole, on Koko Head, is a salt water geyser, caused by rush of the tide.

Ala Moana yacht harbor, at entrance to Ala Wai canal, has boats from afar.

Photos: Hawaii Visitors Bureau

Hawaii

S.S. Lurline passes Diamond Head. Voyage from California is a delightful one.

Girls with bare brown shoulders, flower leis, perform the symbolic Hawaiian hula.

At Kauai island, natives gather round the shores of Nawiliwili bay for a "hukilau" during which they pull in huge nets from the indigo-colored sea, loaded with fish.

Photos: Hawaii Visitors Bureau; top left, Matson Lines

Pineapple fields are colorful part of the Hawaiian landscape, with the green of the leaves contrasting with the brilliant blue of the sky, the reddish brown of the soil.

Pearl Harbor's huge navy base may be seen by boat trip, leaving from Kewalo Basin.

Flower leis, made of colorful and fragrant blossoms, say "aloha" to Hawaii's visitors.

Photos: Shostal Press; bottom left, Rapho-Guillumette

ALASKA IS LAST FRONTIER OF U.S.

Alaska is easily reached by plane, or by Inside Passage as far north as Juneau, and from there across the Gulf of Alaska to Prince William Sound. This beautiful trip visits the main industrial cities. Within Alaska, planes are used for long distance runs, dog teams for short ones. The Alaska Railroad serves the gold mines, coal fields, Mt. McKinley National Park.

ALASKA'S FIRST GOLD RUSH RESULTED IN FOUNDING OF JUNEAU.

Mendenhall Glacier is one of the few that can be reached by automobile road.

Salmon fishing areas are not far from Juneau; fresh water fish are abundant.

Photos: Pan American World Airways

Fairbanks is center for tourists who arrive by Yukon River from Whitehorse.

Eskimo family at Nome keeps busy making shoes from walrus hide, carving ivory.

Started as a supply point for miners in 1890's rush, Ketchikan is usually first Alaska community visited by tourists. Hundreds of fishing vessels use good port.

Photos: Pan American World Airways

Busy Fairbanks, metropolis of interior Alaska, combines pioneer frontier and civilization. The town still has log cabins, but its business district has modern shops.

Photo: Shostal Press

Many of the caribou migrated to Canada when the Eskimos began shooting them with the white man's rifle. Recently the caribou has begun to return to the tundra.

Salmon fishing and canning has been one of Alaska's principal sources of employment.

New apartment building in Anchorage shows cosmopolitan nature of the city.

Photos: Shostal Press, bottom left, Photo Researchers, Inc.

Alaska

Indian Meeting House and totem poles are seen at Totem Village, near Ketchikan.

Cruise steamer, bound north, passes through Lynn Canal in sight of glaciers.

Mt. McKinley National Park is second in size only to Yellowstone. This wilderness is topped by Mt. McKinley, 20,270 feet, the highest point in all North America.

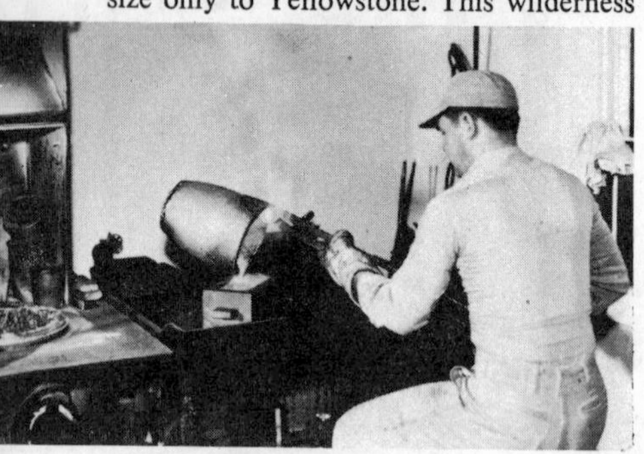

Gold dust and nuggets in the Miners and Merchants Bank are melted into ingots.

This bus is on Alaska Highway, 1527 miles long, Dawson Creek, B.C., to Fairbanks.

Photos: Pan American World Airways; top right and bottom right, Canadian Pacific Railway

INDEX